82
125
140
50
56
95
120
139
171
178
181
185
207
210
213
261
267
274
276

P9-CMS-825

51
56
79 LRK
83 LRK
90 Ion
171
174 Beach
181
203
238
275
276

GREATPLANNED COMMUNITIES

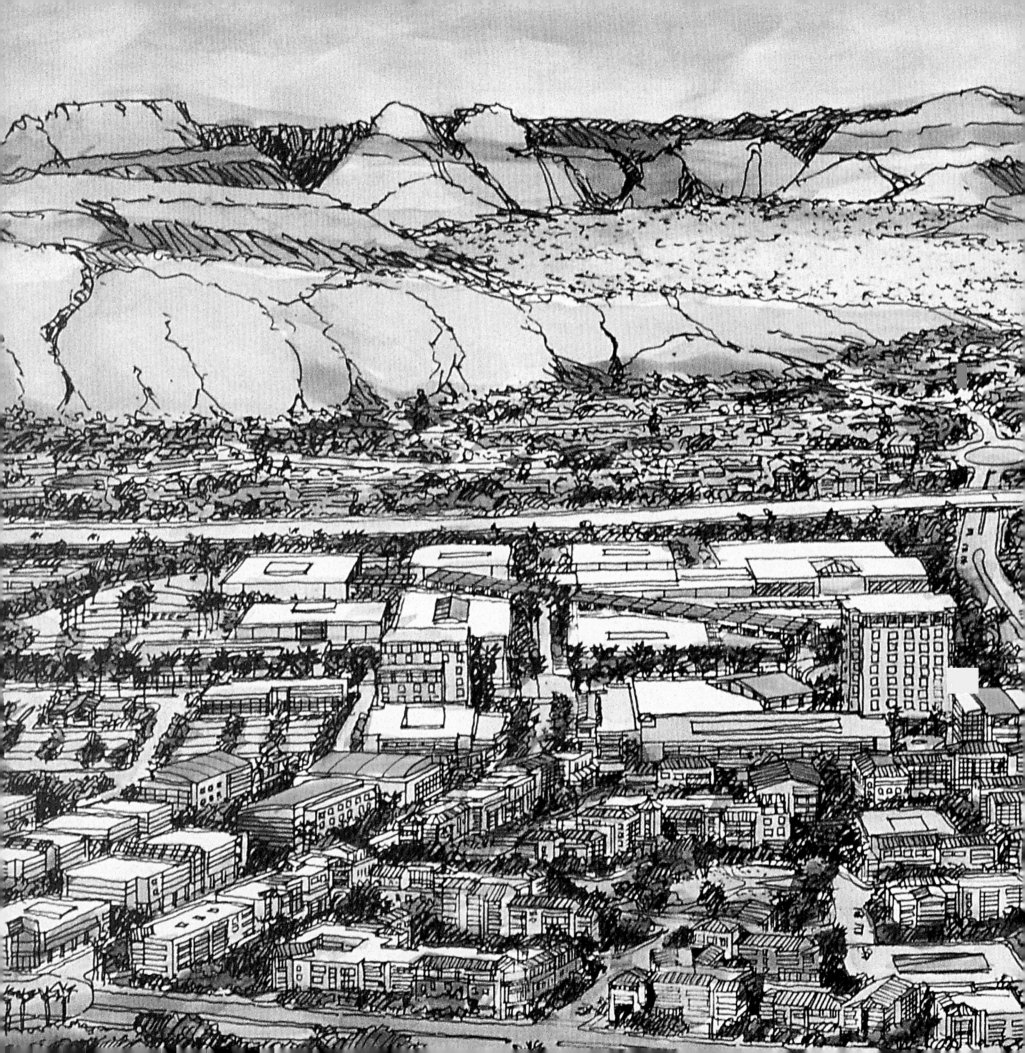

GREATPLANNED COMMUNITIES

Jo Allen Gause, Editor

Alexander Garvin, Introduction · Steven R. Kellenberg, Principal Contributor

THE URBAN LAND INSTITUTE

© Copyright 2002 ULI–the Urban Land Institute
1025 Thomas Jefferson Street, N.W.
Suite 500 West
Washington, D.C. 20007-5201

ALL RIGHTS RESERVED

No part of this book may be reproduced in any form
or by any means, electronic or mechanical, including
photocopying and recording, or by any information
storage and retrieval system, without written permis-
sion of the publisher.

RECOMMENDED BIBLIOGRAPHIC LISTING:

Gause, Jo Allen, et al. *Great Planned Communities*.
Washington, D.C.: ULI– the Urban Land Institute,
2002.

ULI CATALOG NUMBER: D105
ISBN: 0-87420-892-0
LIBRARY OF CONGRESS CONTROL NUMBER:
2002104227

BOOK DESIGN AND PRODUCTION

Meadows Design Office Inc., Washington, D.C.
www.mdomedia.com

Marc Alain Meadows
Creative Director and Designer

Ching Huang Ooi
Assistant Graphic Designer

MANUSCRIPT EDITING

Micaela Porta, Engine Books, New York, N.Y.

PRINTED AND BOUND IN CANADA

06 05 04 03 02 5 4 3 2 1

ULI PROJECT STAFF

Rachelle L. Levitt
Senior Vice President, Policy and Practice
Publisher

Gayle Berens
Vice President, Real Estate Development Practice

Jo Allen Gause
Senior Director, Residential Development
Project Director

Nancy H. Stewart
Director, Book Program
Managing Editor

Betsy VanBuskirk
Art Director

Karrie Underwood
Digital Images Assistant

Diann Stanley-Austin
Director, Publishing Operations

ABOUT ULI

ULI–the Urban Land Institute is a nonprofit education
and research institute that is supported by its members.
Its mission is to provide responsible leadership in the
use of land in order to enhance the total environment.

ULI sponsors education programs and forums to encourage an open international exchange of ideas and
sharing of experiences; initiates research that antici-
pates emerging land use trends and issues and proposes
creative solutions based on that research; provides
advisory services; and publishes a wide variety of materials to disseminate information on land use and
development. Established in 1936, the Institute today
has more than 17,000 members and associates from
some 60 countries representing the entire spectrum of
the land use and development disciplines.

Richard M. Rosan, *President*

FRONT JACKET: Aerial view of WaterColor, Seagrove
Beach, Florida

FRONTISPIECE: Artist's view of Summerlin Centre, Las
Vegas, Nevada

TITLE PAGE: Neighborhood park at Ladera Ranch,
Orange County, California

OPPOSITE: Plan of Celebration, Florida

Contents

Preface

ULI–the Urban Land Institute is pleased to present *Great Planned Communities*—an anthology of case studies featuring some of the best examples of innovation in the design and development of master-planned communities around the world. The book not only explains the visions and presents the plans that guided the development of successful contemporary communities, but also takes readers on a visual tour of the built communities. Together, the text and illustrations highlight the concepts that shaped each project's master plan, the plan's component parts, and the architectural and design elements that unify each community and make it distinctive.

During the postwar suburban building boom years, residential development in the United States began to lose touch with the community design principles that shaped the country's older towns and neighborhoods—a source of nostalgia for many Americans. Indistinguishable subdivisions leapfrogged across suburban landscapes, driven by higher and higher land costs and demand for new housing, and shaped by the suburban model of single-family, segregated use, and low-density, auto-dependent development. The toll that sprawl is taking on quality of life is almost universally acknowledged: consumption of irreplaceable resources, deteriorating public infrastructure, hopelessly long commutes, lack of affordable housing, loss of community.

But soulless subdivisions do not appear to be standing the test of time. Many believe there is a new quest for community, for that intangible sense of neighborhood and belonging that provides the critical framework within which generations can learn and grow, interact and mature, thrive and evolve. Or perhaps it can be thought of as a return to community, albeit one that is geared to the realities of our present day. Developers, planners, and architects are focusing on the physical elements of community design that can enhance livability, facilitate social interaction, and foster a sense of communal satisfaction. Community design is placing new emphasis on the significance of the public realm and of shared open space, and on incorporating higher densities and a greater mix of uses. Community building in the 21st century is looking to its 20th-century roots and rediscovering the planning concepts that shaped the most lasting communities.

The 26 communities featured in these pages include a full sweep of types and sizes—from a compact 91 acres (38 hectares) to a massive 93,100 acres (37,676 hectares). They are built on urban infill sites, suburban greenfields, reclaimed brownfields, waterfronts, deserts, and rural farmlands in every region of the United States and in Australia, Canada, China, England, and Germany.

As different as the communities are from one another, they share a number of features: they were all developed from a comprehensive plan by a master developer; they incorporate a variety of housing types, sizes, and prices; they include a complementary mix of land uses; and they provide ample common open space and a vital public realm.

The case studies in this book are by no means the only examples of exceptional planning and design around the world. Many others that are as good, or even better, were excluded only because of the book's limited space.

The 19 projects included in the Contemporary Communities section of the book are still evolving and responding to changing markets. They represent a wide range of development approaches—traditional neighborhood developments, sustainable communities, high-density urban villages, and traditional suburban community developments—and they have all met with market success.

The seven communities included in the New Visions section are still on the planning boards or in the initial phase of development. These future communities offer models for responding to some of the most pressing issues confronting community development professionals in the coming years—affordability, sustainability, and increasing market diversity—and they illustrate the opportunities that will be found in urban infill and brownfield redevelopment sites.

As shown by the size and scope of the projects highlighted in this book, there is no one correct way to design or develop planned communities. Those that stand the test of time have flexible master plans that are sensitive to their environment and responsive to the lifestyles of their residents.

— Jo Allen Gause, Editor

Acknowledgments

Editor

Jo Allen Gause
Senior Director, Residential Development
ULI–the Urban Land Institute
Washington, D.C.

Principal Contributor

Steven R. Kellenberg
Principal
EDAW, Inc.
Irvine, California

Contributors

Donald K. Carter
Managing Principal
Urban Design Associates
Pittsburgh, Pennsylvania

Alexander Garvin
Professor of Urban Planning and Management
Yale University
New Haven, Connecticut

Adrienne Schmitz
Director, Residential Community Development
ULI–the Urban Land Institute
Washington, D.C.

Many individuals contributed their time and talents to this book, and to each one I would like to extend my sincere appreciation. Although it is impossible to mention everyone who participated in this effort, a number of individuals and organizations deserve special acknowledgment and thanks.

First, very special recognition and thanks go to Steven Kellenberg at EDAW, Inc., who provided the graphics and much of the text and data for 12 of the 26 case studies included in this book. Without his insight into these communities, his breadth of knowledge and experience in town planning, and his considerable contribution of time and effort, this book would not have been possible. I would also like to thank Steve's colleagues at EDAW, Inc., who researched the case study projects and compiled graphics—David Bennett, Greg Ault, Liz Drake, Rick Stoneman, John Leehey, Susan Davison, Helen Cheung, Deana Swetlik, and Stephen Engblom. And a huge thank-you goes to Jeannine Carta-Hanson, who scanned and transmitted hundreds of images from numerous sources, and who was always responsive to our requests to locate and send images, often on very short notice.

I extend thanks to three individuals who wrote significant portions of the text: Alexander Garvin, who wrote the introduction; Donald Carter at Urban Design Associates, who wrote insightful summaries and obtained graphics for several of the projects highlighted in the book, and who provided valuable and much appreciated advice throughout the development of the book; and Adrienne Schmitz at ULI, who turned a great deal of resource material into well-organized, clearly written case study text. Thanks also to the individuals who reviewed portions of the text: Robert Campbell, Marc Weiss, and David M. Schwarz. Their comments enriched the book.

I am indebted to the many developers, planners, and architects who provided photographs, illustrations, and written materials. Without their contributions, there would be no book. The following deserve special recognition: Andrea Finger, The Celebration Company; Peter Neal, The Prince's Foundation; Rob Elliott and Chris Warren, The Irvine Company; Kim Amborse, Terrabrook; Jeff Campbell, Great Seneca Development Corporation; Christian Grahame, Mirvac; Michael Lear, The Bonita Bay Group; Sarah Holt, Holt & Haugh; Sharon Walker, Carma Developers Ltd.; Lia Peterson, DC Ranch LLC; Kevin Warren, Lake Erie Land Company; Susan Vreeland, The Woodlands Operating Company, L.P.; Chuck Kubat, The Howard Hughes Corporation; Peter Denniston, Ken Agad, and Jennifer Fidelman, Playa Capital Company; Mike Mehaffy, Pacific Realty Associates, L.P.; Karen Cooper, Cooper, Robertson & Partners; Roseann Wentworth, The St. Joe Company; Vinayak Bharne, Moule & Polyzoides; Mike Watson and Javier Iglesias, Duany Plater-Zyberk & Company; Janet Sager and Adrian Koffka, Moore Ruble Yudell; Laurin McCracken, Looney Ricks Kiss; Peter Dixon, Robert A.M. Stern Architects; Monika Ruef, Carter Ryley Thomas; Melissa Warren, Faiss Foley Merica Public Relations; and Erling Okkenhaug, Okkenhaug Den Stille Bolgen.

Several others brought their research and writing skills to bear in this effort and improved the quality and content of the text. Thanks go to Geoffrey Booth, David Takesuye, and Leslie Holst, ULI; Abby Bussel, Engine Books; and Dorothy Verdon, Verdon Consulting.

I would like to thank the Urban Land Institute staff for its skill and dedication in bringing this book together: Karrie Underwood for so expertly managing the rather daunting task of cataloging, sizing, and printing the almost 1,000 digital images submitted for consideration in the book; Melissa Weberman for her resourceful pursuit of photographs; Jennifer Good for her meticulous conversion of project data to the metric system; Nancy Stewart for managing the editing process so that every detail was taken care of to perfection, as usual; Betsy VanBuskirk for managing design and layout of the book; Diann Stanley-Austin for coordinating the book's publication; Lori Hatcher for marketing the book; and Rachelle Levitt and Gayle Berens for their support and direction from beginning to end.

Much appreciation and many thanks go to Micaela Porta of Engine Books for her sensitive and careful editing of the entire text, ensuring that the information was clearly written and presented to make it most useful to our audience.

And finally, my deep appreciation and admiration to Marc Meadows of Meadows Design Office for his elegant design and layout of the book and its cover. Marc's creativity, technical skill, and unwavering commitment to excellence are matched only by his warmth and humor.

And to everyone else who had a hand in this work and could not be mentioned in this limited space, I am sincerely grateful.

— J.A.G.

THE ART OF CREATING COMMUNITIES

AN ESSAY BY ALEXANDER GARVIN

During the 19th century, America's cities rapidly outgrew their initial grid plans. Enterprising property owners subdivided land into large lots for houses and gardens that appealed to families who went into town to work, shop, and be entertained. The earliest of these suburban "subdivisions," like New Orleans's faubourgs, were really extensions of cities, located in walking distance of the business district. Later, in large cities like New York, Boston, and St. Louis, they had to be in commuting distance by ferry, railroad, or streetcar.

The earliest examples of planning an America that considered more than streets, blocks, and lots are not urban. They are *suburban*: master-planned communities like Llewellyn Park, New Jersey (1853), and Lake Forest, Illinois (1856), whose creators had greater ambitions than laying out lots that could easily be sold to settlers. The 400 acres (162 hectares), 12 miles (19 kilometers) west of Manhattan, which became Llewellyn Park, were developed by Llewellyn Haskell as a country retreat in which he and 50 neighbors could build large, gracious houses on sites ranging from three to ten acres (one to four hectares). Haskell and Alexander Jackson Davis, the designer he hired to lay out this master-planned community, had the benefit of a lovely site "threaded by mountain streams, pierced with picturesque ravines, rimmed and ribbed with rocks."[1] They cleared trees to open up views, planted thousands of exotic shrubs, created ponds, set aside 50 acres (20 hectares) for a central park, which they called the Ramble, established curving roads, and built a gatehouse to control access.

Lake Forest, 25 miles (40 kilometers) north of Chicago on the shore of Lake Michigan, was a similarly lovely site with picturesque, shallow ravines and small streams. Its rolling topography was different from the miles of open prairie that surrounded Chicago. The site had become easily accessible in 1855, when the Chicago and Milwaukee Railroad opened a station on the eastern edge of the site. The Lake Forest Association purchased the site because of its potential as a commuter suburb. They had been seeking a site for a college and had decided to pay for it by selling property to people who wanted to build country homes that were a short train ride from Chicago. Unlike Haskell, the Lake Forest Association did not spend much

Alfred Loomis

Opening pages: Many of America's earliest planned communities were developed as suburban refuges for wealthy Americans. Tuxedo Park, New York, was developed in 1885 as a hunting and fishing retreat in the Ramapo Mountains for leaders of New York society. The new town included a finished roadway network, a railroad station, a police station, retail shops, a small racetrack, and a private clubhouse.

Right: A gatehouse controlled access to Llewellyn Park, New Jersey, 12 miles (19 kilometers) west of Manhattan. Built in 1853 on a lush, heavily wooded site, planners set aside more than 10 percent of the property for a central park, which they called the Ramble.

on landscaping. The roads they established radiated from the railroad station to the lake following the most obvious routes that required minimal topographic disruption.

The tens of thousands of people in the 19th century who moved to suburban communities like Llewellyn Park and Lake Forest sought more than just charming, country locations. They wanted to own a house. With homeownership, particularly if the house was on a large lot, came the freedom to live life with a greater degree of privacy. These early suburbanites also wanted to live amongst people with whom they felt comfortable. Consequently, developers of master-planned communities often included deed restrictions that specified minimum house prices, land uses, and construction requirements. The inevitable result was to exclude all but the elite few who could afford the price.

Few developers were as open about restricting occupancy as Pierre Lorillard IV, the developer of Tuxedo Park, New York, a hunting and fishing retreat he created for himself and his wealthy friends in the Ramapo Mountains, 28 miles (45 kilometers) north of New York City. In 1885 Lorillard hired architect Bruce Price and engineer Ernest Bowditch to plan his 5,000-acre (2,023-hectare) property as a community for long-established leaders of New York society. They laid out about 300 house sites on heavily wooded sites, many overlooking Tuxedo Park's three lakes. Within nine months, infrastructure, including 30 miles (48 kilometers) of roads, had been built, as well as an entire village with a railroad depot, police station, and retail stores. To get in, you had to pass through an imposing stone gatehouse. Once inside, residents and visitors on their way to their destination passed a small racetrack and the Tuxedo Club, which provided its members with private squash, racquet, and tennis courts, a boathouse, golf course, clubhouse, and even small rental apartments for guests.

These and most 19th- and early-20th-century American master-planned communities share nostalgia for English villages and country estates with houses set back from meandering roadways. They may have included covenants that precluded occupancy by Asians, Africans, Catholics, or

Jews. In most other respects, however, their commitment to relative privacy within a country setting was tempered by democratic principles and a curvilinear aesthetic popularized by Frederick Law Olmsted.

The Olmsted Legacy

In 1868, when Olmsted submitted his plan for Riverside, Illinois, to developer Emery Childs, his reputation was based entirely on designs for the recently completed Central and Prospect Parks in New York City.[2] Riverside was the first venture into the design of an entire community by the landscape architecture firm of Olmsted & Vaux. The principles initiated at Riverside became established practice for hundreds of developers and designers, most of whom probably had never heard of the project.

Riverside's 1,600-acre (648-hectare) site, nine miles (14 kilometers) west of Chicago, was located in what Olmsted described as a "low, flat, miry, and forlorn" prairie. It was too large and undistinguished to be restricted to a small number of elite homeowners. Thus, Olmsted's task was to transform what had been farmland into house lots for middle-class Chicagoans seeking affordable country residences. His solution was a master-planned community that provided residents and visitors with automatic access to amenities similar to those of elite suburbs like Llewellyn Park.

There was no gatehouse. Instead, homeowners (except for those with small lots along the railroad) were guaranteed privacy by covenants requiring houses to be set back 30 feet (nine meters) from the street and 150 feet (46 meters) from one another. Fences were prohibited, yet every property had to have two trees planted between the street and the house.

Olmsted's genius is evident in more than his simple approach to household privacy. Whether on foot, on horseback, or in a carriage, residents made their way along tree-lined streets that offered the promise of something new around the continuing bend in the road. Converging intersections became triangular landscaped open areas. Changing views opened first on one side and then on the other. The trees, when they reached maturity, sheltered passersby from the sun during the summer and opened up to sunlight during the winter.

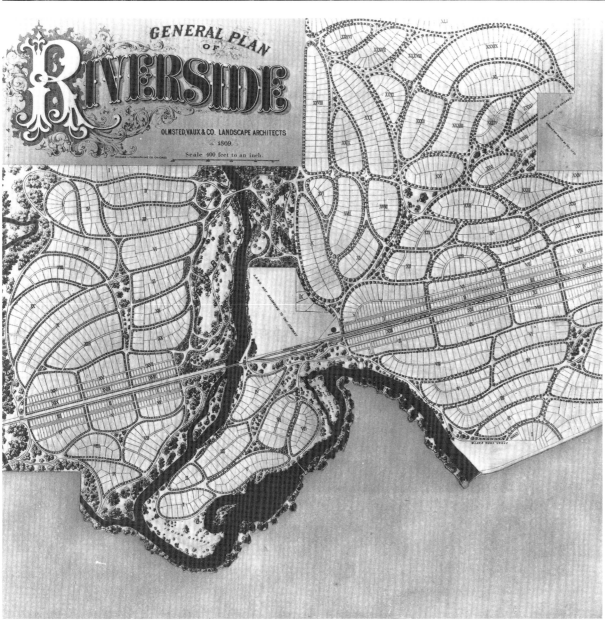

Left: Olmsted and Vaux's 1869 plan for Riverside, Illinois, became a model for generations of developers and planners. Curvilinear streets and clever landscaping transformed this large, flat site into a marketable commuter suburb. The plan turned the site's most distinctive feature—the banks of the shallow Des Plaines River—into a 160-acre (65-hectare) park.

Above: Riverside's deed restrictions provided for an array of controls, from mandatory setbacks, minimum home construction costs, and design review for houses, to prescribed rules for maintaining private lawns.

At the heart of the Olmsted design was the site itself. At Riverside, Olmsted transformed its only distinctive landscape feature into a major component of the public realm. Because the banks of the shallow Des Plaines River flooded during the rainy season, they were inadvisable for development. Instead, they became 160 acres (65 hectares) of parkland that could be used for fishing, boating, or walking.

In 1897, designing the second plat of Roland Park in Baltimore, the Olmsted firm applied its tree-lined street formula to a landscape of rolling hills in which valleys were used for through-streets that alternated with culs-de-sac extending to the end of ridge tops. As at Riverside, development was restricted to one-family houses on large lots, set back at least 30 feet (nine meters) from the street. In 1907, in laying out the Mount Baker section of Seattle, streets were located along the north-south ledges that provided easy access to house sites with spectacular views of Lake Washington. When the firm planned Cherokee Gardens in Louisville, Kentucky, in 1925, it minimized drainage problems by placing streets in shallow valleys, along ledges, or on ridge tops. Drainage rivulets became part of an open space system that ran parallel to the roads.

By establishing the nation's first academic course in landscape design at Harvard University in 1900, Frederick Law Olmsted, Jr., who had joined his father's firm in the early 1870s, spread the Olmsted legacy far beyond the professionals who passed through the firm. One of his more talented students, John Nolen, devised an interesting elaboration on Olmsted's tree-lined street. In 1911, Nolen prepared a plan to transform a former cotton farm into the master-planned community of Myers Park, one and one-half miles from the center of downtown Charlotte, North Carolina. Nolen's plan, like those of the Olmsteds, included a street hierarchy: a 110-foot-wide (34-meter-wide) boulevard with a tree-lined, two-track streetcar median, 80-foot (24-meter) main roads, 60-foot (18-meter) residence roads, 50-foot (15-meter) minor roads, and 40-foot (12-meter) park side roads. A boulevard containing a streetcar median looped through Myers Park so that no house was further than two blocks away. Houses fronting the boulevard were set back far enough from the sidewalk that

the boulevard was enclosed within a tree canopy seven trees wide.

Myers Park was not unique in possessing a streetcar boulevard. The Olmsteds had prepared tree-lined, streetcar boulevard designs for Brookline, Massachusetts, Druid Hills in Atlanta, and Louisville, Kentucky. The most ambitious of streetcar boulevards was created by the Van Sweringen brothers for Shaker Heights, Ohio. In 1920, they purchased an entire railroad so that they could use the tracks to provide commuter service from their master-planned new community of Shaker Heights to downtown Cleveland.

From 1922 to 1923, Frederick Law Olmsted, Jr., working with planner Charles Cheney, designed what is arguably the most beautiful of all master-planned communities: Palos Verdes Estates. The 3,200-acre (1,295-hectare) site wrapped around a spectacular peninsula jutting out into the Pacific Ocean, 23 miles (37 kilometers) southwest of downtown Los Angeles. The peninsula's 25 terraces were the product of the surf slowly washing away rock during the centuries in which the peninsula gradually rose out of the ocean. Olmsted and Cheney placed traffic arteries on these terraces. Thus, from the road the houses on the ocean side of its terrace-streets appeared to be one story high. In fact, they descended several stories below the level of the road, thereby offering their occupants spectacular views. The upper floors of the two- to three-story houses on the inland side had the same spectacular views, only over the red clay tile roofs of the houses across the street.

Beginning with Riverside, the Olmsted firm made an art form of its public realm formula of curvilinear, tree-lined roadways augmented with local landscape features to provide attractive opportunities for recreation. Its approach to the land was based on the principles popularized during the 18th century by English landscape gardener Lancelot "Capability" Brown, who earned his nickname from exploiting the "capabilities" of a site. But as important as Riverside may have been in establishing a design formula for suburban development, it is even more important in disclosing the major financial challenge facing master-planned communities: balancing initial expenditures for infrastructure and community facilities with

revenues from lot sales. Olmsted had set aside 700 acres (283 hectares) for roads, borders, walks, and parks. As a result, between 1868 and 1871, developer Emery Childs had to spend more than $1.5 million on infrastructure and landscaping for Riverside.[3] Land sales, which plummeted during the Panic of 1873, could not cover these costs, and Childs was unable to obtain sufficient financing to carry him through to the time when sales would cover his initial investment. Sixty percent of the design had been executed when he went bankrupt. Unfortunately, too many developers have failed to learn from this experience. The developers of such well-known master-planned communities as Forest Hills Gardens, Radburn, Reston, Columbia, and Kentlands all experienced the very same financial failure.

The Riverside combination of open front lawns, houses set back from the street, and tree-lined roadways remained the formula for innumerable suburban subdivisions built prior to World War II. Yet it proved ineffective in regions that do not easily support deciduous trees. In Maryvale, Arizona, a 2,000-acre (809-hectare) community six miles (ten kilometers) northwest of downtown Phoenix, there are a school and park at the heart of each of its subdivisions, with shopping at their corners. Within each subdivision, the plan repeats what had by then become routine: houses set back from tree-lined curvilinear streets. The trees, however, are not maples, elms, or oaks, which of course have difficulty surviving in Phoenix. They are palm trees that provide no shade from the desert sun and produce a naked public realm that only includes streets and sidewalks.

Few designers and developers of master-planned communities have been as sensitive as the Olmsted firm to difficult topography. The developers and designers of master-planned communities as different as Sea Ranch, California, and the Woodlands, Texas (see page 200), are among the exceptions. They have been as attentive to local landscape characteristics, views, drainage, and site planning as the Olmsteds.

Sea Ranch occupies 5,000 acres (2,023 hectares) along a dramatic ten-mile (16-kilometer) section of Pacific coastline, 100 miles (161 kilometers) north of San Francisco. In 1964, when Lawrence Halprin and Associates

Opposite, top left: Olmsted and Vaux made the most of a site's natural features and minimized its flaws. When the firm planned Cherokee Gardens in Louisville, Kentucky, in 1925, it placed streets in shallow valleys and along ridges to reduce drainage problems. Drainage streams parallel to roads became part of the community's open space system. **Opposite, top right:** Early-20th-century developers began to see the marketing advantage of convenient streetcar access. At Myers Park, North Carolina, just outside of downtown Charlotte, a streetcar median looped through the community so that no house was more than two blocks away. **Top:** The plan for Sea Ranch, California, a dramatic stretch of open, windswept grasslands overlooking the Pacific Ocean, capitalizes on the site's natural beauty. Wind, soil, and natural drainage patterns dictated the placement of housing, roads, pedestrian trails, and other elements of the plan. Recreation facilities are sheltered from the elements by cypress hedgerows planted by logging companies in the 1890s. Houses are clustered in open grassland owned in common by its residents. **Above:** The plan for Palos Verdes Estates by Frederick Law Olmsted, Jr., and Charles Cheney is based entirely on the site. Built into natural terraces on a peninsula overlooking Santa Monica Bay and the Los Angeles Basin, houses look as if they were a natural feature of the topography.

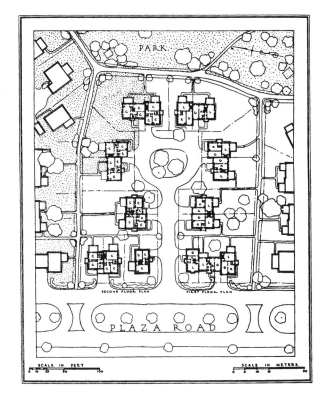

Right: The 1929 plan for Radburn, New Jersey, incorporated many innovative features, such as the use of extra large "superblocks" with interior parks and culs-de-sac to create common open green space, keep automobile through-traffic away from houses, and economize on the typical costs of land and infrastructure development. Pictured is a plan of houses grouped around a cul-de-sac.

Above, right: The Woodlands, Texas, is one of the nation's first large-scale master-planned communities. From its inception in 1974, the Woodlands has pioneered the blending of nature with modern development practices, creating a benchmark in balance and quality of community development.

Opposite, left: The Radburn idea of an open space backbone was taken to a new level at Baldwin Hills Village in Los Angeles. Eighty-acre (32-hectare) superblocks contained hundreds of residences grouped around garden courts that opened onto a half-mile village green.

Opposite, right: Columbia, Maryland, is one of a wave of large-scale new communities developed during the 1960s and 1970s. Envisioned as a place that was more than a real estate venture, developer James Rouse sought to reinvent cities with an emphasis on social interaction and well being, rather than on the structure of the plan itself.

began working on the design of this master-planned community for its Hawaii-based developer, Oceanic Properties, the site consisted of open grasslands interrupted by cypress windbreaks. Although the unpainted wooden houses clustered among the windswept grasses of Sea Ranch could not be more different from the California-Mediterranean red-tiled buildings that lined the streets of Palos Verdes Estates, Halprin's sensitive approach to the site was similar to that of the Olmsteds. Halprin took advantage of natural drainage channels, nestled recreation facilities where the cypresses could shelter them from the elements, and established a pedestrian trail along the edge of the cliffs. Required building roof pitches were based on the slopes that wind erosion had imposed on the cypress trees.[4]

The Woodlands, a 27,000-acre (10,927-hectare) master-planned community 31 miles (50 kilometers) north of Houston, was purchased in 1970 by the Mitchell Energy Company and financed privately with initial assistance federal guarantees.[5] The design, by ecological planner Ian McHarg, though quite different, was as appropriate to its site as Palos Verdes Estates or Sea Ranch. McHarg saved millions of dollars by eliminating the need for storm sewers. Instead, he designed a natural drainage system of wetlands, floodplains, ponds, streams, and ditches that removed sites from development that would otherwise have been costly and difficult to prepare for homebuilders. He identified woodlands that would have been expensive to clear, areas that were suitable as wildlife habitats, and sites with unique local vegetation. By connecting these quite different natural areas, McHarg provided a topographically determined open space framework around which the Woodlands could develop.

The open spaces that the Olmsteds and their followers designed consisted of private property and a public realm. Clarence Stein is responsible for promoting a third element: common open space. Common open space is territory that is jointly used by a group of people. It is not public because those who do not hold it in common can be excluded. It is not private either, because it has to be shared with others. Swimming pools, tot lots, and tennis courts often occupy this third form of open space.

The Radburn Idea

Along with Riverside, another master-planned community that greatly affected the design of new towns is the 149-acre (60-hectare) community of Radburn, in Fair Lawn, New Jersey, 16 miles (26 kilometers) west of New York City. Like Riverside, it succumbed to financial disaster (the Great Depression) before it could be completed; like Riverside, it was based on principles that are often misunderstood; and, like Riverside, it is well known principally to a handful of designers and historians. But, unlike Riverside, its attempt at community building went beyond streets, open spaces, and their relationship with the houses that surrounded them.

Clarence Stein and Henry Wright, the designers of Radburn, were among a group of Americans influenced by the English reformer, Ebenezer Howard. In 1898, Howard had published *A Peaceful Path to Real Reform*, better known under its later title, *Garden Cities of To-Morrow*. The book advocated creating a suburban utopia of "garden cities" that combined the best aspects of city and country.

Stein and Wright adapted Howard's ideas to the demands of America's automobile-based suburban market. They intended Radburn to be an agglomeration of individual subdivisions, called *superblocks*. A landscaped open space spine ran down the middle of each superblock, thereby eliminating through-traffic. Residents drove to a cul-de-sac, where there would otherwise have been a through-street, parked their car, and went into their house. When they walked out on the other side it was into a new living environment that included large amounts of common open space.

The design saved the money that would have been spent installing streets and utilities that otherwise would have extended from one street to the next. It also saved by eliminating sidewalks from both the bounding streets and the culs-de-sac. These savings were used to pay for landscaping, sidewalks, and lighting for common open space, which consisted of three components: (1) sidewalks connecting the backyards of houses whose other side faced a vehicular cul-de-sac, (2) the open space spine that otherwise would have been through-streets, and (3) pedestrian underpasses that allowed residents to walk to stores, school, and playing fields without risking a traffic accident.

Unlike Olmsted, who conceived of tree-lined streets as the locus of community interaction, Stein envisioned an internal open space system that provided a place for "common activities in which all members of the community can or do take part, in which all have an interest, [and] which bring[s] them together."[6] While this open space was owned and managed on behalf of Radburn residents, Stein conceived of it to be every bit as much a part of the public realm as its curvilinear streets.

The Radburn idea of an open space backbone was given its most characteristic expression at Baldwin Hills Village (known today as Village Green) in Los Angeles. In 1941, Stein explained that it combined "the complete convenience in the use of the automobile and a peaceful escape from its dangers."[7] At Baldwin Hills Village Stein switched from detached one- and two-family houses to clusters of two-story buildings, transforming the culs-de-sac into garage courts, turning the pedestrian walks into garden courts, and providing each family with a private patio. The result was an 80-acre (32-hectare) superblock containing 627 residences with three parking places for every family (one in the garage, one in an open-air parking space, and one along the street curb).

Common areas were more generous than at Radburn. Instead of a narrow sidewalk leading to recreational open space, residences were grouped around 100-foot-wide (30-meter-wide) garden courts that opened onto a 250-foot-wide (76-meter-wide) "village green" nearly a half-mile (one-eighth-kilometer) long. As at Radburn, the landscaping transformed a simple idea into a lovely natural area, in this case by clustering trees at two places to create three separate greens. A resident explained the role of the open space backbone, telling Stein: "When I can't sleep nights I walk down the length of the three greens. I can hardly believe I am in the heart of a great industrial metropolis. The quiet sense of security and peace is only broken by an occasional song of a night-singing mockingbird."[8]

During the Depression and World War II, there was little opportunity to adopt the "Radburn idea." After the War it became an integral part of the

Right: In recent decades, leapfrog suburban development has often produced cookie-cutter subdivisions such as this one in the San Francisco Bay area, in which there is virtually no common public space.

Opposite, left: The design for Seaside, Florida, a beachfront resort community on the Gulf of Mexico, triggered an urban design movement known as the new urbanism. Also called traditional neighborhood development (TND), the new urbanism seeks to restore family-centered living, neighborly interaction, and a pedestrian-oriented, community-based public realm.

Opposite, right: The first phase of the Disney Company's new master-planned community of Celebration, Florida, includes a mixed-use town center. The main street, Market Street, is flanked by three- and four-story buildings with retail space on the ground floors and offices and rental apartments on upper floors.

British government's major program of creating planned new towns. In America it took much longer to catch on. The few master-planned communities that tried to emulate Stein's work, such as Park Forest, Illinois, or Reston, Virginia, adopted watered-down aspects of the "Radburn idea." Most developers, unaware of Stein's work, created vehicular culs-de-sac and common open space because they appealed to the suburban market.

Park Forest was one of the first large new planned communities begun after World War II. Elbert Peets, who had worked with Clarence Stein on the design of Greendale, Wisconsin, prepared the first plans for this 3,151-acre (1,275-hectare) community. His 1946 and 1947 schemes for Park Forest were elaborations of the alternating garden and parking courts that Stein had used at Baldwin Hills Village, a project especially admired by Philip Klutznick, President of American Community Builders, developers of Park Forest. In fact, 3,010 of the 8,510 dwellings in Park Forest were two-story, rental rowhouses that easily obtained FHA mortgages because FHA officials were familiar with the scheme from having financed Baldwin Hills Village.[9]

Reston, Virginia (see page 182), an even better known master-planned community 22 miles (35 kilometers) west of Washington, D.C., begun by developer Robert Simon in 1961, also adopted aspects of the Radburn idea. Its 7,400 acres (2,995 hectares) are organized around open space "sinews" that provide play space, jogging and bicycle trails, and a bit of nature. They also provide vehicle-free pedestrian access to shopping and community facilities, via Radburn-inspired underpasses.

Columbia, Maryland, envisioned by James Rouse in the early 1960s as a place for a "more rational way of living," was created around vital "people living areas." Pathways connect Columbia's ten villages and their various components, and each village is surrounded by open space. Stream valleys formed the major element of the open space system and became potential sites along which lakes would be built. As often happens today, though, the desire to make open space more public by incorporating trails—versus more private with maximum home premiums—resulted in a balanced approach with a bias toward greater public access, which ultimately elevates the value of the entire community.

Since the 1960s there has been widespread adoption of Stein's idea of organizing housing around common open spaces, usually containing a swimming pool and community center. Whether these suburban subdivisions and condominium communities are gated or not, unlike Radburn, their pools and community centers are usually fenced in and restricted to community occupants.

The New Urbanism

Designers who used the Olmsted or Stein formula rarely produced the same extraordinary results. Olmsted's lot sizes and setbacks were often cut back to reduce the cost of land per dwelling lot. His topographically determined curvilinear streets were simplified and straightened to allow for faster and cheaper site preparation and house construction. In some cases all that remained of Olmsted's scheme were repetitive rows of little boxes with little front lawns and little backyards. The same thing happened to the Radburn idea. Common open space was devoted to revenue-producing golf courses or reduced to just a fenced-in swimming pool. Culs-de-sac could be extended to every nook and cranny, leaving virtually nothing for the public realm.

One reaction to what threatened to become an ever-expanding landscape of soulless subdivisions came from homebuilders. Many homebuilders—responding to what they had sold in the past, columned Colonial cottages and heavy-handed Spanish haciendas—devoted attention to private property and left the public realm to the government. Despite consumer acceptance, it quickly became evident that increasing house sizes, adding quasi-historical ornaments, and improving finishes did nothing to deal with the inadequate public realm.

Another reaction came from "environmentalists" who claimed to favor new development provided it did not intrude into areas that they did not wish changed. Their opposition to cookie-cutter subdivisions often generated litigation or legislation that substantially increased the time and cost of development. When litigation was finally settled and legislation adhered to, the open land set aside for public use frequently was too steep or too wet for inexpensive house construction or recreation. The resulting higher-

priced development with its difficult-to-use public realm was not the answer, either.

In the early 1980s, while working for developer Robert Davis on the design of Seaside, Florida, an 80-acre (32-hectare) master-planned beachfront community on the coast of the Gulf of Mexico, architects Andres Duany and Elizabeth Plater-Zyberk devised a very different alternative. After more than a century of suburban ticky-tacky, Duany and Plater-Zyberk were not willing to accept Olmsted's view that "we cannot judiciously attempt to control the form of the houses which men shall build, we can only, at most, take care that if they build very ugly inappropriate houses, they shall not be allowed to force them disagreeably upon our attention."[10] Olmsted's mid-19th-century formula for dealing with ugly houses was inappropriate for this beachfront community because the site could not support the large, deciduous trees that he used to shape the character of the public realm and screen out unsightly buildings. Instead, their firm, Duany Plater-Zyberk & Company (DPZ), determined the character of the houses that bounded public streets by instituting design requirements with which property owners had to comply.

At a gross density of four houses per acre (ten houses per hectare) (total site acreage divided by number of units), there was plenty of room for cars on the street. Consequently, there was no need for culs-de-sac or pedestrian underpasses. Nor was there any need for substantial amounts of open space, because recreation took place on the beach. Thus, DPZ had no reason to consider Stein's mid-20th-century scheme, either.

Davis wanted Seaside to have a distinctive, regional appearance. He took a series of trips, with and without his architects, to establish the common characteristics of traditional Florida Panhandle houses. Based on these trips, DPZ established the proportions, architectural details, and construction techniques that provided the basis for the vernacular architecture of picket fences, front porches, and gabled roofs required by the Seaside Code, the main governing document that controls the master plan and establishes the details of the building types on individual lots.

Davis had very little working capital. Consequently, he avoided making

any large initial cash investments. Street widths were kept to a minimum. At first, there was no paving. Paving and a packaged sewage treatment plant were installed after the proceeds from lot sales produced enough money to pay for them. Davis only invested in infrastructure in small increments, timed to coincide with lot sales. In doing so, he achieved what every community builder hopes for: cash outflow that is exceeded by revenues from lot sales.

Like the tree-lined streets of Riverside and the common open space at Radburn, Seaside's design has triggered an urban design movement that has become known as the new urbanism. In 1993, inspired by the promise of Seaside, a group of architects, planners, environmentalists, developers, public officials, academics, and others interested in the practices of traditional neighborhood development (TND) came together to form the Congress for the New Urbanism (CNU). They sparked a movement that has altered the public dialogue and provided marketable alternatives to many of the inadequacies of conventional suburban development.

The CNU favors suburban designs that restore family-centered living, neighborly interaction, and a pedestrian-oriented, community-based public realm (the same goals that Olmsted and Stein thought their designs had achieved). Its principles have been applied primarily to small subdivisions, HUD-sponsored redevelopment projects, and suburban codes adopted in lieu of traditional zoning ordinances. As of 2002, there were only a few new urbanist master-planned communities large enough to support the range of community and commercial facilities that would distinguish them from large subdivisions. The most important of them are Kentlands, Maryland (see page 118), and Celebration, Florida (see page 50).

Because Kentlands was more than four times the size of Seaside, the design goes beyond picket fences, front porches, and gabled roofs to deal with lot patterns and land uses as well. Its designer, DPZ, eliminated curb cuts from the sidewalk, moving driveways and garages to the rear of the houses, and introducing paved alleys that ran down the middle of the block. Opinions vary as to whether rear alleys are a desirable addition to the public realm. They do, however, increase the amount of land that has to be paved, reduce the amount of land available for backyards and, thus, increase the investment per square foot of salable lot.

It is impossible to reduce dependence on the automobile or encourage mixed land use except at the very high densities of major cities. Consequently, at Kentlands retail uses are in one area, institutional uses are in another, and most recreation is separate from both. All three are just far enough away from all but nearby houses that adults choose to drive and children to bicycle, just as they do in most suburbs.

Within the first three years of operation Joseph Alfandre, Kentlands's developer, invested nearly $70 million (including $40 million for acquisition and $20 million for site improvements). Unlike Robert Davis, he had accepted a plan that did not allow him to quickly recoup this investment from lot sales. Worse still, lots were put on the market just as the economy was entering a major recession. There was not enough revenue from sales to pay debt service. The Chevy Chase Bank foreclosed.

For its high-profile town of Celebration, the Disney Company's deep pockets precluded a similar financial catastrophe. It correctly determined that effective marketing of a master-planned community requires stores, schools, recreation, and as many community facilities as possible to be in place when residents move in, years before there are enough people to justify their creation. Because few developers can finance so large an up-front investment, this 9,500-acre (3,845-hectare) new town is a hard act to follow.

One example that may be more instructive is Country Club District, in Kansas City. The brainchild of J.C. Nichols, it became a model for such successful contemporaneous projects as Highland Park, outside Dallas, and Westwood Village in Los Angeles, and more recent ones like the Irvine Ranch in Orange County, California, and Easton and New Albany, Ohio.

Country Club District

Jesse Clyde Nichols was born to middle-income, farmer merchant parents in Olathe, Kansas, in 1880. At the age of 23, after graduating from the University of Kansas and spending a year at Harvard, he decided to enter the real estate business. Like so many other developers who began without capital, he borrowed money from friends, bought a lot, built a house, and

sold it at a profit. At first, the money came from farmers in Olathe, then from fraternity brothers, and in 1905 from two Kansas City investors (Frank Crowell and Herbert Hall) whose relationship with Nichols would generate a fortune and result in a master-planned community none of them initially had intended to create.[11]

They began in 1906 with a ten-acre subdivision. Within two years, it had grown into a 1,000-acre (405-hectare) assemblage. By 1940, Country Club District, as their venture came to be known, included 4,000 acres (1,619 hectares) and by 1980, 5,000 acres (2,023 hectares). Unlike the developers of Riverside, Radburn, or Kentlands, Nichols did not begin with a specific plan. But, like them, he had a planning vision.

The development process usually begins with a developer who obtains government approvals that "entitle" a property to be developed. Some developers subdivide their "entitled" property and sell it to other developers whose business is to erect and market houses. Nichols did both. He also was deeply involved in providing access by public transportation and private automobile, retail stores, community facilities, and every other activity involved in creating successful communities.

Convenient access was central to Nichols's marketing strategy. He was convinced that the key to selling houses lay in improving automobile access. The accuracy of his foresight is remarkable when one realizes that in 1908, there were only 391 licensed motorcars in the city. Nichols and his partners persuaded neighboring property owners that parkway access would improve the marketability of their houses. In 1908, Nichols and other nearby owners deeded to the city the land that became Mill Creek Parkway. Unlike Kessler's early roadways, however, Mill Creek Parkway was dedicated parkland, sometimes several hundred feet across. The rights-of-way that passed through the parkway soon were being used as much by motorcars as by horses or carriages. Nichols had been right. By 1914, there were 9,774 registered automobiles in the city, many of them owned by families who had purchased houses from the Nichols Company.[12]

While the Nichols Company contributed land for Mill Creek and later Ward Parkway as a way of extending automobile access to its property, it

Opposite and left: J.C. Nichols, developer of the Country Club District, a master-planned community in Kansas City, Missouri, engaged in practices that were unusually forward-looking for real estate developers of his day. Nichols saw the potential for developing and owning retail centers as a profitable enterprise and as

a strategy for building community. In 1922, he developed The Country Club Plaza (left), generally recognized as America's first suburban shopping center, in the heart of the community.

did not pay maintenance and operating costs; Kansas City covered the cost of building and maintaining these and other roads that provided access to the Country Club District. The Nichols Company did not have to install the sewers, either. Beginning in 1911, Nichols persuaded the city to annex property his company was planning to develop, thereby transferring responsibility for and cost of providing water and sewer service to the government.

Nichols began referring to his various subdivisions as "The Country Club District" in 1908, due to their proximity to area golf and social clubs. These country clubs, along with schools and churches, provided the basis for the "wholesome home life with relevant neighborliness and closely interwoven community interest" that Nichols believed were essential to a successful master-planned community. He made sure country clubs and schools could afford a location within his subdivisions by contributing land or selling it at a discount. The churches, which had to pay market price for land, were able to locate in the District because Nichols made substantial contributions to their building funds.

In 1921, Nichols added two elements to the development of master-planned communities that would be copied across the country: homeowner associations and shopping centers. The Country Club District Homes Association provided a forum for the discussion of community concerns, a vehicle that could enforce property restrictions, and an elementary form of governance.[13] The more remarkable innovation was Country Club Plaza, one of America's first modern shopping centers. In 1920, plenty of stores in the United States occupied a single structure owned and managed by a single entity. Nichols's breakthrough came in (1) locating a large group of stores where they were visible and easily accessible from the Mill Creek Parkway, (2) giving them a common, distinguishing appearance, (3) providing off-street parking and loading for customers and merchants, and (4) coordinating hours of operation, providing sanitation and security services, and promoting and managing the center as a single business. The Plaza quickly became a significant profit center for the Nichols Company. But the Plaza was also an important way of attracting customers who purchased houses and rented apartments on Nichols's property.

The example of Country Club Plaza was copied by Hugh Prather, one of the developers of Highland Park, a master-planned community four miles (six kilometers) north of Dallas. Its layout followed the Olmsted formula of houses on large lots set back from tree-lined streets. Like the Country Club District, its marketability had been enhanced by the presence of a country club. Prather grasped the marketing significance of adding a shopping center and began to create his complex in 1929.[14]

The Janns Investment Company was developing a similar shopping-center-based community, now known as Westwood, on the western edge of Los Angeles. The site was initially subdivided and sold for single-family houses. In 1925, a 384-acre (155-hectare) portion was selected by the regents of the University of California as the site for its UCLA campus. Like the Plaza, Westwood Village quickly became the community's retail center, as well as one of the city's major regional subcenters.[15]

The Nichols Legacy

In 1936, J.C. Nichols became one of the founding members of ULI—the Urban Land Institute. Hugh Prather and Harold Janns were among its earliest members. ULI showed its growing commitment to master-planned communities when it issued its first book, *The Community Builders Handbook*. The primer presented practical information on community development, as well as Nichols's own thoughts on the matter: "In our early 'single residential' developments we overestimated our market and acquired too much land—creating too large a carrying load in interest, taxes, and maintenance."[16]

Few developers are able to avoid an up-front cash outlay to acquire a site. Some inherit the land, as did Seaside's developer Robert Davis, and some own the land for purposes other than real estate development and later decide to develop it. One of the most notable examples of a large-scale master-planned community that did not become overburdened with large carrying costs was the Irvine Ranch. The 93,100-acre (37,676-hectare) site in Orange County, California, was purchased in 1864 by a consortium including James Irvine, who bought out his partners shortly thereafter. In 1960, when the Irvine Company decided to transform the property into a master-planned community, no cash outlays were needed to cover the cost of carrying the site because its farming activities generated more cash than was needed to cover operating costs and taxes.

Like Nichols's venture, the Irvine Ranch is far more than a subdivision with supporting community facilities. The Irvine Ranch is an important regional employment base and it supports several major shopping centers. Today, the Irvine Ranch includes all of the city of Irvine, portions of the cities of Newport Beach, Tustin, Orange, Laguna Beach, and Anaheim, as well as unincorporated land in Orange County. These communities provide homes for more than 200,000 residents and employment for 250,000 workers. The importance of regional centers in the tradition of Country Club Plaza and the Irvine Ranch cannot be overemphasized. They bring shoppers and employees who provide the street life missing from countless master-planned communities. They constitute a market for residential sales and rentals. And most important, they generate taxes that pay for the schools, parks, and government services that too many new communities cannot afford.

New Albany and Easton, northeast of Columbus, Ohio, are among the most interesting master-planned communities currently underway. Easton is emerging on a 1,300-acre (526-hectare) site adjoining the national headquarters of the Limited, Inc., which purchased the property in the mid-1980s. The 2,750-acre (1,113-hectare) site of New Albany began to be assembled at about the same time by Les Wexner, president and CEO of the Limited. Both projects are the product of a joint venture with the Georgetown Company, organized and directed in 1975 by developer Marshall Rose.

Wexner, Rose, and his associates Edgar Lampert and Adam Flatto are avowed admirers of the Country Club District. Like Nichols, their development strategy is based on the same attempt to avoid "too large a carrying load in interest, taxes, and maintenance." Like Nichols, they have let the planning of Easton and New Albany proceed in response to market demand.

One way in which the cost of carrying the initial investments in infrastructure and public services has been minimized at New Albany has been the emphasis on creating a commercial tax base. As of 2001, ten companies with 8,000 employees had settled on 650 acres (263 hectares) of its 1,200-acre (486-hectare) business park, producing 25 percent of the revenues of New Albany's operating budget. Additional revenues will come from the planned 700-acre (283-hectare) science and technology complex adjoining the business park. Wexner believed the northeast quadrant of metropolitan Columbus, just beyond the airport, was likely to experience major growth. Consequently, he began acquiring property in the area before land prices escalated. Like Nichols, Wexner decided to enhance accessibility to the area by paying for the engineering drawings, contributing land for interchanges leading into Easton from the Interstate-270 beltway, and contributing to the cost of the extension of Highway 161 leading to New Albany, five miles (eight kilometers) further northeast.

Just as Nichols emphasized the point of arrival at Country Club Plaza by erecting buildings inspired by the architecture of Seville, Spain, the points of arrival to Easton and New Albany are carefully controlled. The railings on I-270 overpasses leading into Easton spell out "Easton." Drivers arriving in New Albany encounter white-painted, wooden fences common in horse country. These fences enclose all its major open spaces and distinguish New Albany from ordinary suburban developments.

New Albany might well be called a country club district. At its center are a country club inspired by 18th-century English Palladian–style villas, a tennis club, and a 27-hole golf course. Unlike most golf course communities, the links are not hidden behind houses. Consequently, passersby see large expanses of landscaped open space while taking a stroll, jog, or ride along the golf course.

In fact, 35 percent of New Albany is devoted to open space. Laurie Olin, the designer of its open space framework, identified natural features around which to organize development sites. At New Albany they include creek beds, existing hedgerows, and scenic views tied together by natural area corridors that are designed to sustain use by wandering children and adult joggers, as well as local animals.

The rest of the public realm at New Albany includes a fire station, post office, parks, swimming pools, a village center, a library, and a high school inspired by Jefferson's University of Virginia. At buildout, they will provide

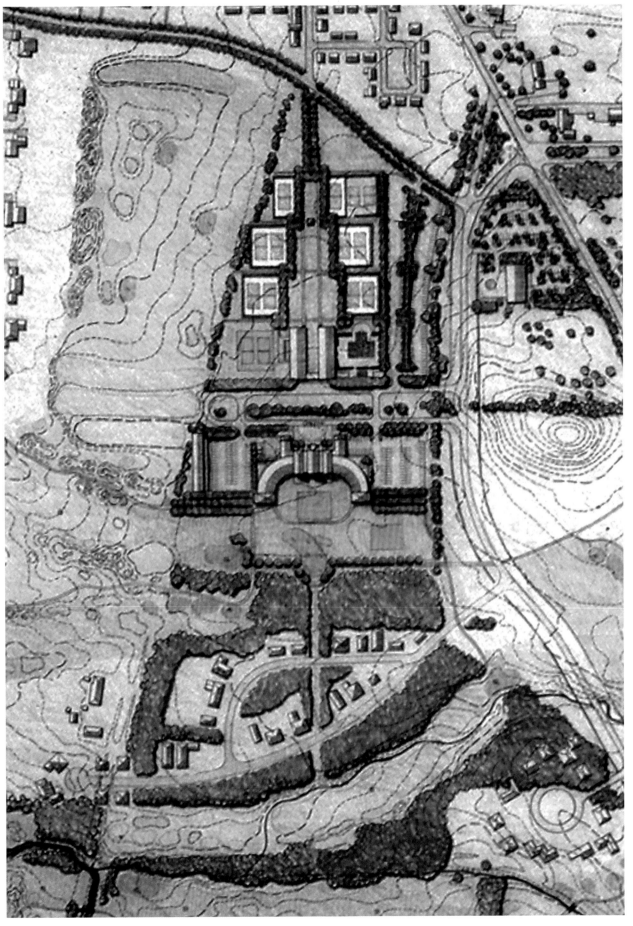

The main elements of the plan 27
for a country club district in
the center of New Albany, a
new master-planned commu-
nity outside of Columbus, Ohio,
are a country club inspired
by English Palladian–style
villas, a tennis club, and a 27-
hole golf course. Views of the
golf course are not hidden
behind houses but are open to
passersby.

Scheme A

MORSE ROAD

INTERSTATE 270

TARGET GREATLAND

THE CHILLER AT EASTON

LOWE'S HOME IMPROVEMENT

WORTH AVENUE

SOCCER BARN

EASTON MARKET

NORTHEAST CAREER CENTER

ALADDIN CONVENTION CENTER

THE LIMITED INC. WORLD HEADQUARTERS

TOWN CENTER

COLLIERY STREET

MORSE CROSSING

EASTON WAY

STELZER ROAD

EASTON BRIDGE

VICTORIA'S SECRET CATALOGUE HEADQUARTERS

EASTON COMMONS

SUNBURY ROAD

HUNTINGTON NATIONAL BANK

LEGEND

TOWN CENTER
RETAIL
HOTEL
RECREATIONAL

Committed / Planned
OFFICE
RESIDENTIAL
OTHER

GRAPHIC SCALE
WALKING DISTANCE

DEVELOPMENT DESIGN GROUP INC.

EASTON.

LIMITED GEORGETOWN STEINER & ASSOCIATES INC.

Opposite and left: A regional-scale town center is at the heart of the plan for Easton, Ohio, a 1,300-acre (526-hectare) master-planned community just within the city limits of Columbus. Surrounded by a mix of residential, recreational, and office development, Easton Town Center recalls the classic American downtown. The town center's 13 buildings are organized along intersecting streets and around a central town square (left).

community foci for the projected 3,160 households living in 46 different neighborhoods, each slightly different in character, house size, and price range.

Wexner and the Georgetown Company are making Easton into a 21st-century, central Ohio version of Country Club Plaza. Only a short drive from downtown Columbus, and an even shorter drive from the airport, Easton is, like the Plaza, fast becoming the "midtown" focus of the metropolitan region. Like the Plaza, it is also far more than a shopping center. As of 2001, Easton already included over 6 million square feet (half a million square meters) of office buildings, hotels, power centers, recreational facilities, housing, and a forest preserve. At the center of it all is the 77-acre (31-hectare) Easton Town Center, a 1.5 million-square-foot (139,355-square-meter) retail complex of squares, streets, and sidewalks. Its site design is the work of the Georgetown Company working with Jaquelin Robertson. The buildings themselves were designed by Development Design Group.

Community Building in the 21st Century
When American cities began outgrowing their initial grid plans in the 19th century, they had to create complex water, sewer, open space, and road systems that were inconceivable at the time they were established. In much the same way Country Club District, the Irvine Ranch, and other successful 20th-century, suburban master-planned communities have opened new territory without adhering rigidly to their initial designs or predetermined property restrictions.

Olmsted understood this need for flexibility very well. In describing his earliest work on Central Park in New York, he explained that the people who come "this year or next are but a small fraction of those who must be expected." For this reason, he advocated planning that considered more than "the land use of the next few years."[17]

Flexible planning requires a public realm that forms the armature around which healthy communities grow. It does not matter whether that public realm consists of tree-lined streets bounded by houses set back from the street (as is the case with Olmsted-inspired subdivisions), or recreational open spaces used in common by the occupants of the residences that surround them (as is the case in Radburn-inspired condominium communities), or the busy commercial district of a regional subcenter (as is the case at Country Club Plaza). Whatever form it takes, the public realm must be appropriate to the location and people who use it.

The minimal roadways at 80-acre (32-hectare) Seaside provide public access to the beach that is the raison d'être for this 326-house resort. Such roadways would be completely inadequate in the middle of Los Angeles, particularly on the 80 acres (32 hectares) of Baldwin Hills Village with double the number of residences. That region's glorious Pacific beaches are six miles away and its large wilderness parks and vehicular arteries provide few gathering places. In Los Angeles, the nearly half-mile-long green provides Baldwin Hills Village with a lovely, tree-lined, community-building asset. But, a village green of this sort would be of little use at a beach resort like Seaside.

In the spirit of such flexible planning this book presents contemporary master-planned communities of every size and variety. They demonstrate that there is no one *correct* way to design or develop such projects. The good ones provide a public realm as compelling to their residents and responsive to their environment as any created by the Olmsteds. Many include shared, common open spaces as useful as those created at Radburn or Baldwin Hills Village. The best of them include a marketable mix of lot sizes and buildings as appealing as those of Seaside. But all of them have, in their own ways, been successful in achieving a wide range of goals—from traditional neighborhood developments to innovative sustainable communities; higher density "urban" villages to scenic, resort-style sanctuaries; retail and commercial hubs to areas with a more residential and recreational orientation. Just as Olmsted, Stein, and Nichols pioneered concepts in planning and development that later became textbook standards, others continue to build on their legacy using ever-inventive strategies. This visual tour of present-day master-planned communities presents a broad spectrum of examples, underscoring the belief that there are as many approaches to creating a community as there are people who live in them.

CONTEMPORARY
COMMUNITIES

BEACON COVE

The historic waterfront of Port Melbourne, once a thriving shipping center, has been transformed into Beacon Cove, a residential community designed with an eye to the site's industrial heritage and its dramatic locale on Port Phillip Bay. The master-planned community, which is 2.5 miles (four kilometers) from the central business district of Melbourne, is a public-private initiative marketed to young professionals who want all the benefits of living in an urban environment, including an easy commute to work.

Developed by Mirvac in a joint venture with the state government of Victoria's Office of Major Developments, the 91-acre (38-hectare) site is to be built out over a 14-year period between 1996 and 2009, with a total of 1,517 residential units and 17 acres (seven hectares) of open space and recreational amenities. The design team worked to integrate the new construction into the existing inland suburban neighborhood, while emphasizing the site's maritime roots. A diverse range of housing types and densities, designed by Mirvac's in-house team, HPA Architects, Planners & Interiors, is organized into a pedestrian-oriented plan with a three-acre (one-hectare) town center and a generous promenade along the bay.

Blending with the Bay

Long after the port's days as a shipping center ended and after a short second life as a petroleum depot, the state of Victoria remediated a large swath of Port Melbourne for redevelopment in the 1980s. After a failed attempt by a private developer to build a mixed-use complex of office towers and housing, the state government stepped in, inviting community residents to take part in a design charrette in 1992 at the Port Melbourne Town Hall. With design parameters influenced by community input, the Victorian government issued a detailed call for proposals, resulting in a joint initiative with Mirvac that became Beacon Cove.

Port Melbourne is not only the site of Melbourne's first seaport and the country's first steam railroad, built in 1854, but it also possesses two of the largest timber-piled wharf structures in the southern hemisphere. With such historic riches, preservation and restoration efforts were important to longtime residents—and a marketable asset for Beacon Cove.

Among the maritime structures preserved by the developers are the Port Melbourne Channel Lights, two historic concrete lighthouses constructed in 1924 to guide the increasingly larger ships plying the waters around Melbourne in the port's heyday. The 78-foot-tall (24-meter-tall) Rear Tower, located about 1,800 feet (549 meters) inland at the far end of Beacon Cove, is still in operation, its flashing lights visible from 20 nautical miles (37 kilometers); the Front Tower, no longer working, is approximately 1,500 feet (457 meters) offshore. Both beacons have been restored, giving the community its name. In fact, a new boulevard named Beacon Vista, which serves as a main artery in the master plan, establishes a view corridor between the two lighthouses.

Creating an Urban Fabric

The developers and planners of Beacon Cove were keen on producing a vibrant and vital public realm, which is played out in the large percentage of parks and open spaces and in the clustered commercial district known as Civic Square. Adjacent to the Princes Pier, one of the original piers in the bay, the square is occupied by a childcare center, a gymnasium, a sports and recreation center, a medical center, neighborhood grocery and convenience store, restaurants, and cafes.

Civic Square is also a transportation hub, with a light rail station for commuters, the restored Port Melbourne railway station, and the terminal on nearby Station Pier, which serves Victoria's trans-Tasman lines, local ferries, and international passenger cruise ships. The square is the organizing element off which can be found the promenade, a network of public parks, public beaches, and open spaces. Directly linked to the promenade, Civic Square is surrounded by high-density residential buildings to maximize patronage for shop owners, restaurants, and other commercial entities.

Stage 1 of development, completed and fully occupied within four years, consists of 469 attached, detached, and semiattached housing units and 368 condominiums in four waterfront apartment towers; three-story townhouses with home offices; and low-rise apartment buildings. Two years later, Civic Square got its light rail station, providing service to Melbourne

P. EDGELEY
DIGITAL 2001

Previous page: An artist's rendering of Beacon Cove when completed. Depicted are the development of two existing piers in Port Melbourne, waterfront high-rise apartment buildings, and low-rise housing behind.

Above: The Stage 2 development concept proposes a mix of high-, mid-, and low-rise housing in the horseshoe-shaped area surrounding Princes Pier, as well as redevelopment of the Heritage-listed pier itself to support apartments and leisure activities.

Opposite, top left: The combination of fashionable new beachfront housing only 2.5 miles (four kilometers) from Melbourne, Australia's second-largest city, proved especially appealing to young, urban-oriented professionals.

Opposite, top right: Stage 1 of Beacon Cove's development is complete and comprises 838 dwelling units and all elements of Civic Square, the community's commercial district. Stage 2, located behind Station Pier, the longer of the two piers, will introduce another 679 units.

Opposite, bottom: Front Light, the restored historic offshore lighthouse, and Melbourne's skyscrapers bracket Beacon Cove's high rises, which offer spectacular views.

and its suburbs. The first stage also included construction of the 1,500-foot-long (457-meter-long) promenade that connects the port's two large piers, Station and Princes Piers, as well as Sandridge, a public beach restored as part of the development agreement between Mirvac and the state government.

The orientation, height, and density of the residential structures give primacy to water views. The plan positions the tallest buildings—four large apartment towers between ten and 13 stories, with their longest facades to the bay—along the waterfront promenade, with a gradual reduction in the height and density of buildings further inland. Three- and four-story terrace home-office-style units are on the inland side of the towers, providing a transition between the high rises on the water to the south and the low-rise housing areas to the north.

Low-rise units come in several different configurations and sizes, from large, semidetached homes and paired courtyard houses to single-story courtyard homes. Many of the units in the low-rise residential buildings have large, open-plan rooms on the ground floor, which are suitable for use as a home office, and living spaces on the second floor with terraces and balconies. Staggered building lines and strategic placement of windows, balconies, and terraces maximize views to the bay and the lighthouses.

Stage 2 of Mirvac's master plan continues the varied density and mixture of housing types that characterize the first stage. And it is equally ambitious in its scope and reclamation of Port Melbourne's industrial heritage. The Cove, built out over the water, is to have four eight-story apartment buildings

that provide a protective arm around a 42-berth marina. Adjacent to Sand-ridge Beach, there is to be a 12-story condominium tower constructed on a landscaped podium over basement-level parking, as are all the towers in the community. The landmark Princes Pier, which is currently closed to the public, would have its historic gatehouse restored and a lookout and kiosk added to its farthest end. New development around the marina and the pier will add 231 apartments. A 1.2-mile (two-kilometer) extension of the prom-enade is also planned, along with a waterfront park.

Location, Location, Location

In the decades following World War II, Australia's suburbs grew rapidly, as they did in metropolitan areas throughout the industrialized world, leaving many port areas to lie fallow. By the 1990s, significant changes in lifestyles and family structures refueled an interest in city life. Beacon Cove was posi-tioned to capitalize on this cultural shift. Indeed, the largest demographic group among Beacon Cove's population is the 25 to 34 age range, single or

Above, left and right: With a predominance of multifamily product—high and medium-rise apartments, low-rise attached (terrace) housing, low-rise attached (mews), and semidetached (courtyard) housing—Beacon Cove met the demand of a residential market that has shifted dra-matically in the last decade from suburban back to urban living.

married but without children, who were attracted to the metropolitan location, short commute to downtown Melbourne, and low-maintenance living quarters (no lawns to mow). The romance of waterside life, the convenience of shops and services in Civic Square, and the plentitude of park and recreational spaces were also appealing.

   A study by a real estate research firm found that 22.5 percent of residents in the Beacon Cove area did not own a car, while the corresponding figure for the Melbourne metropolitan area was only 11.8 percent. Similarly, 21.6 percent of Beacon Cove residents live in detached houses, as compared to 76.3 percent for metropolitan Melbourne. The statistics speak to the success of the master plan to provide a walkable community, where building density is used as a tool to create an active street life, both along the waterfront and in the commercial district.

Above: The demographic attracted by Beacon Cove favors apartment or terrace housing because of its low maintenance, urban waterfront setting, and proximity to big-city commerce, culture, and conveniences. Contemporary architectural styles reflect the urban setting.

Right and below: To promote walking within the community and reduce the time spent on yard maintenance, private open space was minimized in favor of landscaped public areas with pedestrian linkages.

Opposite: Civic Square, Beacon Cove's mixed-use district, is a public transportation hub and the nexus for retail, commercial, and civic facilities, including (top) a recreation center; (bottom, left) a grocery/café; and (bottom, right) a childcare center.

BONITA BAY

BONITA SPRINGS, FLORIDA

In 1979, David Shakarian, chairman of Bonita Bay Properties, Inc., began assembling land just north of Naples in Bonita Springs, Florida, for environmentally responsible development. Shakarian wanted to create a luxurious, self-contained ecological sanctuary for active adult and second-home buyers where "people and nature could live harmoniously." He had no professional background as a planner, developer, or designer, but he championed concepts of sustainability before they became guiding principles of community planning. After his death in 1984, David Lucas, Shakarian's son-in-law, was named chairman of Bonita Bay Properties, Inc., now the Bonita Bay Group (BBG), and charged with implementing his vision.

Bonita Bay is a 2,400-acre (971-hectare) master-planned community with an ecologically based plan that preserves or enhances multiple ecosystems. Unlike many other sites in south Florida, the Bonita Bay site was unspoiled; it had not been farmed or otherwise altered by human activity. Water—Estero Bay, Imperial River, and Spring Creek—surrounds the site on three sides and incorporates a range of delicate ecosystems, from fresh- and salt-water marshes to mangrove stands, hardwood hammocks, a pristine river, and a creek. At an overall density of only 1.4 units per acre, fewer than 3,300 residences are woven into a series of intimate enclaves that overlook the Gulf of Mexico, the bay, lakes, golf courses, and nature preserves.

Preservation Drives Design

Planning for Bonita Bay was done in the early 1980s, before the environmental movement gained significant momentum. BBG performed the most thorough site assessment ever undertaken in southwest Florida, identifying 40 different habitat types and mapping 22 different drainage basins on the property. Preservation of these natural features and the sensitive ecosystem has been the primary focus of design.

The master plan for Bonita Bay does not rely on a strong geometric pattern, axial, loop, grid, or other formal structure. Rather, it is based on evaluating the natural systems of the site and then identifying suitable development areas. The resultant development pattern reflects the complexity of the underlying natural systems. By saving or moving many specimen trees and selectively clearing land, BBG preserved hundreds of acres of wildlife habitat, including a bald eagle's nest discovered in the early 1980s where a pair of eagles has since reared roughly 20 chicks.

Twelve miles of bicycle and walking paths, which encourage residents to avoid automobile use, crisscross the community and lead to three waterfront parks, the marina, the tennis and fitness center, and the golf clubhouse. Community parks were designed to accommodate a variety of residents' interests and activities. Spring Creek Park includes a playground, secluded picnic areas with grills and hiking trails, and a canoe launch. Estero Bay Park features an 800-foot (244-meter) boardwalk to Estero Bay and parallels the original North Naples pier, which dates back to the early 1900s. A butterfly garden, screened pavilion for nature lectures, playground, and picnic sites are also inside the park. Riverwalk Park overlooks the Imperial River and includes a playground, multiple picnic sites, two lighted tennis courts, a 12-station Parcourse, fitness trail, basketball court, boat ramp, and day slips.

Bonita Bay opened for sales in 1985 with one golf course and 9,000 units in its master plan. But as interest in golf and lower-density housing intensified, BBG revised the master plan to convert commercial and residential property into two more on-site golf courses, reducing the unit count to 3,300 and eliminating a proposed regional mall concept. These adjustments resulted in a more upscale and less dense character and better met changing market conditions. It is notable—and rare—that a developer would make such a dramatic mid-course correction in response to the market, especially when it means reducing the unit count by two thirds.

Visual Harmony

Within the framework of extensive waterways and golf courses, 53 single-product neighborhoods are situated to maximize views and emphasize Bonita Bay's pastoral character. Each neighborhood has a specific product and architectural theme, ranging from European cobblestone streets with Mediterranean architecture to "Old Florida" style with tin roofs and pastel color schemes. Neighborhoods can contain from 18 to 120 homes.

Opening page: The Marina Club, offering 125 wet slips and 350 dry slips, has direct access to the Gulf of Mexico via the Imperial River.

Above, clockwise from top left: The award-winning Bonita Bay West Club is at the heart of the community's social infrastructure, offering an array of golf, tennis, swimming, and fitness options in addition to dining, banquet, meeting, and retail facilities. The Crossings and Greenbriar, Bonita Bay's two condominium neighborhoods, offer a multitude of housing choices in a variety of settings, all of which stress views, amenities, and convenience.

The project relies on extensive design review and landscaping requirements. Strict architectural standards were established to ensure that the diverse mix of single-family and attached residences was designed and built consistent with the company's ecologically sensitive principles. The result is a clearly apparent harmony between man and nature throughout Bonita Bay. Views from streets and trails always seem to have a foreground of natural landscape with architectural massing subservient to vegetation. This is achieved, in part, by siting houses back from collector roads, requiring an extensive buffering system, and preserving natural features within each neighborhood. Landscaping incorporates existing vegetation and is supplemented with native species. The community's primary thoroughfare is lushly landscaped to reinforce the natural beauty of the site.

BBG has worked to coordinate efforts with local planning and zoning officials to shape signage and architectural design standards for new development along the U.S. 41 corridor, the entry highway to the community. The product of this collaboration is a corridor of aesthetically appealing character that is distinct from other areas in the region.

Sustainability in Action

An extensive site assessment was analyzed to ensure that lakes were properly positioned with respect to the natural water flow on site. To protect the delicate Estero Bay ecosystem, natural wetlands were preserved and a storm water system created to allow plants to filter out silt, nutrients, and pollutants. After 20 years of water quality monitoring, there have been

Environmentally ahead of its
time, the guiding principle of
this early-eighties master plan
was to preserve and enhance
the area's natural, historical,
and archaeological features.
Neighborhoods were planned
around the natural topography
and vegetation, and one-half
of the 2,400-acre (971-hectare)
site is open space.

43

44   **Right: Five Audubon-certified 18-hole golf courses represent just one of the many outdoor activities available at Bonita Bay, which also boasts more than 200 lakes, four water-front parks, ten miles (16 kilometers) of bicycling and jogging trails, and educational programs dedicated to environmental stewardship.**

46

Above and opposite: With one of the lowest densities of any community in the area, the 51 distinctive, intimate neighborhoods of Bonita Bay offer a mix of housing types responsive to diverse lifestyles. From single-family estate homes to luxury high-rise condominiums, villas, patio homes, and carriage houses, all are situated to take full advantage of the site's natural and man-made attributes.

no significant long-term effects due to land development or golf course maintenance at the community.

In fact, all five of Bonita Bay's golf courses have received the Audubon Sanctuary certification, which means they are maintained according to Audubon International's strict standards to preserve and enhance the natural ecosystem. The courses have a very small percentage of turf and maintain indigenous plant materials. A wildlife survey was performed prior to construction of the Bonita Bay East courses and again seven years later. The number of listed species observed increased by 50 percent postdevelopment.

An integrated program of environmental management has been established that includes a natural pest-management program, recycling natural materials, leaving snag trees undisturbed to provide habitat, restricting pesticide application anywhere on the property, making hand-pulling of weeds standard procedure, and planting native grasses to reduce maintenance and to provide for wildlife.

A sophisticated dual-line water delivery system was created to separately provide high-quality potable and treated reuse water for irrigation to homes. Xeriscape principles were implemented throughout the property before the concept was even widely understood, and the South Florida Water Manager District named Bonita Bay the region's first Xeriscape demonstration site in recognition of its innovative water-conservation practices. The community's irrigation practices save nearly 11 million gallons of water per year.

BBG held on to the commercial sites until the mature stages of the project, allowing the firm to draw upscale retail with an above average lease rate. The Promenade, an upscale shopping and dining center, is built around outdoor waterfalls, a sprawling amphitheater, domed gazebo, and rich, Mediterranean colors. It contains five restaurants, more than 20 boutiques and upscale apparel shops, and an art gallery. In addition, Bonita Bay includes a hotel, an adult living facility, and a medical center. The array of support services is such that residents don't have to drive outside the community unless they choose to.

Clustered neighborhoods of single-family, coach, and carriage homes, as well as luxury high-rise condominiums (some reaching 24 stories), overlook the gulf, bay, lakes, golf courses, and nature preserves. Home prices range from $200,000 for an attached carriage home to $4.7 million for a custom single-family home. Of the total 3,300 residential units planned, 2,810 have been built.

Bonita Bay's water management system, which follows the natural contours of the land, employs indigenous vegetation to filter silt and pollutants from storm water runoff. The community's governing documents mandate use of Xeriscaping, the planting of hardy, drought-tolerant native plants.

49

CELEBRATION

CELEBRATION, FLORIDA

When the Walt Disney Company purchased 27,000 acres (10,927 hectares) of undeveloped land near Orlando, Florida, in the mid 1960s to build a theme park, part of Walt Disney's vision was to develop a futurist community called EPCOT ("Experimental Prototype Community of Tomorrow"). Plans were drawn up for the new town, but when Walt Disney died in 1966, the idea for EPCOT evolved instead into a futurist theme park.

Getting to Square One

Walt Disney's vision for a new town remained dormant until the mid 1980s when Disney CEO Michael Eisner recognized that after the current planned attractions were built, approximately 10,000 acres (4,047 hectares) of undeveloped land would still remain. Eisner created the Disney Development Company, headed by Peter Rummell. One of the projects undertaken was to design and build a new town of 5,000 to 6,000 housing units and over 2 million square feet (185,806 square meters) of commercial development. Planning began in 1991, after the Celebration Company was established to plan, manage, and develop the community's buildout. Construction started in spring 1995.

The major road infrastructure and office park were completed first, followed by the town center and adjacent residential area which was known as Celebration Village. The buildout of other planned residential neighborhoods is now under development. The Celebration Company is the community's master developer as well as builder and owner of the town center, golf course, and some of the initial office buildings. The residential areas are planned, developed, and marketed by the Celebration Company. For the largest lots, individual house lots were sold to homeowners who then contracted with approved homebuilders. All other lots were sold to approved builders, who built houses under the aesthetic review of the Celebration Company and resold them to homeowners.

For the town's master plan, Disney held an invited competition involving four nationally known architectural firms (Gwathmey Siegel & Associates, Duany Plater-Zyberk & Company, Robert A. M. Stern Architects, and Edward D. Stone, Jr., and Associates). Of the four firms, three submitted

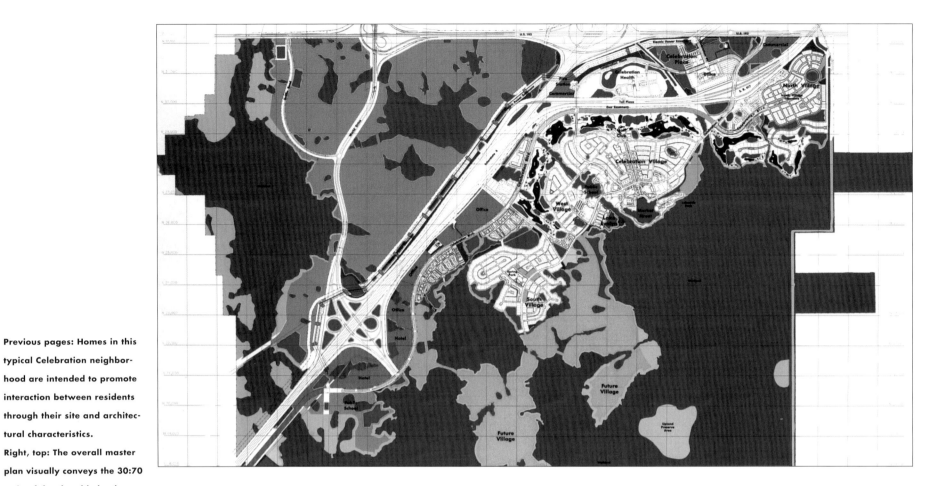

52 Previous pages: Homes in this typical Celebration neighborhood are intended to promote interaction between residents through their site and architectural characteristics.

Right, top: The overall master plan visually conveys the 30:70 ratio of developable land to preserved open space.

Right, bottom: As depicted in the site plan, Celebration Village is encircled by a 4,700-acre (1,902-hectare) greenbelt and features an extensive network of walking and bicycle trails.

Below: A footbridge adorns
one of the many natural water
features found in Celebration,
where the landform and environmental integrity were key
factors in establishing development areas.

designs based on new urbanist concepts. A consensus plan was subsequently prepared in a design charrette with those three firms. The Celebration Company then embarked on the complicated process of securing entitlements for the project from local and state authorities. Environmental concerns and program changes resulted in three more master plan competitions. The final plan was completed by a joint venture of one of the original invited firms, Robert A. M. Stern Architects, and a new firm, Cooper, Robertson & Partners. EDAW became the landscape architects and Urban Design Associates (UDA) prepared the Celebration Pattern Book.

Deferring to the Site
The master plan responds to the ecological features of this virtually flat site, conserving 5,000 acres (2,023 hectares) of Central Florida natural habitat. Valuable wetlands, tree stands, and water areas were preserved, with development sites confined to 4,900 acres (1,983 hectares) of environmentally nonsensitive land. Because of the meandering form of the protected natural

areas, the portions earmarked for development consist of peninsulas and islands in a sea of natural vegetation, connected by landscaped boulevards, parkways, and trails.

Celebration Village (including the town center) and the golf course are located on the largest piece of developable land. Other residential villages are sited on smaller adjacent parcels, but are connected to the town center by the street network and trail system. An office park, a health center, and highway-oriented large-scale retail development are located near new interchanges with Interstate I-4 and Route U.S.192.

Celebration's hierarchical street system ranges from wide, landscaped boulevards connecting the development areas to narrow streets and alleys in the residential villages. The road layouts in the residential villages vary from neighborhood to neighborhood, but the general strategy is a curving grid punctuated by parks that act as focal points.

Creating a sense of place was a major effort of the master plan design team, both for the town center and the residential villages. The resultant

Less than a ten-minute walk from every Celebration Village residence, the town center features signature civic and commercial buildings that Disney commissioned world-famous architects to design.

Clockwise from left: preview center, town hall, hospital, post office, school.

54

Within this downtown business
district, modeled after traditional, small-town America, a
variety of uses coexists along
a wide promenade that rims
picturesque Celebration Lake.

From mansions to apartments, Celebration Village offers a wide variety of housing types. An egalitarian planning approach ensured that each neighborhood contains a mix of products as well as parks and squares that establish a unique identity.

High-density housing predominates, whether it is attached (condominiums, left) or detached (single-family, below). The street system ranges from wide boulevards to narrow residential streets and alleys.

58

The Celebration Pattern Book was developed to guide the design of custom and production homes. Architectural, landscape, and community patterns are addressed. In Architectural Patterns, detailed guidelines are provided for six different styles. Opposite: Community Patterns establishes the general criteria for how houses are placed on five different lot types and includes landscape guidelines for plant materials, fencing, driveways, walks, and paving options.

CLASSICAL

Continuing the grand tradition of Classical American houses, Celebration's Classical Style uses the principles found in eighteenth and nineteenth century pattern books. Inspired by the gracious houses of the Old South, many of the elements are derived from nineteenth century Greek Revival architecture. All the elements of the facade are harmonious and balanced. Often the main fronts are symmetrical. Columned porches, pedimented facades, and vertically proportioned windows are composed in regular bays. The result is both gracious and formal.

Celebration houses will be designed in one of the six styles described in the Celebration Pattern Book. These are based on traditional styles found in Central Florida and throughout the Southeast.

COASTAL

The environmental conditions of the low country and coastal regions of the South produced a unique house form. Large verandahs, wrapping around the houses provided a breezy place to escape the heat. The basic form absorbed many different architectural traditions, all of which were adapted to the house type. Celebration's Coastal Style is based on both the French Colonial and Low Country traditions. Simple, large houses will have one and two story porches. Windows, sometimes reaching to the floor, may have a different spacing than porch columns and roof dormers. The character of the houses is at once stately and related.

VICTORIAN

During the second half of the nineteenth century, pattern books were published that enabled builders to create elaborate and eccentric houses with fanciful compositions and ornament. Celebration's Victorian Style is based on the principles in these pattern books. The form of the house is asymmetrical and picturesque. Porches and verandahs wrap around corners. The steeply sloped roofs often have dormers. Elaborate ornament and details give character to the porches and eaves. Their character is whimsical and cheerful, with inviting porches.

MEDITERRANEAN

Much of Florida's architectural legacy is either Spanish, Spanish Colonial, or Italian Eclectic. Although St. Augustine has original Spanish Colonial architecture, most of Florida's Mediterranean Style is an invention of twentieth century architects who were able to create well-composed and eclectic houses by combining a number of styles. Celebration's Mediterranean Style is based on this approach and includes relatively simple stucco forms with asymmetrically placed windows, doors, and arcades. Porticos or loggias face the street. Tile roofs provide color and character.

COLONIAL REVIVAL

Much of the character of the traditional neighborhoods of Orlando, Tampa, and other Florida cities and towns, is created by houses built between 1900 and 1940 in the 'Colonial Revival' style. Celebration's Colonial Revival Style continues this tradition. As with other revivals, it draws its inspiration from a 'younger America'—the Colonial Period. Although it follows classical principles of balanced and symmetrical compositions, it has rather broad proportions and simplified details for columns and eaves. Its character is cheerful, optimistic, and somewhat less formal than the Classical Style.

FRENCH

Many veterans who had served in France during the First World War were intrigued with the character of French architecture and, upon their return to the United States, built their homes based on French country houses. Celebration's French Style is based on the 'French Country' Style in which there are stuccoed walls with deep reveals for windows and relatively steeply pitched roofs. Tall, well-proportioned windows on simple rectangular forms create an elegant house. The character of the house is simple and elegant.

ARCHITECTURAL STYLES   A - 5

strategy addresses the scale and location of parks, and the relationship of buildings to common spaces and streets, to create memorable addresses within each neighborhood.

The Town Center

Lining the north shore of Celebration's Town Center Lake, the town center is a compact, pedestrian-oriented, mixed-use complex, located within a ten-minute walk from every house in Celebration Village. The main street, Market Street, is flanked by three- and four-story buildings with retail space on the ground floors and offices and rental apartments on upper floors. Surface parking is located behind the mixed-use buildings in the middle of the blocks.

Unique to Celebration's town center is the collection of signature civic buildings, which were designed outside of the town's pattern book. The post office, town hall, preview center, Celebration School, Celebration Hotel, a church, university facility, and cinema were designed by a constellation of star architects including Michael Graves, Philip Johnson, Charles Moore, William Rawn, Robert Venturi, Graham Gund, and Cesar Pelli, who critiqued each other's buildings in order to assure a certain compatibility. Far from just fitting in, each of these landmark buildings has become a widely recognized icon that stands out from the fabric of Celebration.

Celebration Village

Celebration Village, which surrounds the town center, follows the design strategies of traditional American towns. Houses with front porches set close to narrow, tree-lined streets impart the feeling of a traditional "hometown," that being the prevailing image of Celebration. Several neighborhoods make up Celebration Village, each with a mix of housing sizes and types, and each with a unique park or square as a focal point and identifier.

Nearly all the single-family houses have rear-alley access for parking. Larger lots and houses line the golf course parkway and the boulevards, while smaller lots and houses are located in the center of the Village. Where possible, like-size lots and houses face each other across streets. Townhouses with rear alleys face squares or collector streets. In addition to the upper-floor apartments in the town center, rental apartments line Water Street, which leads north from the town center through the

Village to the golf clubhouse. The golf course is public and is bounded by a parkway and trail, making it an integral part of the Celebration open space network, rather than a privatized amenity lined with fairway housing.

Celebration Pattern Book

Disney wanted Celebration to have the character of a traditional small Southern town and retained Urban Design Associates to develop a design code for the custom and production builders who would be building the houses. UDA visited 22 Southern cities, including Charleston, Savannah, Beaufort, New Orleans, Winter Park, Coral Gables, and St. Augustine, to identify architectural styles, residential building types, and street and community patterns. Using as a model the almost extinct device of "builder companions" or "pattern books," which guided the development of many of America's great neighborhoods between the Civil War and World War II, UDA prepared the Celebration Pattern Book in three sections: Community Patterns, Architectural Patterns, and Landscape Patterns. The Community Patterns and Landscape Patterns provided guidelines for how the houses relate to the street, the neighborhood, and each other.

The Architectural Patterns, the most widely known section of the pattern book, laid out six architectural styles (Classical, Victorian, Colonial Revival, Coastal, Mediterranean, and French) that could be used for the houses. A kit of parts for each style was illustrated to facilitate flexibility in the design of the houses, including massing options, alternative door and window proportions and profiles, and porch and facade treatments.

The street-facing facade of each house was the most important design element because of its contribution to the character of the street. Plans for every home are submitted to the Celebration architectural review manager to ensure their conformance with the intent of the Pattern Book. Townhouse sites and multifamily sites are sold to independent builders and developers who also are required to submit their designs for review by the architectural review manager.

Celebration is one of the most successful communities based on the principles of the new urbanism. It includes a diverse mix of housing types, with prices ranging from $160,000 to over $2 million; a walkable town center with residences above street-level shops; office development; and all of the soft and hard infrastructure that make up a living, working town.

DC RANCH

SCOTTSDALE, ARIZONA

At the foothills of the McDowell Mountains northeast of Phoenix is the 8,281-acre (3,351-hectare) DC Ranch, a master-planned community that seeks to respect the beauty and ecology of its site while providing a technologically advanced, architecturally diverse, family-friendly environment. The project is at the forefront of several trends, from communitywide access to high-speed intranet and a health care "concierge," to land use and building design parameters that stress the preservation of indigenous landscape and regionally inspired architecture.

Though its developer, DC Ranch LLC (an affiliate of DMB Associates), planner, Swaback Partners, and architect, Dale Gardon Design, take great pains to put nature first, DC Ranch, when complete in 2010, will be a large community, with 5,000 dwellings (attached, detached, and multifamily), two golf courses on a total of 400 acres (162 hectares), a mixed-use town center, a community center, two schools (K–8 and 9–12), a recreation center, several places of worship, and 700 acres (283 hectares) of open space. Construction started in 1997 and the first families moved in by the end of that year. The first phase of construction includes approximately 1,200 acres (486 hectares) and 1,200 homes, one golf course, the country club, the recreation center, the elementary school, and a mixed-use main street.

Guiding Design

Common to all development at DC Ranch is a set of design, construction, and landscape guidelines, which seek a middle ground between conformity and individual expression. Acceptable architecture styles—there are 14— must be consistent with the region's building history and traditions. The styles range from Western (ranch- and farmhouse-inspired designs) to Spanish (Mission, among others), Prairie, and contemporary. Significantly, the guidelines are meant to produce "four-sided architecture," in which the design and detailing is visible from all vantage points and consistent with the topography of the land. House design, be it a production home or a custom-built residence, must conform to site slopes with stepped rooflines and interior level changes. The garage must be turned 90 degrees from the

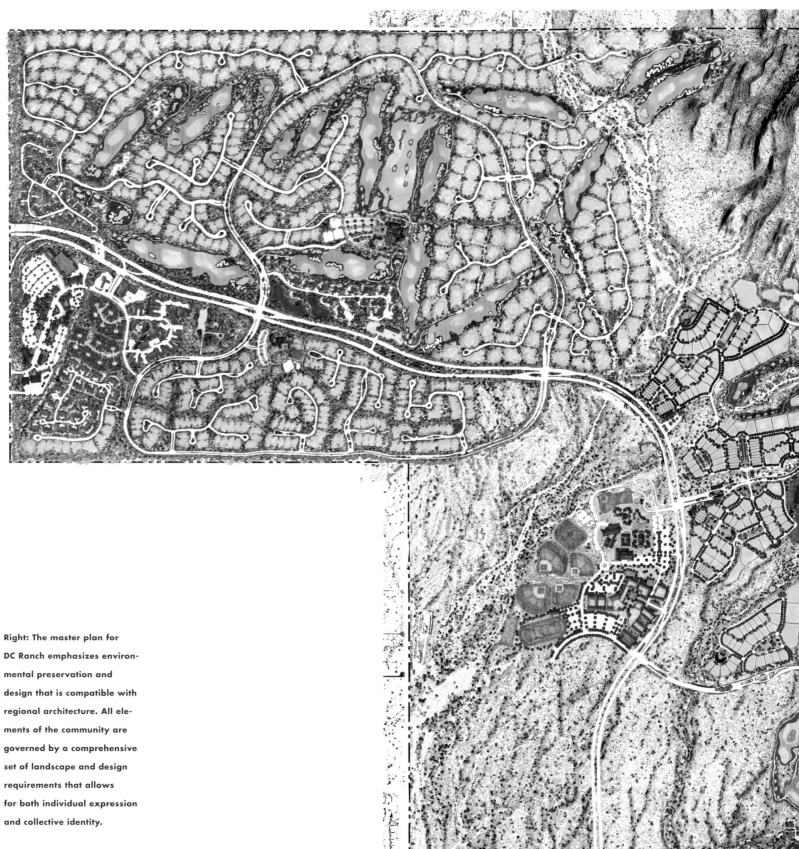

Opening pages: The DC Ranch Country Club is a private, family-oriented club that includes swimming, tennis, fitness, and dining facilities, as well as space for social events.

Right: The master plan for DC Ranch emphasizes environmental preservation and design that is compatible with regional architecture. All elements of the community are governed by a comprehensive set of landscape and design requirements that allows for both individual expression and collective identity.

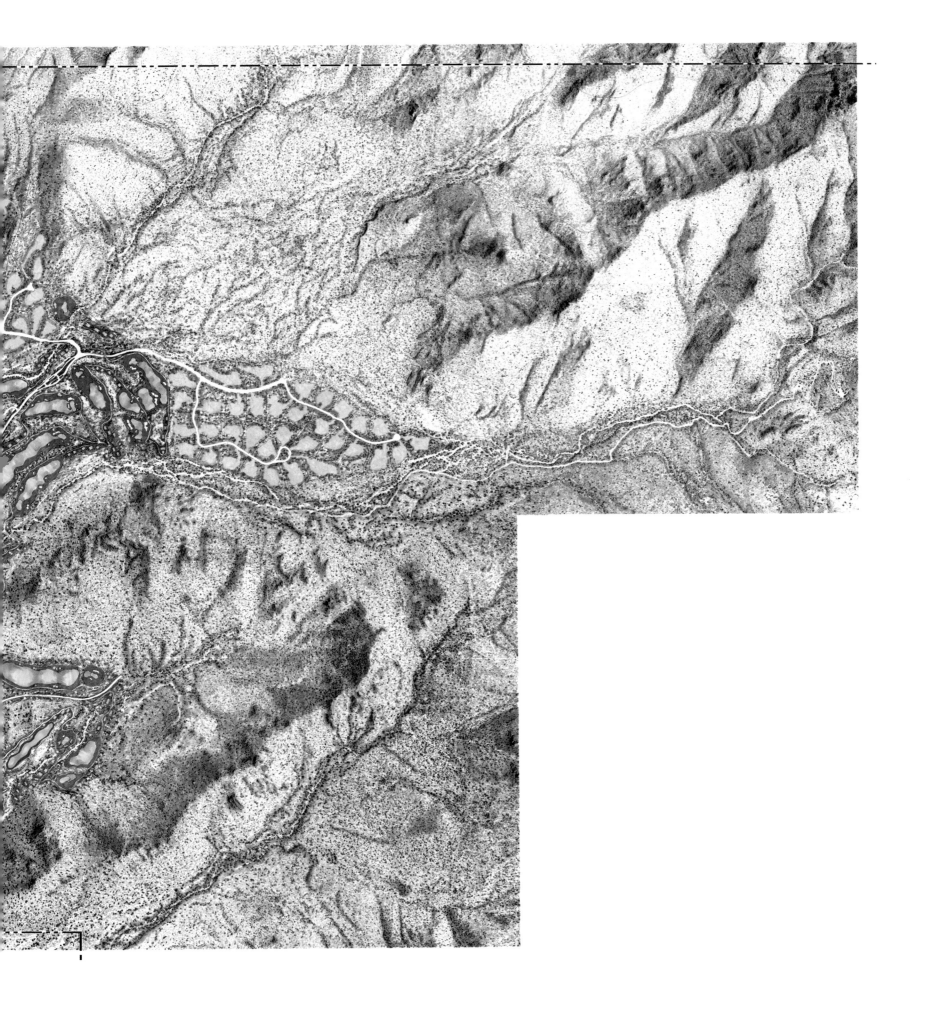

street or set behind a portion of the house to minimize its profile from the street. And front porches are strongly recommended, as part of the developer's strong interest in community-building measures. Homes range in size from 900-square-foot (84-square-meter) rental units to 2,400-square-foot (223-square-meter) attached villas to custom homes up to 8,000 square feet (743 square meters).

Respecting and Celebrating the Land

Sited on what was once a 40,000-acre (16,187-hectare) cattle ranch spanning four vegetation zones (from Sonoran Desert lowlands to snow-capped mountains), the master plan evolved from both an analysis of land use constraints and a philosophical commitment to the "neighborhood" as the primary building block of the community. The highest elevations (up to 4,000 feet, or 1,219 meters), where premium lots are typically found in planned communities, were ruled out of bounds, ensuring that the site's dramatic vistas would belong to everyone, both DC Ranch residents and those living in the surrounding areas. Protection of the washes—broad, flat seasonal drainage areas—mandated by the U.S. Army Corps of Engineers were also off limits. Within the remaining area, neighborhoods of approximately 60 houses are defined and linked by a continuous system of paths and open spaces, which is designed to join Scottsdale's regional path system and the McDowell Mountain Preserve.

The layout of roads and individual lots and the allotment of open spaces were guided by several principles. The entry to each neighborhood must be marked by an open space, on which no driveways can be seen. The end of each residential cul-de-sac is a common open space, in lieu of the pie-shaped housing lots that typically terminate such streets in planned communities. A continuous thread of open space separates lots and provides continuity for the pedestrian path system. The path and open-space system—13 miles (21 kilometers) long in the first phase of development—is rendered in both paved and unpaved walking surfaces. Pedestrian underpasses maintain path continuity at major street crossings and provide safe passage for children.

In accordance with DC Ranch policy and a Scottsdale ordinance, all significant vegetation on a building site must be inventoried, boxed, saved, and reused. The developer's in-house regulations also establish acceptable plant palettes (native, Sonoran, Southwestern, arid, and exotic) and specify landscape zones (natural, transition, private, and streetscape), where each may be used. Turf is permitted for front yards, but is limited in its scope of coverage because of its water-intensive maintenance. Even the golf courses were designed to respect the natural contours and features of the terrain.

Thompson Peak Parkway, the four-lane arterial road that operates as the primary corridor through the master-planned community, is designed to follow the natural undulations of the land. Beyond its meandering route, the road incorporates a median that continuously changes width, providing an organic sense of form and capturing many different views as it winds its way through the Sonoran Desert. As with the residential lots, construction of roads and paths occurs only after the desert "carpet" is lifted and stored for safe keeping until grading is completed. Landscape specialists hand-plant desert grasses, flowers, and cacti in the same orientation and habitat density as occurs naturally. Streetlights, bridge abutments, drainage structures, street signs, railings, and bollards are custom designed to blend into the natural environment.

Keen to minimize water use, the developers employ a high-tech irrigation system that controls the amount and location of water application. The computer-controlled system is outfitted with extensive information on plant species, water use data, and planting zones and densities, recognizing that turf, trees, cacti, Saguaros, wildflowers, and desert shrubs each require different quantities and frequencies of water. The irrigation system receives information daily from an on-site measuring station, which tracks wind, solar radiation, rainfall, humidity, and temperature. Ambitious plans to use 10 percent of the water that is typically consumed by master-planned communities in the area have not been met, holding at 18 percent higher than original projections, which may be attributable to the establishment period of new plantings.

Opposite: Like the residential neighborhoods, the two 18-hole golf courses were designed to respect and capitalize on the natural features of the terrain.

Top, left and right: Great care was taken to preserve and protect the beauty and integrity of the Sonoran Desert landscape. Development was prohibited on both the highest slopes and primary drainage washes. Much of the native vegetation has either remained untouched or was faithfully reconstructed after being disturbed.

Left and above: Bridges, drainage structures, walls, and paths are often built with natural stone found on the site. Landscape regulations, which apply to all project components, reinforce the integration of architecture and natural features.

66 Clockwise from above: Among the variety of housing products offered are custom and production single-family detached homes, attached villas, and luxury rentals. Stone and other non-stucco materials are used authentically.

Opposite, left: Market Street is an upscale shopping, dining, and entertainment district based on a traditional main street model, with on-street and off-street parking, storefronts, and vertical mixed-use buildings. Anchors include a public safety facility that houses the local police and fire stations and a national chain supermarket.

Opposite, right: Copper Ridge School (K–8) complements the desert setting.

Activating Community Life

Open spaces and pathways connect residents physically just as sophisticated wiring at DC Ranch is used to connect them electronically. With the purchase of each house comes an advanced communications package that allows residents to use a single line for phone, fax, Internet, and cable, thanks to the broadband fiber-optic lines that were installed in place of standard telephone and cable lines. Described as one of the first "telecommunities" in the United States, the development's communications system includes high-speed wiring within each home and an intranet (called RanchNET®) that links residents to all the facilities and services offered at DC Ranch, such as the health care referrals and information system, the swimming pool, library, schools, and arts and social programs.

A town center is planned for a site near the mountains, but there is a downtown area already underway on a different site. Market Street is part convenience center and part main street, with shops, restaurants, and entertainment venues. It is also home to essential services like the fire and police departments. Designed as a traditional, mixed-use town center, Market Street is intended to look as though it had grown and expanded over a long period of time. Buildings have retail on the ground floor and offices above. Shopping is only one part of the social mix. The Country Club is meant to be family friendly with special events for groups and children. Likewise, Desert Camp, the local community and recreational center that occupies nine acres (four hectares), includes a fitness center, two heated pools, and courts for tennis and basketball; the camp also offers social and cultural programs.

FAIRVIEW VILLAGE

FAIRVIEW, OREGON

Traditional small-town America was what the developers of Fairview Village had in mind in 1994 when they purchased a 96-acre (39-hectare) site just outside of Fairview, Oregon, 12 miles (19 kilometers) northeast of downtown Portland. Fairview Village is an expansion of the city of Fairview, an existing bedroom community with little in the way of amenities or nonresidential uses. Rick and Sarah Holt of Holt & Haugh, Inc., envisioned a community with the warmth and security of a small town and the energy, diversity, and convenience of an urban area. They believed their new village and main street would serve the needs of the existing town and create a variety of housing opportunities in a gracious setting, making the whole a more complete community.

For inspiration, the developers looked to notable pre–World War II garden suburbs—Mariemont in Cincinnati, Shaker Heights in Cleveland, and Country Club District in Kansas City—famous for their continuing livability and timeless beauty. They also looked to established Portland neighborhoods, where main street shops wrap around residential blocks, and where real estate values have climbed well beyond Portland's general marketplace.

The overall design for Fairview Village incorporates many of the ingredients of traditional neighborhood development (TND)—a diverse mix of land uses within walking distance of each other, smaller lot sizes, public gathering spaces, and distinctive civic buildings, all interconnected by a comprehensive street and pedestrian system. When complete, the project will contain more than 500 new single-family houses, duplexes, townhouses, rental apartments, and live-work units; 219,000 square feet (20,346 square meters) of retail space; and 183,000 square feet (17,001 square meters) of office space. All of the houses have porches and are placed at the front of small lots, with garages located at the back to eliminate driveway cuts along the tree-lined sidewalks. Homes feature vertical, street-facing windows, allowing views of public areas.

Connecting with and Caring for the Environment

Creating a walkable environment was a primary goal expressed to Lennertz & Coyle, the town planners for Fairview Village. Their plan features sidewalks and walking paths that connect virtually everything in Fairview Village, allowing residents to walk or bicycle to the school, post office, and gym, and when completed, the shops. Although most residents will still own cars, access to public transportation makes it possible to live in Fairview without one. Two bus lines serve the Village with access to MAX—the regional light rail system stop two miles away. On MAX, downtown Portland is a 35- to 40-minute ride.

Lot sizes have been minimized; instead, a series of small parks throughout the project provides outdoor space for interacting with neighbors. Most homes are within a two-minute walk of a park and each park is distinguished by a special landmark feature—a brick plaza, a fountain, or special tree variety. While private yards are more compact, the resource of these parks and 30 additional acres (12 additional hectares) of adjacent conservation lands more than compensates as an amenity for joggers, walkers, and outdoor enthusiasts.

Holt & Haugh was determined to rehabilitate the environment as well as build an urban fabric. The development incorporates natural flood control, which increases the value of the property by allowing nature to refresh its own amenity. The community preserves four and one-half acres (two hectares) of upland forests and forested wetlands, plus 11 acres (four and one-half hectares) of conservation easements. A regional trail system links these resources with some 30 acres (12 hectares) of city-owned wetland-upland park areas adjacent to the community. Preserving and enhancing these resource lands has led to air and water quality benefits, reclamation of wildlife habitat, native feedstock for migrating birds, and has created recreational and educational opportunities.

Housing Variety and Mixed-Use Development

Like older towns that accommodate the housing needs of a full range of the population, Fairview Village offers a variety of housing choices—garden apartments, accessory rental units, townhouses, single-family houses, and senior living opportunities—which can accommodate people's needs at every stage of life. But for the developer, having a range of housing types

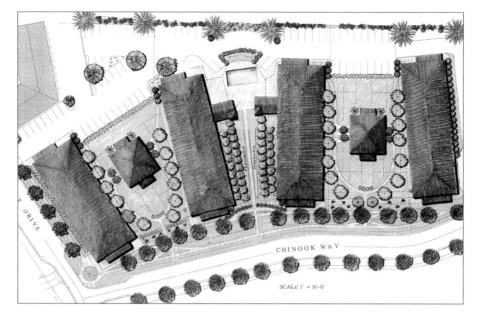

was not enough; the mixed-use configuration was also key. One problem Holt & Haugh encountered in developing its mixed-use community was the city's typical suburban zoning, which segregates retail and office space from residences, and large residences from small residences. Rather than amend the existing code, the city approved Fairview Village as a special plan district with its own code. Since then, the city has rewritten its base code, incorporating much of the Fairview Village code.

So instead of isolated rental units, Fairview Village's rentals are scattered throughout the community and well integrated into its physical fabric. Rental units include flats over stores, carriage houses over garages, as well as a 124-unit luxury apartment complex with elevators and underground parking, making it suitable for elderly and handicapped residents. The challenge of enticing homeowners to live across the street from rental apartments is met by establishing detailed architectural and design guidelines that require the same high standards for apartments as for single-family homes. The guidelines draw from the town of Fairview's Craftsman style, favored from the 1890s to 1940s, and specify such items as the pitch of the roof, scale of the chimney, window types, and ceiling heights. Materials include shingle and clapboard siding, wood-framed windows, and quality details like copper gutters and downspouts. Holt & Haugh felt that maintaining control of the development process was the only way to control the quality of the project. Ultimately, to maintain the quality of planning, building, and design, the developer became its own builder.

Rowhouses are targeted to two distinct markets. Brickyard Rowhouses are a live-work model, ranging from 1,100 to 3,264 square feet (102 to 303 square meters) and located adjacent to the town's square. This product attracts buyers seeking an urban environment. Zoning allows these units to be used for commercial, retail, and residential uses. By contrast, Langley Park Rowhouses are located closer to the single-family neighborhoods and are aimed at families, empty nesters, and single-parent households. They range from 1,250 to 2,725 square feet (116 to 253 square meters) and some include a carriage house apartment that can be rented out. Charles Court Townhomes are zero-lot-line units of 2,000 to 3,000 square feet (186 to

Previous page: Chinook Way Apartments represent nearly one-quarter of the dwelling units in Fairview Village, whose thoroughly integrated housing mix features apartments, carriage units, rowhouses, townhouses, duplexes, and single-family homes. Above: The four large apartment buildings on Chinook Way were set perpendicular to the street to minimize their mass and create opportunities for garden courts between buildings. Underground parking contributes to the openness of the site.

Left: A trail system—some of which was built by community volunteers when public funds dwindled—links 4.5 acres (two hectares) of upland forests and 11 acres (four hectares) of conservation easements with 30 acres (12 hectares) of city-owned wetland-upland parks adjacent to Fairview Village.

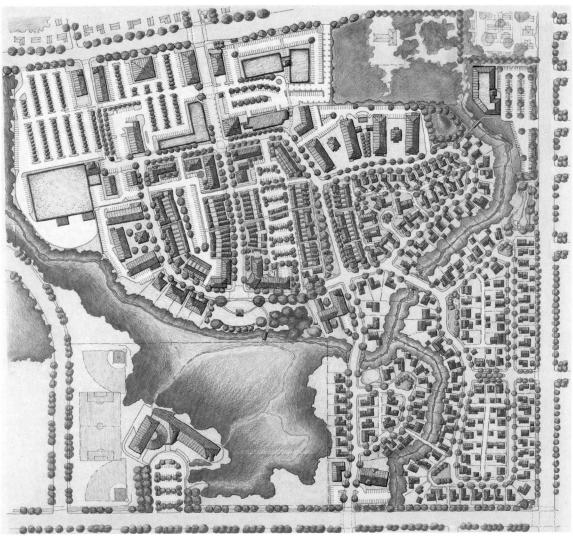

Right, top: Fairview Village was one of the first new urbanist master-planned communities in the Pacific Northwest and compact mixed-use infill developments within Portland's urban growth boundary.

Right, bottom: Cleverly designed water detention areas masquerade as neighborhood parks and serve a dual function by using wetland vegetation to naturally condition storm water and feed migratory birds.

71

Diverse housing products were conceived to accommodate every generation of a family in the same neighborhood. To ensure architectural cohesiveness throughout, all housing types adhere to Village design guidelines drawn from the region's rich craftsman heritage.

Above: Although designed as a housing product that promotes higher density, Brickyard live-work rowhouses have private courtyards with decks and gardens. The units, located in the Village Market Square, take advantage of mixed-use zoning by including a study or potential separate office space in the front of the home.

Opposite: Each distinct neighborhood is served by one of nine pocket parks—each with a unique landmark feature—strategically located within a two-minute walk of every home.

279 square meters), targeted to empty nesters. Single-family homes range from about 1,200 to 3,100 square feet (111 to 288 square meters) and occupy lots averaging a compact 5,300 square feet (492 square meters).

In keeping with the concept of a village, and not a subdivision, the developer of Fairview Village included all the facilities that day-to-day living requires. Civic buildings include a U.S. post office, elementary school, public library, and city hall with attached police department. These completed facilities, as well as the partially completed retail and commercial components, will serve the needs of the village and surrounding neighborhoods. All civic and commercial buildings are constructed with the same high level of design standards as the residences, fostering a cohesive ambience.

Fairview Village hopes to attract a broad mix of middle-income buyers, including young families, empty nesters, older and younger singles, and single-parent households—segments which are often poorly served by typical suburban subdivision housing. The marketing challenge has been twofold: to sell finely crafted homes through a sales network accustomed to selling lower quality tract housing; and to educate the consumer about village living before enough of the fabric was built for the advantages to be readily apparent.

Though hesitant, early customers showed a certain sustained interest in the new concept, returning time after time to learn more about the project. Realtors balked at selling the higher cost-per-square-foot product. It soon became clear that the developer would have to market the project itself in order to properly convey the message. The results have been positive. At this writing, about 80 percent of the homes are built and occupied.

76　Amenities and institutional uses were vital to the master plan. These included parks, trails, and nature conservancy areas as well as a post office, city hall (top), library, and new elementary school (opposite, bottom), all of which were built.

Fairview Village's master plan combines elements that evoke small-town nostalgia with those that reflect urban energy and convenience. Examples of the latter include South Market Square (opposite, bottom), a neighborhood retail center in a plaza setting, and the Boulders (top), an adjacent retail and commercial office center.

HARBOR TOWN

MEMPHIS, TENNESSEE

Harbor Town is a 136-acre (56-hectare) master-planned community located on Mud Island, virtually in the shadow of downtown Memphis. Now mostly built-out, Harbor Town embodies the principles of a traditional town: gridded streets with wide, radial boulevards, a strong pedestrian orientation, formally planned squares, and architectural forms based on historical prototypes. The project's land plan is based on a grid pattern of narrow streets, many of which terminate in small parks fashioned after village squares. The plan provided for a broad, highly integrated mixture of housing types, sizes, and price ranges.

Harbor Town is the vision of Memphis-based developer Henry J. Turley, Jr. In the late 1980s, Turley saw an opportunity to build a new downtown community, one much like the Memphis neighborhood where he grew up. Turley recalls, "Right there in my neighborhood, there seemed to be everything—a hint of all of life's possibilities mixed with all kinds of people." He sought to re-create this neighborhood ethos, and the sense of community it engendered, in Harbor Town.

Interconnected Neighborhoods

The master plan, originally designed by RTKL Associates and later modified by Memphis-based Looney Ricks Kiss, incorporates three distinctly organized, yet interconnected neighborhoods. A wetlands detention feature, designed to look like a stream and ponds, runs through the center of the site and serves as a natural, but distinct boundary between neighborhoods.

The garden district, which lies at the center of the community, includes a mix of attached and detached houses that are integrated with three parks, a wetlands bird sanctuary, and a nature trail winding through a central wooded area punctuated by six ponds. The most formal of the parks is Settlers Point Park, which includes a pavilion area for resident gatherings and for such community activities as the regular jazz concerts that take place on Sundays during the summer. The garden district provides approximately 250 residential lots, including townhouses, zero-lot-line houses, and larger detached units. Lot widths generally range from 30 to 40 feet (nine to 12 meters) for zero-lot-line products to 50 feet (15 meters) for the larger,

more expensive homes. Most lots average 90 to 120 feet (27 to 37 meters) in depth.

At the northern end of the site is the village district, which is the more densely configured of Harbor Town's neighborhoods. The village district contains rental apartments and a variety of for-sale homes such as townhouses, semiattached homes, and single-family houses. An apartment complex (similar to one in the harbor district at the southern end of the project) features three-story stacked flats and townhouse flats.

The harbor district at the southern end of the community contains the town center, whose retail core is fashioned after a traditional main street. Planned for 55,000 square feet (5,110 square meters) of restaurant and specialty retail uses, the town center will also include 42 rental apartments above retail.

Product Design and Mix

During the first phase of construction, the developer discovered that written design standards were difficult for designers, builders, and buyers to understand. To counter this, Looney Ricks Kiss established a set of visual design guidelines that translated the developer's vision into an accessible format of "do's" and "don'ts."

The visual guidelines do not prescribe any particular architectural style, but they do set the basic ground rules for street facades, scale and proportion, materials, and key details. In support of the traditional architectural vernacular, the guidelines require, for example, that windows be oriented vertically, rather than horizontally, and that porches be raised 24 to 30 inches (61 to 76 centimeters) above grade. In addition to establishing an overall aesthetic for the community, the intent of the design guidelines is to ensure that lower-priced homes on narrow lots maintain a level of design compatible in quality to the more expensive homes.

In accordance with these guidelines and the development of many older towns, there is a mix of housing types; in Harbor Town, one can find $800-per-month rentals just a few steps from $800,000 riverfront houses. While the original master plan divided each block into 50-foot-wide (15-meter-wide)

Opening page: Located on an island in the Mississippi River, the new community of Harbor Town is just a bridge-span away from downtown Memphis.

Right, top: The master plan for Harbor Town employs traditional neighborhood planning principles. Dense, intimate streets, sidewalks, neighborhood parks, and neat wooden houses on small lots are key planning elements intended to create small-town interaction and a pedestrian-oriented street life.

Right, bottom: A wetland detention area ringing the center of the site is designed to look like a stream and ponds. It creates a buffer between neighborhoods.

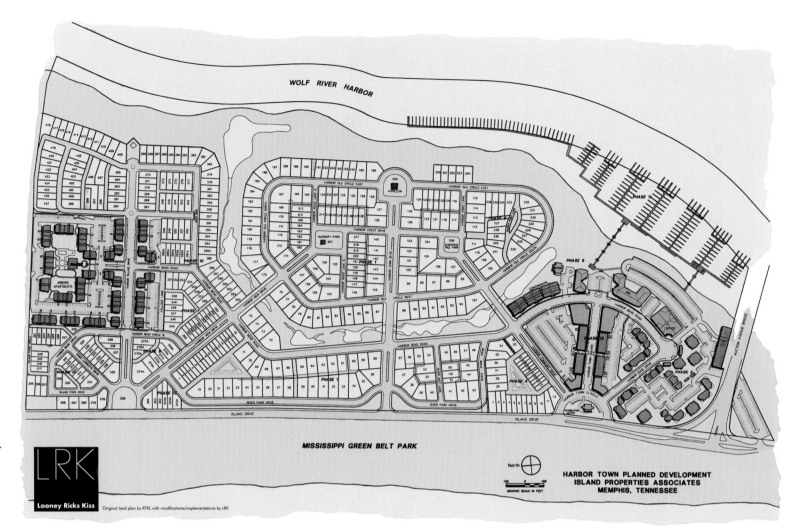

WOLF RIVER HARBOR

MISSISSIPPI GREEN BELT PARK

LRK
Looney Ricks Kiss

Original land plan by RTKL with modifications/implementations by LRK

North

GRAPHIC SCALE IN FEET

HARBOR TOWN PLANNED DEVELOPMENT
ISLAND PROPERTIES ASSOCIATES
MEMPHIS, TENNESSEE

Left: Harbor Town is composed of a series of radial boulevards superimposed on a grid of streets.

Below, left: The plan includes three neighborhoods and a town center. A small downtown has a grocery store, restaurant, other businesses, and a private neighborhood school.

Below, right: Harbor Town's developer, Henry J. Turley, Jr., wanted to create a community that was dense but not urban, and with small streets that would encourage intermingling. His vision was to recreate the spirit of the Memphis neighborhood where he grew up.

81

Above and center: Harbor Town includes a variety of housing types—single-family, townhouses, apartments, and condominiums—in a wide range of prices. These townhouses (center) are in a single building, intended to look more like a classic Southern Colonial mansion than new development.

lots with front-access driveways, the plan was subsequently amended to provide for rear-access alleys and the diversification of lot widths. Lots as narrow as 25 feet (seven meters) were created for the smallest detached homes.

Most of the residential designs are updates of local vernacular forms, ranging from Charleston side-yard houses to simple shotgun cottages, although some units are more modern in detail. The small houses are among the most interesting and innovative. Situated on lots as small as 25 to 30 feet (seven to nine meters) by 100 to 110 feet (30 to 34 meters), these dwelling units typically are side-yard designs, one room wide (occasionally two) with alley garages. In many instances, the units have raised front porches and second-story balconies to engage the street. In some designs, the porches wrap around to the side yard, creating a sheltered extension to the outdoors. The yards themselves are laid out with an eye toward maintaining privacy, and are enhanced with courts and patios. Architectural details, such as eight-foot-high (two-meter-high) doors and ten-foot-high (three-meter-high) ceilings, are used to offset the small footprints and give the units a sense of spaciousness that belies the actual numbers.

Above: Design guidelines do not prescribe a particular architectural style but instead set basic ground rules for street facades, scale, proportion, materials, and details to maintain an overall aesthetic and level of quality. Most of the residential designs are updates of local vernacular forms, ranging from Charleston side-yard houses to simple shotgun cottages.

Left: A park gazebo provides a perfect vantage point for gazing at the nearby harbor.

The project was initially a hard sell because of its location on the eastern side of Memphis and its mix of housing products. Developer incentives ultimately attracted a diversity of buyers, from empty nesters and professional couples to singles and young families. Right: Duplex housing. Below, left to right: Streetscape of single-family houses; houses lining a neighborhood park; rear elevations of townhouses facing wetland water feature with Pyramid Arena in background.

84

Pedestrian-Oriented Planning

The plan for Harbor Town envisions an intimate, pedestrian-scaled community where streets are narrow and short and building setbacks are minimized. Local street rights-of-way are 44 feet wide (13 meters wide), with a 28-foot (nine-meter) curb-to-curb distance, including parking on both sides of the street. The traffic-calming effect is evident: it is difficult to drive more than 15 miles per hour (24 kilometers per hour) almost anywhere in the community.

Single-family residential setbacks are typically ten to 15 feet (three to five meters) from the property line. Garages, in most instances, are kept off the street, accessed via rear alleyways that were established as easements carved out of adjoining properties. Where parking is accessed directly from the street, garages are set back—and in some cases covered by second-story porches—to minimize their visual impact.

Selling a Hard Sell

Initially, Harbor Town was a hard sell to builders and buyers alike. New growth was occurring on the eastern side of the Memphis metropolitan area, while there was little to none happening adjacent to downtown. Considerable effort and expense were required to persuade builders to construct houses speculatively, and to persuade realtors to bring prospective buyers to see them. Expecting that sales to families would be among the most difficult to close—given the local school choices available—the developer initially offered lot price concessions of $1,200 per child. Also, an on-site Montessori school was organized, which has been expanded twice.

Through these efforts, and through the design of the community itself—from front porches to neighborhood parks—Harbor Town has been able to win over a substantial number of families with children. Because of the wide variety of housing sizes and prices offered, the project has also attracted a broad spectrum of buyers that includes empty nesters, singles, and professional couples. Under the umbrella of the community's design guidelines, Harbor Town has been able to integrate a mixture of custom homes, plan-book homes, and production housing.

85

Above and center: Houses are on relatively small lots and are set close to the street. Garages are placed in the rear of houses to preserve the architectural integrity of the streetscapes. Service alleys provide homeowner access. Right: With the intent of creating a more intimate and pedestrian-scaled community, Harbor Town's streets are narrow and short, and building setbacks are minimized.

Left: Harbor Town's smallest houses are among its most interesting. Traditional Southern shotgun houses and two-story cottages serve as models for single-family houses on narrow lots. While the form is traditional, the interpretation is contemporary. Whenever possible these homes were oriented toward neighborhood parks, with communal open space compensating for minimized private yards.

I'ON

MOUNT PLEASANT, SOUTH CAROLINA

Along the deep-water marshes of Hobcaw Creek in Mount Pleasant, South Carolina, is I'On, a new 244-acre (99-hectare) master-planned community inspired by traditional neighborhood development (TND) concepts. The community, a mere six miles (9.7 kilometers) east of Charleston, features a pedestrian-friendly, relatively high-density environment. When fully built-out it will include over 700 single-family custom-built homes as well as community facilities and a small-scale commercial area near its entrance. The development is divided into six residential neighborhoods, each of which is planned around a community space.

Regional Inspiration

I'On's founders, Tom and Vince Graham, began with the concept of a mixed-use development that would include single- and multifamily housing units, commercial space, and public areas. The Grahams and the planners they had retained—the firms of Duany Plater-Zyberk & Company and Dover Kohl and Partners—first visited regional models of urban planning and design, including Savannah and Charleston, South Carolina, as well as such historic areas of lesser-known South Carolina coastal towns as Beaufort, Rockville, and Mount Pleasant.

Based on their observations the designers chose the classic Lowcountry vernacular style as a reference for the new development. This style, borrowed from Mount Pleasant Old Village and Historic Charleston, is characterized by deep front porches, tall windows, and a strong verticality (homes taller than they are wide). The style also embraces natural exterior finishes such as wood, clapboard, brick, or stucco; balconies; shuttered windows; simple, symmetrical rooflines; fences, walls, and gates; and out-buildings such as garages, potting sheds, and workshops.

Individual residences at I'On are built by members of the I'On Guild, a group of 18 builders who have been selected by the developer based on experience, craftsmanship, client and trade references, financial strength, and enthusiasm. The purpose of the Guild is to ensure high-quality, sustainable construction. By encouraging a variety of builders and craftsmen to participate in the development process from the very beginning, the community has acquired a level of visual diversity and a sense of authenticity in an unusually short period of time.

A Neighborhood Focus

I'On's six neighborhoods—Shelmore, Eastlake, Ponsbury, Ionsborough, Westlake, and Montrose—are connected by a network of narrow streets and view corridors. Each neighborhood, planned around a preserved civic space such as a lake, park, or square, contains 80 to 150 homes, with lot sizes ranging from 3,500 to 12,000 square feet (325 to 1,114 square meters). House sizes are anywhere from 960 square feet (89 square meters) to more than 6,000 square feet (557 square meters), with the average at about 2,400 square feet (223 square meters).

The neighborhood streets are also narrow (17 to 22 feet/five to 6.7 meters) and designed with twists and turns to add visual interest and slow vehicular traffic. I'On's connector streets are wider (30 feet/nine meters), but granite-block curbs are used to narrow the size of intersections so that drivers slow down in response.

Eight sites throughout I'On have been reserved for civic buildings to be built in the future, including small churches and other community buildings. I'On Square, a commercial center for retail and office uses, will eventually house just over 30,000 square feet (2,787 square meters) of commercial space. The first phase includes a gourmet food-to-go shop, a restaurant, salon, spa, the I'On Company's sales office, and several professional offices. Other amenities include the I'On Club, a private swim and tennis club, and the Creek Club, a 5,000-square-foot (464-square-meter) facility for parties and community gatherings.

Putting the Landscape to Work

Integral to I'On's design are the quantity and quality of public space. I'On's two lakes (created by a former owner) are not concealed behind a barricade of expensive homes. Instead, the entire shoreline is community owned. So are more than two miles of walking trails around a marsh and wildlife preserve, numerous playgrounds, and a multipurpose athletic field.

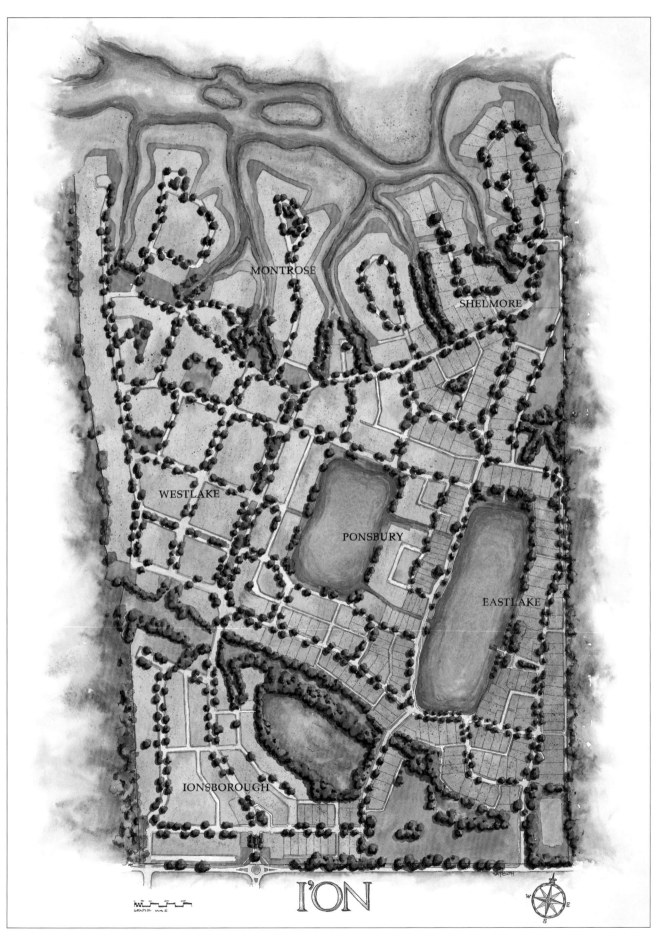

MONTROSE

SHELMORE

WESTLAKE

PONSBURY

EASTLAKE

IONSBOROUGH

I'ON

GRAPHIC SCALE

Opening pages: The Creek Club facility is a place for neighborhood events and is available to I'On residents for private functions.

Opposite: I'On's two lakes are focal points for premium residential development as well as numerous aquatic and land-based recreational activities. Their shorelines are community owned and completely accessible.

Left: Divided into six boroughs comprising 80 to 150 single-family homes each, I'On's master plan creates a balanced relationship between the position of each home and the public and civic realms, with an emphasis on shared amenities. Twenty-five percent of the site is dedicated open space.

Above: Residents in all six boroughs have direct access to the miles of lakefront parks and walks throughout the community. Streets are intentionally narrow and sidewalks wide to encourage pedestrian circulation as the primary mode of transit.

Above: The I'On Club, located between Ionsborough and Eastlake boroughs, is a private swim and tennis facility dedicated to providing a quality environment for recreation, exercise, and social interaction.

Opposite: A leisurely stroll down interconnected tree-lined streets leads residents to I'On Square, an intimately scaled commercial area featuring shops, offices, and restaurants.

The Rookery, a five-acre (two-hectare) pond used by wading birds as a nesting site, was enhanced as a freshwater wetland preserve. Careful planning and monitoring has protected the area, enabling the nesting population to increase while allowing residents to view the birds without disturbance from blinds. Sensitive freshwater ecosystems have been preserved through the dedication of wetland areas and undisturbed buffers surrounding them. These freshwater springs are the headwaters of I'On's tidal creeks and home to a wide variety of Lowcountry plants and wildlife. Other on-site green areas include a two-mile Marshwalk along the Hobcaw and Shelmore creeks, a soccer field, and intimate pocket parks scattered throughout the development.

Planners made the most of the two-block-wide strip of land between the two lakes in the center of the site. Two canals were dug to connect the lakes, and specially designed houses flank these canals in "an almost Dutch relationship between buildings and water," according to Victor Kohl of Dover Kohl and Partners. The canals are bridged at key points to preserve street continuity.

Opposite: The Rookery, a slough at the southern end of I'On, is a special place where walking paths and discreetly placed observation stands provide dramatic yet unobtrusive glimpses of hundreds of native birds and wildlife in their natural habitat. The South Carolina Department of Natural Resources bestowed its Stewardship Award on the I'On Company for protecting the natural environment and adhering to smart growth principles.

Left and above: Inspired by traditional neighborhood design concepts, I'On is characterized by an exceptionally lush and verdant natural environment in harmony with the built environment of tree-lined streets, shady lanes, and attractive homes.

Above and opposite: Forming the I'On Guild, 18 builders are responsible for the unique appearance of the community, characterized by classic Low-country architectural styling found in such Southern coastal towns as Charleston and Savannah. They may look historic, but these homes were designed to meet the requirements of today's discriminating buyers.

Winning Approval

The I'On Company faced many hurdles in its two-and-one-half-year pursuit of rezoning and permitting. The initial rezoning application was rejected by the Mount Pleasant town council in the face of considerable opposition from local residents, who objected to the scale and density of the proposed development. For the next 14 months, the developer worked with the town council to turn the plan into one that could be approved. By the time I'On got its approval, the plan had been shorn of its most controversial features. I'On's commercial space, for example, was sharply reduced. Another disappointment for the developer was the council's refusal to allow apartments and "granny flats," inexpensive housing that would have attracted residents with a mix of incomes. I'On does, however, include some tiny lots, on which small houses can be built.

The developer began infrastructure development for the first phase of the project in August 1997. By summer 2001, about 45 percent of the total number of homesites were sold or under contract. Plans call for all homes and commercial areas to be completed by 2005.

THE IRVINE RANCH

IRVINE, CALIFORNIA

The Irvine Company is developing one of the largest and most successful master-planned communities in the United States. Following a comprehensive master plan created in the 1960s, a series of large villages within incorporated cities is being built on the 93,100-acre (37,676-hectare) Irvine Ranch. These communities provide homes for more than 200,000 residents and employment for 250,000 workers.

Established in 1864, the original Irvine Ranch consisted of about 120,000 acres (48,562 hectares) reaching 22 miles (35 kilometers) inland from the Pacific Ocean at Newport Beach to the edge of the Cleveland National Forest. It encompassed more than 185 square miles (479 square kilometers) and represented nearly one-fourth of Orange County's total land area. Today, the Irvine Ranch includes all of the city of Irvine, portions of the cities of Newport Beach, Tustin, Orange, Laguna Beach, and Anaheim, as well as unincorporated land in Orange County. The city of Irvine is the geographical and historical heart of the Irvine Ranch. Incorporated in 1971, it now has a population of more than 143,000.

Development over the Long Term
From the beginning, the transformation of the Irvine Ranch has been a continuous sequence of innovation and experimentation. Conceived by William Pereira in 1960, the original master plan consisted of a series of villages connected by mixed-use activity corridors and buffered with agricultural lands. Led by Ray Watson, now the Irvine Company's vice chairman, the original planning team sought to create unique "lifestyle environments" by capitalizing on Southern California's climate and regional recreational and educational resources. Villages like University Park, Rancho San Joaquin, East Bluff, Woodbridge, and Turtle Rock demonstrate that high-quality neighborhoods can be built of mixed housing types in a range of densities.

The Irvine Company leveraged the value of nonresidential components, like the University of California, Irvine, to accelerate growth and to provide the full range of uses and services a city requires. The 5,000-acre (2,023-hectare) Irvine Spectrum business park, begun in 1985, is a series of master-planned centers for research, technology, and business that is home to

Few new communities, especially of this size, have the topographical and environmental diversity of the Irvine Ranch. Some of the more dramatic land features include rolling hills, steep slopes, rock and limestone canyons, arroyos, and salt and freshwater marshes, not to mention miles of Pacific coastline.

were the most environmentally sensitive areas, so almost all of those formations were preserved. Residential enclaves were built on some of the ridges to take advantage of the magnificent views and the ocean breezes. The canyons establish the community's open space structure as well as its predominant character.

A large part of the Newport Coast was preserved when land there was sold to the state of California for the creation of Crystal Cove State Park. In order to ensure that other areas of the coast would be protected, the Irvine Company entered into an alliance with the Nature Conservancy, a national land conservation organization, to manage wildlands and restore natural habitats.

A series of important design elements helps establish the overall character for the community and link the physically separated residential enclaves. Architectural guidelines specify classical Mediterranean architecture for all aspects of development: production and custom homes, monuments, gatehouses, light fixtures, walls, and fences. A coordinated palette of colors further unifies the residential enclaves. An evergreen plant palette is used to blend new development harmoniously with the adjacent coastal sage scrub plant ecosystem.

Although planning of the Newport Coast began during the 1960s, the project did not start in earnest until 1969, when a contingency of the Irvine Company's planners toured the Mediterranean Coast, an area with the same latitude and similar water temperature and climate as Orange County. Ray Watson recalled the impact the visit had on the group: "To do justice to the Newport-Irvine Coast we needed to build it into a timeless place of longevity and boldness. There were roots and a sense of heritage to preserve and build on, a sense of unfolding generations, and architectural presence and color from the Mediterranean hill towns ... to blend into our own country's early California missions. All of which, if combined properly, could conceivably become a New World resort for 21st-century California."

The resulting Mediterranean-style architecture relies on forms and materials that provide relief from the sun and that work with the natural terrain. Deep-set windows, doors, and balconies are used to diffuse direct sunlight, and interior courtyards and covered arcades create cool shadows. Sensitivity to the landform is achieved by designing structures that terrace down the hillsides and by clustering development within the generous expanses of open space. The concept was to decrease the developable acreage by clustering the houses, changing them from a custom lot/custom house community to a blend of custom and builder houses. The benefits were major. In doing so, the Irvine Company could increase the number of housing types, decrease the actual land area devoted to building, and dramatically expand the open space.

The planners concluded that the best use of the coastal land was a combination of resort and residential development. The area adjacent to the Pacific Coast Highway was reserved for golf and hotel uses to meet requirements for visitor services. Inland from the coast highway and above the resort area, a mixture of custom residential lots and houses was planned. The homes were organized into a series of enclaves, each with its own identity, but all part of the Newport Coast. It was decided that only a quarter of the Newport Coast would be developed; the remainder would remain undeveloped natural areas.

Because of his reputation for preserving natural resources and incorporating courses into the natural setting, renowned golf course designer Tom Fazio was selected to design the golf courses on the Newport Coast. In order to achieve subtle transitions between natural areas and landscaped yards, native vegetation is used extensively in landscaping and in wildfire safety zones, an important land function in Southern California.

Northpark

In 2001, the Irvine Company opened the Northpark village portion of Irvine Ranch. The intention with the 392-acre (159-hectare) community was to evoke the small-town feeling found in some of California's classic towns, where residents still know their neighbors. Northpark was planned and designed around existing natural features, particularly the rows of mature eucalyptus trees that had been planted on the former agricultural land decades earlier to slow down the Santa Ana winds as they roared through

Left: Mediterranean architecture distinguishes housing in four luxury home neighborhoods. Choices include condominiums, townhouses, and single-family homes.

Top and above: Overlooking the coastline between Laguna Beach and Newport Beach, Newport Coast is one of Irvine Ranch's most visually compelling communities. Of its 10,000 acres (4,047 hectares), 80 percent is open space that includes Crystal Cove State Park as well as neighborhood parks and trails. Residents of Newport Coast, which has 2,600 housing units planned, enjoy assorted amenities, such as the two-course Pelican Hill Golf Club; community recreational facilities; a school district; shopping and dining at Fashion Island; and the excitement of adjacent Newport Beach.

Above: The San Joaquin Wild-life Sanctuary encompasses 300 acres (121 hectares) of coastal freshwater wetlands, half of which have been restored to their natural state through the innovative stewardship of Irvine Ranch Water District and the Irvine Company. The remaining acres were not in need of restoration.

Right: Home to more than 800 businesses—including the Irvine Company—Newport Center is a 600-acre (243-hectare) commercial, retail, and entertainment complex overlooking Newport Harbor.

One of the newest villages at the Irvine Ranch, Northpark reflects new urbanist planning and design principles through its architectural heritage, pedestrian orientation, neighborhood parks and landscaped common space, streetscape enhancements, town center, and above all, sense of community.

the nearby mountains. These "windrows" planted at 700-foot (213-meter) intervals served as windbreaks to protect the citrus trees that once occupied the site. Visually compelling, these windrows established a strong sense of place. They were incorporated primarily into the public rights-of-way, the street parkways, medians, and parks. The largest windrow—and, the only one running north-south through the community—serves as the dramatic focal point for the central park and a paseo, or walkway that runs through the heart of the village and also serves the needs of the area, linking trails to the south with those in the northern foothills.

Each neighborhood in Northpark has its own distinctly different park. Two of the parks include swimming pools, tennis courts, and clubhouse facilities connected by a graceful promenade. The community has its own neighborhood shopping center, Northpark Plaza, and an elementary school that can be accessed without leaving the community gates. The community also is minutes away from major shopping and employment centers and transportation corridors.

Borrowing from new urbanist planning concepts, Northpark has an extensive pedestrian network featuring wide tree planting strips along streets. Nostalgic street lamps are an additional amenity for residents and shoppers. As part of a traffic-calming effort, and to increase the area for planting trees, "chokers," places where the curb is bumped out into the street, are included on all of Northpark's streets.

Whenever possible, planners also minimized paving to increase landscaped areas. For example, Northpark's culs-de-sac include landscaped islands in their centers, breaking up the usual sea of asphalt. Instead of being terminated by a house, culs-de-sac are linked with pathways to the adjacent streets, encouraging community interaction. Loop streets that run parallel to the many parks in the village have houses on one side only—facing the park— avoiding the undesirable rear-lot view that park users might otherwise see.

Northpark embodies the evolution of planning and design that has taken place at Irvine Ranch. A prototype for the master-planned community of the 1960s, the Irvine Ranch continues to grow and engender new ideas, and to be a major influence on Southern California community development.

Top: Northpark's central loop street ties together the various neighborhoods and their focal parks.

Center: Through extensive research, the developer learned that residents liked a variety of sizes of parks, and that given the same acreage, they preferred to have more small parks distributed throughout the community than one large park. Northpark is known for the paseos and promenades linking its 11 parks.

Bottom: Unique street and landscape design elements reinforced the identity of the village and helped establish a pedestrian environment. All streets are the same width, with parkways, sidewalks, and parking on both sides. To further enhance the streetscape, many Northpark homes feature porches and balconies in the front and garages in the rear.

Left: Northpark Plaza serves residents with larger grocery and drug stores, a dozen shops, and many service-related businesses.

Above: Single-family houses, townhouses, and apartments in Northpark are organized into neighborhoods, each with its own park. Densities range from 3.4 units per acre (8.5 units per hectare) to 20 units per acre (50 units per hectare). Strong architectural orientation to the street is common to all housing types.

KAROW NORD

BERLIN-WEISSENSEE, GERMANY

The unification of Berlin in 1990 brought with it a pressing need for new housing in the city, housing that had to maneuver through a complex political and cultural climate. In this environment, commissioning architects from California to design a master plan for 5,200 units of subsidized housing on the outskirts of Berlin, in what was once East Germany, would seem risky at best, untenable at worst. But Moore Ruble Yudell (MRY), based in Santa Monica, had a great familiarity with the terrain, having designed the master plan for Tegel Harbor on a former industrial port northwest of Berlin in 1980, as well as a variety of housing in the city since then. That the edges of Los Angeles and Berlin are similarly dispersed is a commonality not lost on the architects or their developers.

MRY's competition-winning proposal for the 243-acre (98-hectare) town in Weissensee, just north of Karow, a historic agrarian village northeast of Berlin, combines the idiomatic language of the old village and the contemporary functions of a modern satellite suburb. The planners emphasized "qualities of habitation at every scale," hoping to make a memorable place, despite the necessarily small size of the subsidized residential units in the new community.

Karow Nord, as MRY project manager Adrian Koffka wrote in a 2001 report of the Congress for the New Urbanism, is "a government-subsidized, low-income, rent-controlled project reflecting the high ideals of the society it was conceived for." ARGE Karow Nord (an abbreviation for Arbeitsgemeinschaft, or "work team") included several developers, local and regional planning agencies, the municipality of Weissensee, and the state government of Berlin. Funding came from the federal government as well as the private developers, including Groth + Graalfs, the firm that commissioned MRY for the plan of Tegel Harbor, among other projects.

Fueled by a determination to avoid the often artificial qualities of instant city design and construction, MRY's development of set typologies for housing, open spaces, streets, and pedestrian walkways set a goal of diversity within a coherent whole. Where strict design guidelines are often used for master plans—many times with great success—Karow Nord's planners opted for strategic recommendations. The gradation of scales between the four-story perimeter blocks around the new town center and the existing one- and two-story buildings of historic Karow played a pivotal role in easing the transition from old to new.

Cultivating Community

Karow Nord occupies two large sections of agricultural fields and open meadows connected to the north end of Karow. The principal aim was to produce a town-like setting derived from the site's agrarian character and the modest scale of old Karow's tree-lined streets and historic core, where simple buildings are clustered around intimately scaled courts. The planners deferred to the small-scale quality of Karow and accommodated the higher density of the new town, establishing a new but related identity for Karow Nord. Siedlungen, the German tradition of producing large-scale housing developments, was overlaid with the principles of the Garden City movement—natural setting, healthy environment, and easy access to work.

MRY studied Karow and other towns on the outskirts of Berlin. They found streets lined with a range of housing types, from the humble to the grand in scale, many individual buildings in need of repair, but all most often with carefully cultivated gardens. The architects admired "the broad regional scale of the agricultural fields," the "marriage of landscape and building (both in the tree-arched streets and the delightful hodge-podge of summer gardens)," the mix of architectural scales, and the variety of block sizes and diagonal streets.

Understanding the critical role time plays in the place-making process, the architects drew a plan in which the areas between the old village and the new development would "evolve and adapt over time." One way to encourage a fluid evolution defined by sensitive infilling was to integrate the new street system into the old in an organic fashion. Similarly, a series of linear parks and green boulevards extends the surrounding farmland deep into the new residential areas. Indeed, the network of green spaces organizes the plan, delineating neighborhoods and establishing a pedestrian-oriented fabric.

Open spaces are wide-ranging, from the artificial lake with its associated wetlands and the arboretum to the vernacular market garden and the

Opening page: Karow Nord integrated 5,200 new government-subsidized housing units and requisite schools, child-care centers, and retail facilities into a largely rural setting on the outskirts of Berlin. Pictured are perimeter apartment blocks of four-story buildings with as many as 100 units each.

Opposite, top: The traditional farm configuration of house, stables, and barn was a design inspiration for housing in Karow Nord.

Opposite, bottom: Karow Nord's mixed-use town center echoes the look and feel of the old village center of Karow.

Right: The master plan, by Moore Ruble Yudell of Santa Monica, California, endeavored to create a dense but human-scaled, mixed-use environment that references the small farm village of Karow and the Communist-era housing blocks that flank the 243-acre (98-hectare) site. Drawing from the traditions of English Garden Cities, the plan is organized by a network of green spaces that weave through the community with linear parks extending to the fields beyond. Two parcels are connected by a main dividing road.

Right, top: Street typology varies from small boulevard to country lane. Automobiles are intended to function but not dominate. Parking is on-grade only, with on-street spaces and small car courts. Pictured are mixed-use buildings along a narrow, curved street behind the town center.

Right, bottom and opposite, top: Functional and aesthetic green space deeply infiltrates neighborhoods in the form of parks, squares, and garden courts. A hierarchy of pedestrian pathways winds through the community: sidewalks along the streets, mid-block paths, mews through-blocks, and pathways along the lake.

mannered residential oval and forum-shaped plaza of the town center. The high water table and surrounding natural landscape call for sensitive management of surface runoff. Hardscaped areas are minimized and paving is made permeable. Landscaped swales and trenches funnel rainwater toward the new lake. Sustainability guidelines, long a part of the German building codes, are met at Karow Nord through the use of healthy building materials, responsible waste management, and recycling.

Dispersed Densities

Unlike the nearby Communist-era housing blocks, with their grim sameness, the housing stock at Karow Nord is relatively heterogeneous, despite a set of design guidelines established by MRY that encourage both coherence within neighborhoods and distinctive differences between neighborhoods. Color guidelines, also based on typology, were established. With designs by some 20 architectural firms, the diverse housing stock is expressed through the parameters of five basic building types: perimeter blocks, mixed-use terraces, villas, courts, and agrarian rowhouses.

Four-story perimeter blocks, a long-established building typology in European cities, are the densest and most urban housing type at Karow Nord and sit in the heart of the town plan, farthest from the low-rise agrarian buildings of Karow. Mixed-use terraces are just that: apartments above retail and office spaces found mostly in the town center but also sprinkled throughout the community. Their shape inspired by the farm typology of dwelling, stable, and barn, the courts are defined by a villa-type structure and two L-shaped buildings, all with multiple housing units grouped around a semiprivate courtyard. Larger villas are freestanding buildings set at focal points in the plan. Agrarian rows are small-scale townhouse mews, which serve a transitional role between the new town and the old one. No matter the shape or size, all residential units have a terrace, a balcony, or a corner patio, but no private gardens.

Left, bottom: A spatial sequence of axial streets and diagonals punctuated by an occasional traffic-calming roundabout visually connects and imposes order on Karow Nord's main public venues. As evidenced by the high school library pictured to the left of the traffic circle, the community has strong public infrastructure that incorporates 17 childcare centers, a high school, a church, and two youth centers along with other public facilities.

Above: Karow Nord has five different housing types varying from two to four stories. Large perimeter blocks (top, left) are the most urban in scale and are located the farthest from the low-rise farm village of Karow. Mixed-use terraces are apartments above office and retail found mostly in the town center. Karow Courts are clusters of multi-family buildings grouped around courtyards (top, right). Larger villas are single buildings grouped at focal points in the community, such as a pond or park (above, left and right). Mews of townhouses are the smallest-scale housing type.

Above: Karow Nord's design guidelines are based on building types and are intended to encourage coherence within and contrast between residential areas. Color guidelines for building types and a hierarchy of public spaces create visual harmony and coherence. Pictured are large villa-type apartment buildings of varied architectural styles.

Walking and Talking

The making of a cohesive community begins with the establishment of an armature for social exchange, be it informally on the street corner or the park bench, or more organized as on a playing field or in a civic building. MRY established a hierarchy of potential social spaces in its plan. Like the housing at Karow Nord, for example, the streets also come in a variety of styles and sizes, from boulevards to lanes, although the general rule is that roadways are narrow to ensure that pedestrians, not automobiles, are a dominant presence. (Parking is on-grade only, with on-street spaces and small car courts.)

Pedestrians, in fact, have a selection of common pathways: sidewalks along the streets, passages between the housing blocks, mews through the blocks, and pedestrian walkways along the lake. The most dominant circulation routes, axial streets and diagonals, link the town's main public spaces, like Karow Strasse, the village's central spine, with its curvilinear central plaza. The diagonals are sometimes discontinuous, with streets turning into parks, gardens, or pedestrian pathways.

Schools, youth centers, and childcare centers are located on prominent parcels throughout the community, all with direct connection to green spaces. Public buildings must be faced in brick. Some of the individual firms designing housing chose to clad the bases of their buildings in brick, initiating a dialogue between the public and private realms.

Opposite, top, left and right: Twenty different architectural firms were responsible for the design of Karow Nord's residential, retail, and civic buildings. The varied size of units within each residential building accommodates a healthy mix of age groups and incomes. Each apartment has a balcony, terrace, or corner patio. Building heights and the pitch of the roofs are varied throughout the community. Pictured are two-story agrarian rowhouses located at the edges of the project, which ease the transition from the surrounding farm village to the dense new community.
Opposite, bottom: Housing above retail.

Left: The plan gives significant position to public spaces and civic buildings. Schools such as this one, and other civic buildings, are located throughout the project rather than being concentrated in one area.
Below, left and right: Karow Nord's 20,000-square-foot (1,858-square-meter) town center, anchored by two schools at either end, is an urban-scaled, mixed-use area with ground-floor retail plus one floor of office and two floors of housing above.

117

KENTLANDS

GAITHERSBURG, MARYLAND

Kentlands was the first large-scale new urbanist master-planned community designed and built for year-round residents in the United States. It has served as a kind of laboratory for new urbanist theories, becoming one of the most visited and studied examples of the new urbanism in the nation. Kentlands is located in Gaithersburg, Maryland, a suburban locale 23 miles (37 kilometers) northwest of Washington, D.C.

Collaboration Yields Results

Homebuilder and developer Joseph Alfandre optioned the 352 acres (142 hectares) of farmland in 1987. Deciding against a conventional cul-de-sac subdivision plan for the property, Alfandre sought out the firm of Duany Plater-Zyberk & Company (DPZ) because of its pioneering work in neotraditional planning, most notably in Seaside in Florida. To develop a master plan and design guidelines for the site, DPZ conducted an unprecedented seven-day public design charrette in Gaithersburg in June 1988. Local citizens, business-people, and city of Gaithersburg officials participated in the charrette, along with Alfandre and DPZ. The goal was to create a self-sufficient community where all daily needs could be met. The plan that emerged was adopted by the city and became the zoning document for the development.

The Kentlands plan achieved higher densities and reduced street widths beyond what the existing zoning permitted. Rear alleys were implemented as a way to keep the messy, utilitarian aspects of daily life separated from the front streetscapes. In addition to its over 1,869 housing units, the plan incorporated 2 million square feet (185,806 square meters) of retail and office space, helping to make the development a destination for shoppers and workers from outside the community as well.

In 1991, Alfandre was forced by slow economic conditions and rising development costs to submit to a friendly foreclosure by his primary lender, Chevy Chase Federal Savings Bank, which took over the project, retaining Alfandre as a development consultant. A new development company, Great Seneca Development Corporation, was formed by the bank to complete the project.

Less Is More

The master plan divides the site into three components: a series of residential neighborhoods; an apartment district; and a retail district. The layout was dictated to some extent by the streams, lakes, wetlands, and wooded ravines that traverse the site and now serve as amenities for the residents. These natural features help to identify the various neighborhoods while serving as a resource for storm water management.

Kentlands's most distinctive aspect, and the one most studied, is the design of its residential neighborhoods, which is based on streets in a connecting grid pattern, with most blocks also having rear alleys for garages and service access. Over 16 percent of the site, or 56 acres (23 hectares), is set aside for common open space, which includes common greens, five tot lots, a recreation complex, three lakes, and a connected trail system. Because lot sizes in Kentlands are smaller than in conventional subdivisions (5,000 square feet/465 square meters versus 10,000 square feet/929 square meters on average), the common open space was seen as compensation for the

reduced size of yards and reduced distance between houses. Quality of open space has been emphasized over quantity, with all of the open space being well integrated into the community. Another 20 acres (eight hectares) of the site is reserved for civic uses, including Rachel Carson Elementary School, a church, a daycare center, cultural center, and meeting hall.

Bordered by three major arterial roads, Kentlands is an island in a sea of sprawl. Two internal boulevards connect it to the arterials, creating three primary entrances. Within Kentlands there are four classes of streets: boulevards with planted medians, street trees, and parking on both sides; primary streets with street trees and parking on both sides; secondary streets with parking on one side and trees on the other; and rear alleys. There are no culs-de-sac. Extensive on-street parking helps Kentlands meet city of Gaithersburg parking requirements. In addition, the on-street parking on the primary and secondary streets serves as a traffic calming device in the residential neighborhoods and contributes to a safer pedestrian environment.

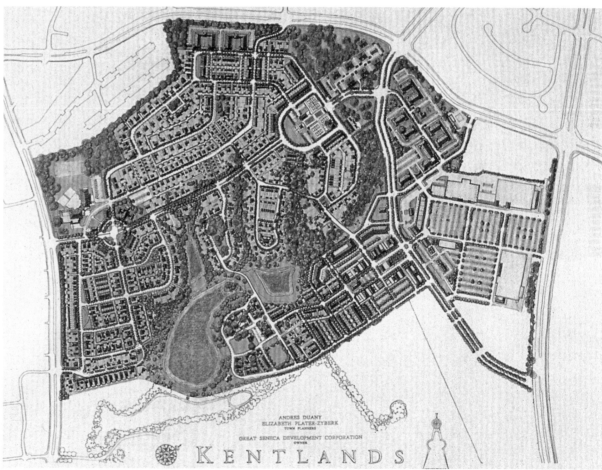

ANDRES DUANY
ELIZABETH PLATER-ZYBERK
TOWN PLANNERS

GREAT SENECA DEVELOPMENT CORPORATION
OWNER

KENTLANDS

Opening pages: Numerous examples of Kentlands's neo-traditional planning concepts are in evidence on Main Street within the mixed-use town center.

Left and above: Kentlands's plan envisions a small suburban town. Key design elements include: coherent circulation, well-defined neighborhoods, a healthy ratio of residential to commercial development, sub-stantial open space, civic facilities, and a spectrum of housing choices.

Houses set close to the street, smaller lots than traditionally offered in the suburbs, and narrow, tree-lined streets interspersed with shared open spaces—and in some cases garages—were key elements in the creation of a pedestrian-oriented environment.

The Traditional Neighborhoods of Kentlands

Kentlands is made up of seven districts: Old Farm, Lower Lake, Middle Lake, Upper Lake, Hill District, Gatehouse, and Market Square, which is a mix of townhouses, live-work units, apartments, and commercial development. Each neighborhood has a unique design and is within five to ten minutes walking distance of a major community amenity.

The Old Farm neighborhood is centered around the original mansion and barn of the Kentlands Farm, which are now used as cultural facilities by the city of Gaithersburg. The mansion and barn face a town green which is flanked by townhouses on two sides.

The Lower Lake, Middle Lake, and Upper Lake neighborhoods comprise the Lake District and are located on three fingers of developable land separated by wooded ravines and streams. The neighborhoods, primarily single-family with a few townhouses in Upper Lake, are connected to each other and to the three adjacent lakes by footbridges and trails. Because of the topography, the Lake neighborhoods have few alleys, but garages are set

Architectural styles at Kentlands reflect the history of
the region, including Georgian,
Colonial, Arts and Crafts,
Victorian, and shingle styles.
To alleviate visual and socio-
logical tedium, the plan enabled a mix of housing types
and designs by several
builders to be constructed on
the same street.

back from the street so that garage doors are not a dominant feature. The
largest and most expensive lots and houses in Kentlands are in this district.

The Hill District is built on a sloping site that required long streets
running parallel to the slope and connected vertically by streets at only a
few places. Further connections are made with picturesque pedestrian ways,
mews, and steps transecting the slope. The Hill District neighborhood is a
mix of cottages, single-family houses of varying sizes, and townhouses, providing a rich mix of house types, sometimes all in one block. One of Kentlands's innovations was to bring back accessory units—generally over a
garage—as a way of providing rental housing within the context of a
mixed neighborhood.

The Gatehouse neighborhood spans from the Rachel Carson Elementary
School to Lake Inspiration, the largest of the three lakes at Kentlands.
Gatehouse was the first neighborhood to be developed and it features brick
sidewalks, later deleted for cost reasons from all but the Old Farm neighborhood. The first houses built in the late 1980s were large, finely detailed,

Right: Apartments and condominiums, which account for about half of all housing units, provide the multifamily component of Kentlands.

Below: Townhouses and live-work units are the denser of the single-family types. What distinguished the townhouses at the time was that architectural variety was achieved by varying a unit's height and width within each grouping, rather than by altering the style and setbacks.

and expensive, followed by somewhat more modest detached houses and townhouses during the economic turndown in the 1990s.

Eclectic Design, Authentic Materials

Kentlands's entire design code is depicted on a two-page graphic. One page is the Urban Standards Code, which specifies the placement of the house on the lot, setbacks, building height, parking locations, porches, and building extensions. A hedge, fence, or low wall is required along sidewalks.

The second page is the Architectural Standards, which specifies forms and materials for building and landscaping. No specific architectural style is dictated, but materials, massing and proportions, and design elements are spelled out. Only authentic exterior materials are permitted, such as brick, stone, or wood—no aluminum or vinyl siding. Initially this led to high costs and to the loss of some production builders who did not want to abide by the code. Because wood has not held up well at Kentlands, the code is being revised to include some composite materials that simulate wood. Tra-

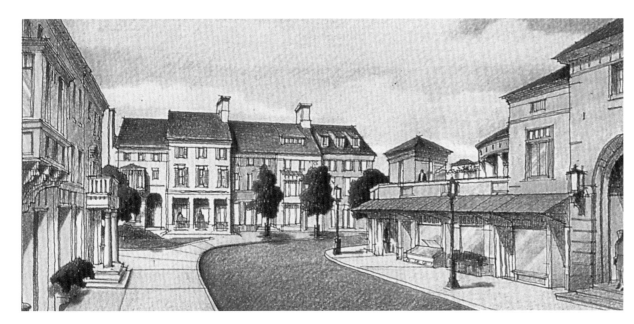

ditional Maryland architectural styles predominate. Homes are mostly Georgian, with a mix of Victorian, shingle, and other historic styles.

By rethinking how mixed uses should be integrated into communities and reintroducing the urban concept of combining housing types, sizes, and price points on single blocks, Kentlands has made a major impact on new master-planned communities everywhere. Among its most imitated advances are its open town squares and townhouses sited on streets as they are in cities, rather than the suburban model of surrounding homes with parking lots. Kentlands has proven that a more urban-style community can be successful in a suburban locale.

So successful, in fact, that today Kentlands is a highly sought-after address, where home values have escalated well beyond those of neighboring communities. The residential neighborhoods have been fully developed according to the master plan. The retail and office components have been scaled down to 745,000 square feet (69,213 square meters), reflecting market realities following the recession.

Top, left: An early rendering shows the mix of retail, office, and residential uses envisioned for Kentlands's Main Street.

Top, right: Public and civic facilities include the 800-student Rachel Carson Elementary School (pictured), the Kentlands Children's Center, and a church.

Above: Community amenities include jogging and bike trails, three lakes, tot lots, parks, squares, and picnic areas. The recreation center (pictured) features three pools; tennis, basketball, and volleyball courts; and a clubhouse.

LADERA RANCH

ORANGE COUNTY, CALIFORNIA

In 1996, Tony Moiso, the second biggest landowner in Orange County, and Drew Brown, president of DMB Associates, decided that it was time to build something meaningfully different. Brown believed that the cookie-cutter, mass-produced subdivisions of Southern California did not meet consumer demands.

Enter "neighborhood as amenity." That is the concept around which Ladera Ranch, a 4,000-acre (1,619 hectare) master-planned community adjacent to Mission Viejo and San Juan Capistrano, is being built. Developed on land holdings from the massive Rancho Mission Viejo, the 8,050-dwelling-unit community has been organized and designed around a hierarchy of community, village, and neighborhood planning concepts. At the community level, Ladera Ranch is linked by a communitywide intranet. Within the community, five villages are planned, each with its own core of social and recreational facilities. Each village, in turn, is composed of a series of neighborhoods, with their own complement of open space and amenities, and linked via pedestrian pathways to the village core and the nonresidential districts of the community.

Despite its large size, the site might be considered infill because it is surrounded by existing development on three sides. The site's greatly varying topography was so challenging that it required a major regrading effort. The resulting site preparation costs were such that a relatively high density of development is required for a cost-effective project.

Legacy of the Land

Rancho Mission Viejo has, for the last 120 years, been a major presence in the region due to its vast land ownership, ranching, farming, public service, political, and land stewardship activities. The desire to develop the site in a manner reflecting its ranching history led to in-depth research and the identification of nine historic town types that had evolved locally between 1900 and 1930. Mission towns, beach towns, agricultural towns, and urban satellite towns were evaluated as possible models for site planning, architecture, and landscape design. Several of these typographies were chosen to provide cues, if not models, for villages and districts within the community.

In order to create a buffer for the planned community, and to leave a legacy of the ranch, approximately 1,600 acres (648 hectares) of the site's 4,025 acres (1,629 hectares) have been set aside as permanent open space.

Distinctive Village and Neighborhood Design

The planners of Ladera Ranch believed that although a strong identity for the overall community was important, a development of 8,050 dwellings required a smaller planning unit to ensure a reasonable sense of geographic identity, and convenient access to recreation and social activities for residents. Six villages and four districts were planned, varying from 600 to 1,400 homes, and sized so that every home is within a 12-minute walk from a village core. A village core consists of various community facilities, such as a village club, recreational facilities, schools, daycare, and churches. Each village also projects a subtle shift in site plan and architectural character drawn from one of the nine town types identified in the planning process.

The most significant innovation was to focus on the neighborhood as the primary amenity for the community. Early studies tested the economic feasibility of such expensive, high-profile amenities as golf courses and artificial lakes, but the high cost of land preparation resulted in only marginal financial returns. Instead, a long list of neighborhood design elements were identified and tested for financial feasibility. From that process, several distinct neighborhood prototypes evolved. Some hillside locations are based on conventional suburban plans with cul-de-sac streets and single housing types. Others are based on intersecting street grids with a mix of housing types. Yet all neighborhoods incorporate a number of concepts new to the region. For instance, tracts of detached housing generally do not exceed 50 homes in one location, with each home located within two blocks of a neighborhood park or open space. For a more organic, "unplanned" look, each product line has a minimum of five architectural styles, and no elevation can be repeated on a single block face. Ladera's designers have also introduced curb-separated sidewalks—sidewalks separated from the curb by a planting strip that provides a continuous tree canopy.

Opening page: Ladera's neighborhoods were designed to
provide amenity value by incorporating rich architectural
and landscape details. Residential units, such as the

courtyard homes pictured, are
oriented to promote social interaction between neighbors,
an underlying planning goal.

Bottom, left: The rural
character of the site is reflected in understated entry
signage constructed of native
materials.

Bottom, right: Portions of the
town green have been re-
served for special community
icons such as the gazebo
bandstand and rose garden.

Commercial Districts

The Bridgepark and Township districts are established multiuse districts with, respectively, ten- and 15- acre (four- and six-hectare) neighborhood-serving shopping centers. Bridgepark Plaza is the first retail center to be completed. It carries an agrarian/ranch architectural theme and has provided early residents with shopping and food court services.

The Urban Activity Center is an 85-acre (34-hectare) mixed-use development consisting of a modest medium-box retail center, an office park, a multitenant service/commercial area, and rental apartment sites. Also included are government and community facilities consisting of a fire station, a church site, daycare, a self-storage facility, and a fitness club.

The Township Downtown will be a 15-acre (six-hectare) main street pedestrian-oriented retail center that will include storefront shops and cafés adjacent to the town green and information center.

Design of Homes

Although the DMB development team felt a more new urbanist approach was not appropriate for the site or scale of the project, there was a strong interest in creating more walkable, social, and visually rich neighborhoods than typically found in Southern California subdivisions. The question was: To what degree could the design techniques of the new urbanism be brought into a high-velocity, merchant builder environment and not adversely affect the economic performance of the project?

One way was design. As important as the design of the neighborhood was the design of the homes themselves. Three primary concepts have guided the residential design at Ladera Ranch: architecture forward, diversity, and authenticity. "Architecture forward" is the design team's shorthand for emphasizing and articulating a residence's living areas while recessing the parking garage. The planner's goal of being able to look down a sidewalk and see only porches, stoops, windows, and entries, but not a single garage, has been generally achieved.

"Diversity" is Ladera's response to Orange County's red-tile Mediterranean subdivisions. Seventeen styles have been identified and distilled by William Hezmalhalch Architects for use by builders at Ladera Ranch. Supplementing the Mediterranean style with its tile and stucco finishes are more traditional styles reflecting the region's early period, derived from Midwestern precedents, including California ranch, Monterey, American farm, Prairie, Cottage, Craftsman, and others.

The concept of "authenticity" deals with the appropriate expression of a given architectural style The execution of the style, rather than the floor plan, must drive the design of the house, so that the style is authentically expressed in massing and roof forms rather than through "paste on" details so often found in production housing.

The inevitable questions of cost impacts were addressed through a detailed analysis of each style and the authenticity criteria. This analysis identified those elements too expensive to be absorbed by either higher prices or reduced land costs. Only those architectural elements that had a reasonable cost-benefit ratio were retained in the guidelines. The resulting neighborhood character succeeds in being different from that found elsewhere in the market, with rich variation in architecture, authentic detail,

Below, left: An illustrative plan shows the variety of village and neighborhood patterns. Because it is surrounded on three sides by existing development and an arterial roadway, Ladera Ranch can almost be considered an infill site—a rarity in Orange County.

Below, right: The challenging topography of the 4,000-acre (1,619-hectare) site yielded six villages and four districts. Each has a distinctive identity derived from the setting, residential products, and urban design form.

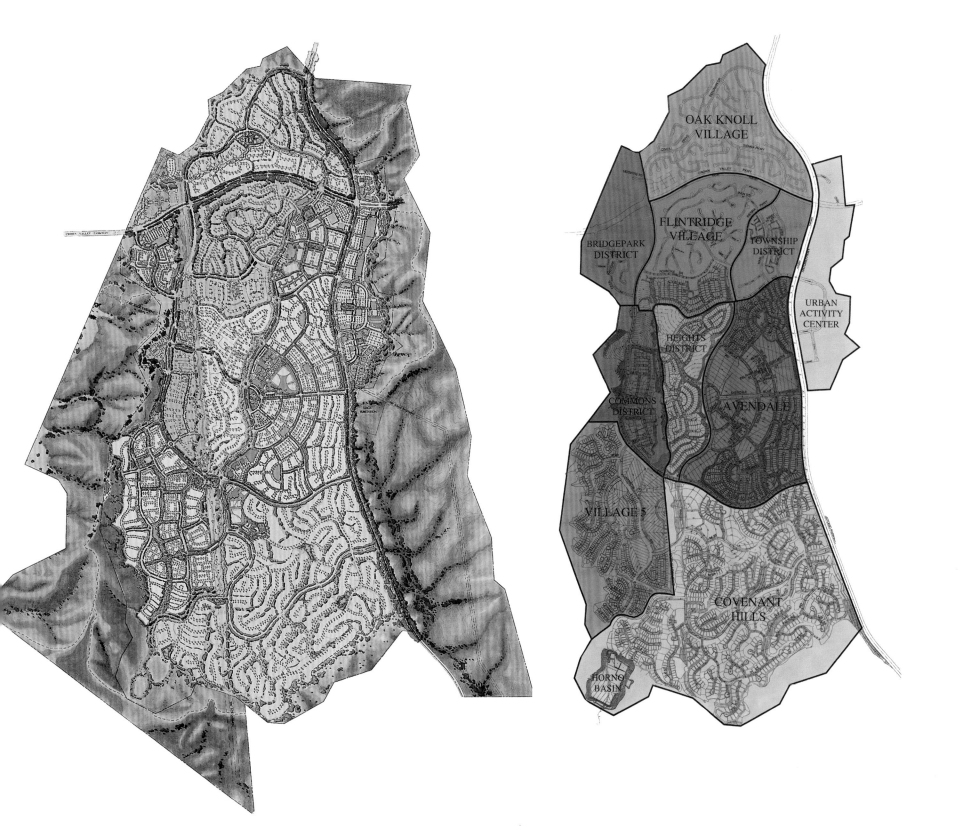

Below: The town green is centrally located and serves as a venue for concerts, festivals, and other community activities.

Bottom, left: Roundabouts calm traffic and provide signature landscape elements in the villages. Each contains a heritage live oak transplanted from elsewhere on the site.

Bottom, right: Children's playgrounds are among the numerous shared recreational amenities at Ladera Ranch, where many young families have settled. Almost every home is within two blocks of a neighborhood park or open space.

Below: Corner lot homes are given special treatment because of their visibility. Each must have fully articulated elevations facing both streets, and wraparound porches are prevalent.

Bottom: Common open space, including an off-street trail system, occupies 7 percent of the total site area. The trails link residents with community facilities and other villages.

Housing along the trails lends architectural interest and a sense of security.

visually minimized garages, and continuous street trees.

An underlying goal of the Ladera approach to neighborhood and village design is to promote the opportunity for neighbor-to-neighbor social interaction. Soft infrastructure and governance structures at Ladera Ranch build on experience at both the Irvine Ranch (see page 98) and Rancho Santa Margarita (see page 170) and are among the most ambitious and sophisticated in the country. A highlight of the program is LaderaLife.com, the community intranet, which services an online community network exclusive to Ladera Ranch. It links residents to one another, local businesses, community, social, civic, recreational activities, and the World Wide Web via high-speed Internet access.

From a market perspective, the site is in one of the strongest housing markets in the country, with steadily increasing prices. Strong demand is due not only to pent-up demand from the early and mid 1990s, when Southern California was in a deep recession, but also to the shortage of developable land and dwindling housing supply in the region.

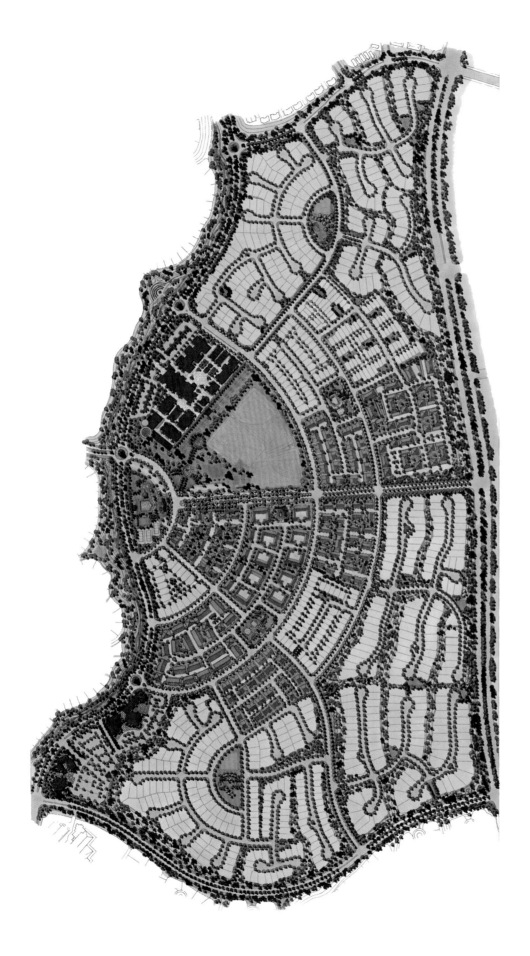

The villages of Avendale (left) and Covenant Hills (above) incorporate interconnected grid and cul-de-sac street patterns, neighborhood parks, architectural variety, and a village core.

Oak Knoll Club is a typical clubhouse, featuring swimming pools, a tot lot, special event area, and community services office (top).

Village homes are located within a 12-minute walk from their respective cores. Each village core contains a private social club for residents, recreational facilities, school (above), childcare and/or a church, and convenience retail (left).

Two concepts, authenticity and diversity, guided the design process in a merchant builder environment. Fourteen different styles were derived from a rich regional heritage, and each product line has a minimum of five styles. The execution of that style must be expressed through an authentic rather than decorative application of architectural details.

Typical street scenes capture the diversity of homes, with some demonstrating the "architecture forward" design concept widely embraced at Ladera Ranch. The idea is to enhance the pedestrian environment by eliminating elements that interfere with safety. Planting strips separate sidewalks from the street, improving the overall ambience.

McKENZIE TOWNE

CALGARY, ALBERTA, CANADA

McKenzie Towne was Calgary's and, indeed, Canada's first master-planned new urbanist community, with sales beginning in 1995. Located in the southeast quadrant of the city, approximately 30 minutes from the downtown core, McKenzie Towne is surrounded by conventional suburban single-family houses ranging from $175,000* to over $500,000. In the early 1990s, extensive market research was conducted before finalizing concept plans for McKenzie Towne, and results indicated some dissatisfaction with prevailing subdivisions of the time. The challenge for Carma Developers was to create a community that would incorporate the attributes of the new urbanism while also achieving broad market acceptance. Upon buildout, expected in 2015, the community will have approximately 6,500 housing units with over 20,000 residents.

The developers selected the firm of Duany Plater-Zyberk & Company (DPZ) to design the master plan and conduct a number of charrettes with the city of Calgary, surrounding landowners, builders, and the public. DPZ also completed a concept plan for the first village—the village of Inverness. Stantec Consulting completed the planning approvals, and initially was the engineering, transportation, and landscape consultant on the project. Stantec had to resolve the engineering issues of street widths that were narrower than local standards, narrower rear lanes, and a traffic roundabout.

The site's flat topography presented both practical and aesthetic challenges—for servicing, because natural drainage flows in a different direction from that of the nearest storm outfall, and for design, in terms of building a visually appealing development. The 960-acre (389-hectare) community is laid out as a series of four villages, each with a central park and many smaller parks. Streets are in a grid pattern and are about three feet (one meter) narrower than in conventional subdivisions, with shorter curb returns to reduce the crossing distance on a roadway. High Street, a commercial main street featuring a full array of shops, services, and public facilities, is the heart of the community.

McKenzie Towne's design concept embodies traditional town planning principles. Each village has its own village square or park that is central to the neighborhood and within walking distance for residents. The village size is therefore determined not by population, but by its distance from the village square. These open spaces, focal points of the community, are additionally used to terminate vistas. Rear lanes throughout McKenzie Towne permit garages to be located behind houses, removing the front driveway and garage to let the architecture be fully expressed. All streets have tree-lined sidewalks, improving pedestrian safety and creating an appealing streetscape. McKenzie Towne Centre, located on High Street, provides a range of commercial and recreational activities. Extensive open spaces and roadways, including a traffic circle at the entryway, connect all villages with each other and with Towne Centre.

Many Opportunities for Homeownership

Residential designs and building types suit a wide range of preferences and market segments, from renters and first homebuyers to estate homebuyers. Single-family detached homes include bungalows, two-story models, and split-level designs, and are available in three market segments—entry-level (from the $150,000s), move-up (from the mid $160,000s), and estate homes (from $250,000 to $400,000). A variety of attached products offer condominium ownership townhouses, bungalow villas, and apartments ranging from the $120,000s to over $180,000.

Each village features architectural detailing that gives it a distinct character. The first two villages, the village of Inverness and the village of Prestwick, offer single-family homes in one of four architectural styles—national, Craftsman, Georgian, and Queen Anne. The latest village, Elgin Village, offers six European styles—English Cottage, Greek Revival, French Eclectic, Italianate, English Tudor, and Arts and Crafts—but continues the uniform streetscapes for which the community has become well known. Front porches that span the width of houses and ornate architectural detailing accent most homes in the community.

As distinctive as are McKenzie Towne's houses, its condominium townhouses, bungalow villas, and apartments are not mere afterthoughts. The brownstone rowhouses that surround Inverness Square in the village of Inverness were introduced at the beginning of the development. Today, they are a signature design element of the village and the overall community.

All dollar values in this case study are Canadian dollars.

Previous page: In Inverness, the first of McKenzie Towne's four villages, stately brownstone townhouses and condominium apartments flank Inverness Square. Each village features a central park or square within walking distance of all residents.

Right: Extensive open spaces and roadways, including this traffic circle at the community's entrance, connect all villages with each other and Towne Centre.

Right: "Generations in the making for generations to come" was the tagline for McKenzie Towne when marketing for the 960-acre (389-hectare) community began in 1995. The concept, which informed the master plan, was to look to the past for inspiration in creating a traditional small-town atmosphere with today's modern conveniences and amenities.

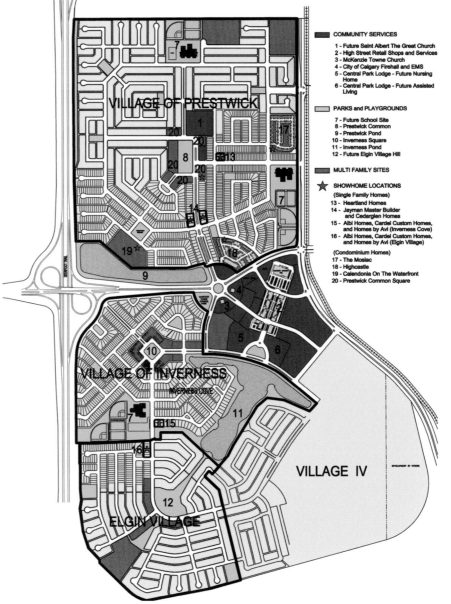

COMMUNITY SERVICES

1 - Future Saint Albert The Great Church
2 - High Street Retail Shops and Services
3 - McKenzie Towne Church
4 - City of Calgary Firehall and EMS
5 - Central Park Lodge - Future Nursing Home
6 - Central Park Lodge - Future Assisted Living

PARKS and PLAYGROUNDS

7 - Future School Site
8 - Prestwick Common
9 - Prestwick Pond
10 - Inverness Square
11 - Inverness Pond
12 - Future Elgin Village Hill

MULTI FAMILY SITES

SHOWHOME LOCATIONS
(Single Family Homes)
13 - Heartland Homes
14 - Jayman Master Builder and Cedarglen Homes
15 - Albi Homes, Cardel Custom Homes, and Homes by Avi (Inverness Cove)
16 - Albi Homes, Cardel Custom Homes, and Homes by Avi (Elgin Village)

(Condominium Homes)
17 - The Mosaic
18 - Highcastle
19 - Caledonia On The Waterfront
20 - Prestwick Common Square

VILLAGE OF PRESTWICK

VILLAGE OF INVERNESS

VILLAGE IV

ELGIN VILLAGE

Left: The Gables in the village of Prestwick was the first phase of townhouse development that completely surrounds Prestwick Common, the village square. To broaden market appeal, 12 different models were offered.

Below, left: Inverness Square is distinguished by a 92-foot-high (28-meter-high) clock tower that chimes on the hour. The building initially housed the community's information center.

Below, right: The Victorian gazebo in Inverness Square is one of the landmarks that give each village its singular identity. Its function as a gathering place for residents is indicative of McKenzie Towne's focus on establishing community spirit and neighborliness.

INVERNESS SQUARE

Ten different architectural styles can be found in McKenzie Towne's housing mix. In order to maintain consistently high-quality design and construction standards throughout the community, strict architectural guidelines were established and adhered to by builders.

Below and opposite, bottom: Social interaction is promoted through neighborhood design. Tree-lined boulevards, a traditional grid street pattern, garages in back, porches out front, village squares, and small parks are just a few of the community's people-friendly gestures.

Opposite, top: Inverness Pond is a 30-acre (12-hectare) pond and park that provides recreational opportunities, wildlife habitat, and serves as an integral part of McKenzie Towne's storm water management system.

Build-to Line

In harmony with classic architectural styling, the streetscape is an important design element. The streetscape is established by a "build-to line," rather than the more typical setback requirements. The build-to line specifies that buildings must be no more than 12.5 feet (3.8 meters) from the front property line. This creates a uniform building wall that frames the street and sidewalk. Further enclosure is created by street trees, which are planted at regular intervals along boulevards. Details such as specialized street lighting and textured sidewalks are also incorporated. Garages located at the rear of houses are accessed from paved rear lanes, except for those lots that back onto Inverness Pond, where the lots are wider and garages are allowed to protrude a maximum of six feet (two meters) from the front of the house.

A small-town atmosphere prevails in each of the villages, augmented by carefully planned public space (as illustrated in Prestwick Commons, opposite, bottom), but urban conveniences such as retail shops, services, and eateries are only minutes away on High Street in McKenzie Towne Centre (below). A church and fire station (opposite, top, left and right), strategically located at the entrance to the community, respond to the spiritual and physical well-being of residents.

McKenzie Towne Centre

McKenzie Towne Centre, the community's commercial component, is a mixed-use downtown area that contains shops and services not normally found at this early stage of development. (Development of Towne Centre began in 1998, just three years after the initiation of the project.) The first phase features a 37,000-square-foot (3,437-square-meter) grocery store and over 20 retail shops and services along pedestrian-oriented High Street, the town's most notable feature. Developers believe this amenity will draw prospective homebuyers.

Zoning allows for a variety of uses in the 46-acre (19-hectare) Towne Centre, including office space, yet the market will dictate what is ultimately built. High Street, with a land area of 11.6 acres (five hectares), now has 107,000 square feet (9,941 square meters) of development. Towne Centre also includes two seniors' facilities encompassing seven acres (three hectares) and a 6.4-acre (2.5-hectare) multifamily development. The remaining 9.7 acres (four hectares) of commercial land could accommodate an additional 100,000 square feet (9,290 square meters) of retail space, a 7.1-acre (three-hectare) site designated for a transit park-and-ride lot, and 4.5 acres (two hectares) of future multifamily land. Carma Developers constructed High Street rather than engage a commercial developer, thus ensuring that the new urbanist architectural controls were maintained. The cost of construction was approximately 10 percent higher than a high-quality strip center would have been, due to the higher quality streetfront facades, higher volume spaces on the corners, and the fact that the on-street parking is complemented by rear parking, which requires a secondary access.

Market demand for McKenzie Towne's retail space is already strong, due, in part, to the surrounding population of 16,000 in the nearby community of McKenzie Lake, which is undersupplied with retail services. Of the four villages, the village of Inverness is almost completely built out with over 1,000 homes. The village of Prestwick opened in 1998 and currently has 1,500 homes. Elgin Village opened in September 2000 and has almost 100 homes. The fourth village, currently unnamed, is in preliminary planning stages and will be introduced as buildout occurs in Prestwick and Elgin villages.

ORENCO STATION

HILLSBORO, OREGON

Originally zoned for industrial use and later rezoned for higher density housing, Orenco Station was born when the site was designated a "town center" in the Portland Metro Area 2040 Plan. The plan for Orenco Station, a 209-acre (85-hectare) master-planned community in the western suburbs of Portland, Oregon, established residential density targets at varying distances from the Orenco light rail stop and mandated mixed-use development.

Developer Pacific Realty Associates (PacTrust) planned the pedestrian-oriented community for 1,906 housing units, 350,000 square feet (32,516 square meters) of retail, and 60,000 square feet (5,574 square meters) of office space. The compact design includes a wide range of housing types. Everything from single-family detached houses to accessory dwellings built over garages, live-work townhouses to lofts over retail shops, is included in the mix. What binds it all together is a formal system of open spaces and mini-parks terminating in the Orenco Station stop of the Tri-Met MAX light rail line, which connects the community to downtown Portland, about 45 minutes away.

With little precedent for either higher density or mixed-use development in the area, PacTrust and Costa Pacific Homes assembled a team to explore the locally uncharted waters. As part of the exploration, market research was conducted among workers in surrounding high-tech companies to establish design and housing preferences and define affordability issues. The survey and subsequent focus group research revealed an attraction to the older Portland suburbs, with their Craftsman- and Cottage-style architecture, picturesque rose gardens, and neighborhood-oriented shops. The research reflected a somewhat nostalgic outlook, but one that fit well with the concept of a higher density, transit-oriented development.

Two years of discussions, design studies, and negotiations with city, Metro, and transit officials ensued, culminating in a custom-tailored zoning ordinance for Orenco Station. Dubbed a "Station Community Residential Village," or SCRV district, the new zoning established design guidelines that would allow for—and ensure—the sort of heterogeneous and urban mixing of housing types and land uses not typically found in the suburbs.

Transportation Drives Design

The light rail station, located at the southern edge of the development, is the generative element of the community's site design. Orenco Station Parkway is a main street that provides the primary circulation network for vehicles and pedestrians leading from the station to the town center and culminates in a formal central park. Secondary circulation and open spaces branch laterally from this ceremonial spine. The open space and circulation framework have a processional quality, meant to induce a sense of place and community. Vistas are terminated by strong visual elements, such as the classically inspired pergolas at each end of the central park. The village green provides a transition from the town center to the adjacent single-family neighborhood. By these means, and by the judicious placement of smaller mini-parks, the developer and architects have sculpted a plan intended to encourage walking—and a more community-oriented way of life.

In the residential areas, several design devices were employed to reinforce the pedestrian and community orientation of Orenco Station. Residential street widths were minimized (25 feet/seven and one-half meters, with parking on one side), and sidewalks are bulbed to narrow intersections and slow traffic. To further reduce the impact of the automobile, Orenco's site design provides alley parking access through drive lanes, thereby eliminating the usual garage-door-dominated streetscape and ubiquitous curb cuts and driveways. To minimize costs, drive-lane paving was held to a width of 16 feet (five meters), with turn-ins expanding to the full 24 feet (seven meters) from garage face to garage face. The space between the garage turn-ins is used for plantings, which soften the drive-lane appearance.

Urban Street Life

The town center is the community's focal point both visually and functionally. It lies at the intersection of Orenco Station Parkway and Cornell Road, a quarter mile (one-half kilometer) from the light rail station. Designed by Fletcher Farr Ayotte Architects (FFA), the first phase of the town center provided space for small neighborhood shops and restaurants, including a

Opening pages: Anchored by a gazebo, the village green provides a transition from the town center to the residential neighborhoods. This central park and several smaller pocket parks form a "string of pearls" throughout the community.

Opposite top, left and right: Single-family houses are built on relatively small lots and are set close to narrow, tree-lined streets. Architectural styles are based on Portland-area Craftsman and English Cottage precedents, and most have front porches.

Opposite, bottom: The brick-clad exterior and bay windows of the live-work units highlight the architecture of the nearby town center. The units feature a split entry that goes up to a main living area and down to a home office or commercial space.

Below: Orenco Station's compact plan occupies a 190-acre (77-hectare) site. The density of the pedestrian-oriented community is mitigated by a system of neighborhood parks and pedestrian routes. The open space and circulation framework have a processional quality, meant to introduce a sense of place and community.

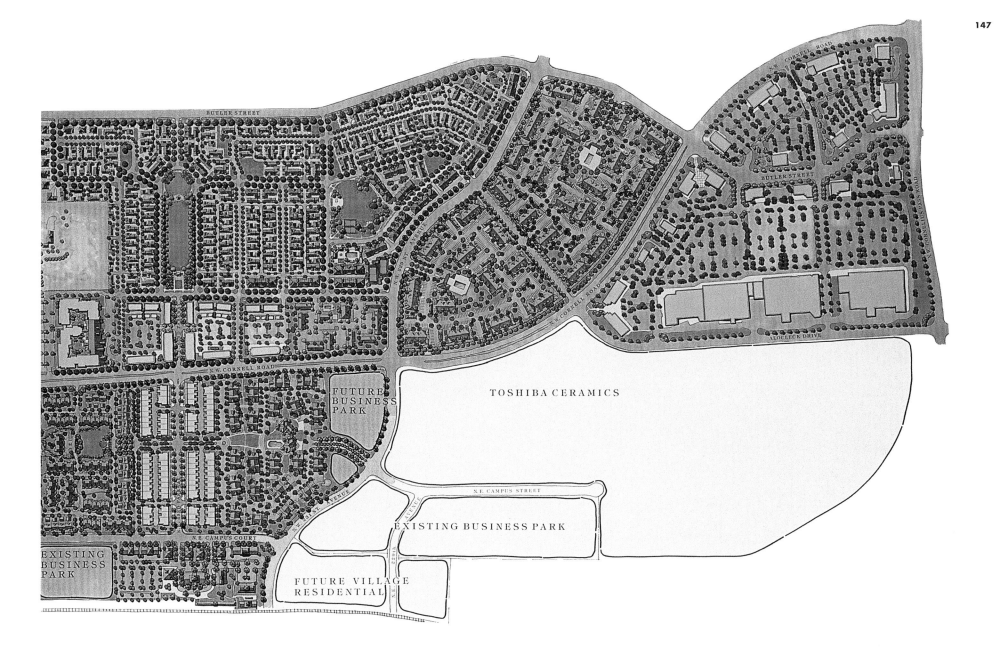

148   Clockwise, from top: Small front yard setbacks, as in this English-style stucco house, encourage a more active and engaged street life. The pavilion at the village green provides a shady spot and space for public functions. Garages are located behind the homes along landscaped alleys. Some of the garages feature carriage houses, with the option of either a studio or apartment. Opposite: Townhouses and condominiums at Orenco Station are integrated with the single-family detached houses, often anchoring the ends of single-family blocks. The Morello Place condominiums shown here feature balconies, porches, and numerous large windows, complementing the traditional neighborhood architecture that surrounds them.

coffee shop, Italian and Indian restaurants, wine and cigar shops, a dentist, and an optician. Some storefronts have roll-up glass doorfronts to allow for outdoor dining along the extra-wide 17-foot-wide (five-meter-wide) sidewalks. Condominiums above the retail are designed as industrial-style lofts. Commercial space is located on the corners above the stores. On-street parking and wide sidewalks create a strong urban character along this main street, and additional parking is provided behind the buildings.

FFA also designed three-story live-work townhouses adjacent to the main street. These mixed-use dwellings offer a ground-floor professional office-studio combined with a two-story loft residence. The brick buildings feature bay windows, echoing the architectural detail of the nearby shops. Recessed, "tucked-under" parking is located at the rear. A New Seasons community grocery store and an additional 44,000 square feet (4,088 square meters) of retail anchor Phase II of the town center, which recently opened. Twenty-two for-sale loft units were constructed over the retail.

Nearby is Crossroads shopping center, offering a grocery store, sports store, video rental store, banks, and a restaurant in easy walking distance from most residences. Crossroads provides shops and services to meet the needs of Orenco Station and other residents of the surrounding area.

Flexible Housing Configurations

Single-family lots at Orenco Station are small by local standards, ranging from 3,680 to 4,500 square feet (342 to 418 square meters). Homes are held close to the street with eight-foot (two-meter) maximum setbacks for townhouses and 13- to 19-foot (four- to six-meter) setbacks for detached housing units. While the smaller-than-typical front yard setbacks and the front porch elements are intended to encourage a more active and engaged street life, the dwelling units are raised above the sidewalk, as in many older Portland neighborhoods, to afford a vertical measure of privacy.

Traditional facade designs are based on Portland-area Craftsman and English Cottage precedents, and most homes have front porches. Designed by Iverson Associates, housing units at Orenco Station are relatively small: single-family detached models range from 1,400 to 1,700 square feet (130 to 158 square meters). Designs include two- and three-bedroom models, although some have flexible spaces allowing for conversion to three- or four-bedroom residences. Responding to emerging lifestyle patterns and preferences, all units have a dedicated home office space, typically an alcove or open area off a second-floor stair landing. Dwelling units are constructed with high-speed wiring for computer communication as well.

The decision to include accessory units or carriage houses over garages was approached cautiously by the development team, because the market for these spaces, as well as the impact of mixing smaller residential units with the larger main residences, was relatively untested at the time. The 514-square-foot (48-square-meter) carriage houses were offered as a buyer's

Below: The town center includes small retail shops on first levels, with offices and housing above. Some of the buildings have roll-up glass doorfronts that open to outdoor cafés along wide sidewalks. Brick facades, bay windows, and balconies echo the architecture of nearby neighborhoods, creating a strong urban enclosure.

option, with two different plan configurations: a studio option (one large room, a bath, and a small closet) and an apartment option (living room, sleeping alcove, kitchen, and bath). About one in four buyers has purchased the accessory space; most of these have taken the apartment version, currently priced at $59,900.

Use of the added space has been varied; some owners have used it as office space or as a guest suite, and others have rented it as an apartment. The accessory units have separate legal addresses and are entered directly from the drive lanes via an exterior stair. One parking space is carved out of the rear portion of the homesite for each accessory unit. The dwelling units have windows that overlook the drive lane. They also have a small covered porch at the top of the stairs, providing activity and oversight to the drive lanes.

Unlike more conventional subdivisions, the three- and four-unit townhouse structures are integrated with the single-family detached housing, often sited at the ends of single-family blocks. From the exterior, the town-

house structures are designed to look like larger cousins to the adjacent single-family houses, with asymmetric and varied facades and entryways.

Sales at Orenco Station have exceeded projections. Absorption has averaged 7.5 units per month, and prices are running about 20 to 30 percent above the area average. The project's sense of community, town center, traditional architecture, and pedestrian orientation have been cited in post-purchase focus groups as primary reasons for purchasing a home in Orenco Station.

The experience of Orenco Station has demonstrated that higher densities and mixed housing types can be successful in suburban markets. The success, according to PacTrust and its design team, is due in large part to the attention paid to the public realm and to the creation of a strong sense of place, which offset the smaller private space offered to buyers.

Below, left: Orenco Station Parkway is the project's back-bone, a main street promenade leading from the light rail station through the town center and terminating at the village green.

Below, right: The town center site plan illustrates the street and circulation grid that defines the urban character of the community.

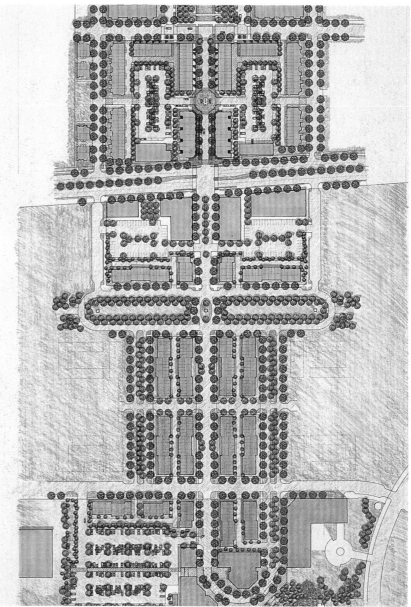

PARK DuVALLE

LOUISVILLE, KENTUCKY

Park DuValle in Louisville, Kentucky, was once one of the city's most blighted inner-city neighborhoods. Dominated by a massive public housing project, it had become an isolated pocket of poverty, crime, and hopelessness. Today, Park DuValle is being transformed into a 132-acre (53-hectare) mixed-income, mixed-density community of more than 1,200 new homes, townhouses, and apartments, with a blend of public housing, market-rate rental, and homeownership units.

The metamorphosis of Park DuValle began in 1995 when the 1950s barracks-style public housing project was razed to make way for new development. The major impetus behind the new development was a HOPE VI grant to the Housing Authority of Louisville (HAL) from the U. S. Department of Housing and Urban Development (HUD). The goal of the HOPE VI program is to replace public housing projects with new mixed-income neighborhoods that integrate public housing residents and communities into mainstream city life. The redevelopment of Park DuValle has been and continues to be a collaboration between local, state, and federal agencies with community-based organizations and private sector partners. The Community Builders, Inc., based in Boston, was chosen to be the master developer.

The Challenge
The overall goal for the redevelopment of Park DuValle was to provide public housing for families in need while simultaneously attracting middle-income renters and homebuyers to the new neighborhood. Essentially, prospective homebuyers were being invited to invest their life savings in a house on a site with 40 years of bad newspaper headlines, and to live next door to public housing residents—an ambitious plan given the condition and reputation of the neighborhood at the onset of the project.

To overcome the negative realities of the site and program, the urban design and architecture of the new mixed-income neighborhood had to be based on strategies that would instill confidence and, ultimately, create a safe, stable, sustainable neighborhood. By using the images and forms identified with successful, traditional Louisville neighborhoods, the design

has served to reassure residents, to turn initial skepticism into support, and to foster the rebirth of the area as a community in which residents can take pride.

The master planning process involved extensive public participation by public housing residents, adjacent neighborhood residents, city officials, and others. A public design charrette was held during which the initial concept plan was developed.

The master plan by Pittsburgh-based Urban Design Associates is based on principles of traditional neighborhood development (TND) as found in Louisville. The plan creates a new community consisting of small-scale neighborhoods, compact residential blocks with a mix of housing types, street-facing houses, and a clear delineation of public and private space. The master plan also calls for providing a mix of community-serving amenities, including schools, parks, and a town center, as well as making the new neighborhoods of Park DuValle walkable, connecting them to each other, and weaving them into the surrounding urban fabric of Louisville's West End.

Building a Neighborhood on Olmsted's Tradition
The master plan extended the site beyond the boundaries of the public housing projects to include adjacent vacant properties and publicly owned parkland. A network of new streets meets the street grid of the surrounding neighborhoods, seamlessly connecting Park DuValle to the larger community.

The configuration of streets and parks within Park DuValle continues the forms established in Louisville by Frederick Law Olmsted in 1891. The Algonquin Parkway and Algonquin Park, both part of the Olmsted plan, form two edges of the new community. New residentially scaled parkways lined with houses connect all of the public buildings, parks, and recreation amenities in the project. Smaller streets connecting to the parkways frame a series of neighborhoods and public open space. The community's connections to Olmsted's "emerald necklace" of Louisville parkways further serve to create a memorable and marketable image for the neighborhood.

154 Creating a Mixed-Income Community

Owned and rented units are mixed together throughout the community, although rental units are clustered in small groups for ease of maintenance. No distinction is made between subsidized and market-rate rental units; the units may change from one to another classification. The unconventional relationship between market-rate and subsidized housing was a concern to lenders, as was the need to price new for-sale houses substantially higher than surrounding neighborhoods because of the disproportionately high ratio of rental to for-sale homes. The challenge was to convince homebuyers who had other options to buy houses in a neighborhood with lower-income rentals.

To overcome the stigma of government housing, Park DuValle houses are 5 to 10 percent larger than homes in surrounding neighborhoods and offer more varied designs. To conform to financing requirements, it was decided that owned homes would face each other and that rental homes would face other rentals.

The plan also calls for many of the functions of daily life to be available within walking distance. A closed school in the center of Park DuValle was renovated and reopened and new recreation facilities are being built in the parks. A mixed-use town center is the key element of the third phase of development and will include a 40,000-square-foot (3,716-square-meter) medical center, 25,000 square feet (2,323 square meters) of convenience retail, and an assisted living facility.

Louisville's Architectural Legacy

The architectural design of the houses, as well as the character of each neighborhood within Park DuValle, is based on a carefully crafted pattern book developed in conjunction with the master plan by Urban Design Associates. The UDA Pattern Book establishes architectural design guidelines based on traditional Louisville housing. The book is divided into three sections: Community Patterns, which sets the relationship of buildings to one another and to the streets and parks; Architectural Patterns, which sets the style palette and key design elements such as massing, windows and

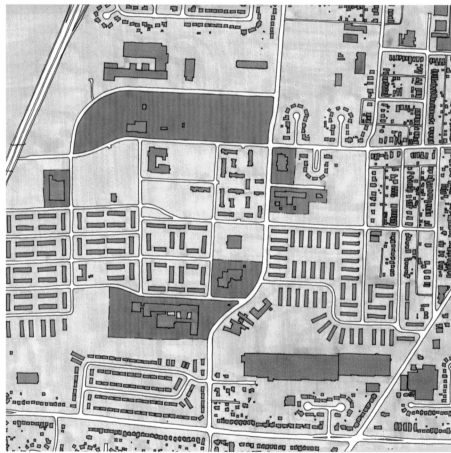

Opening page: A page out of the Park DuValle Pattern Book, a tool provided by the master planner to the development team to set the character of each neighborhood and guide the architectural design of all housing types.

Top and above: Before Park DuValle, two crime-ridden public housing projects and a deteriorated apartment complex dominated the 132-acre (53-hectare) site.

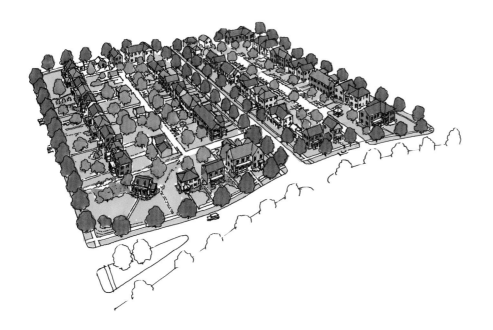

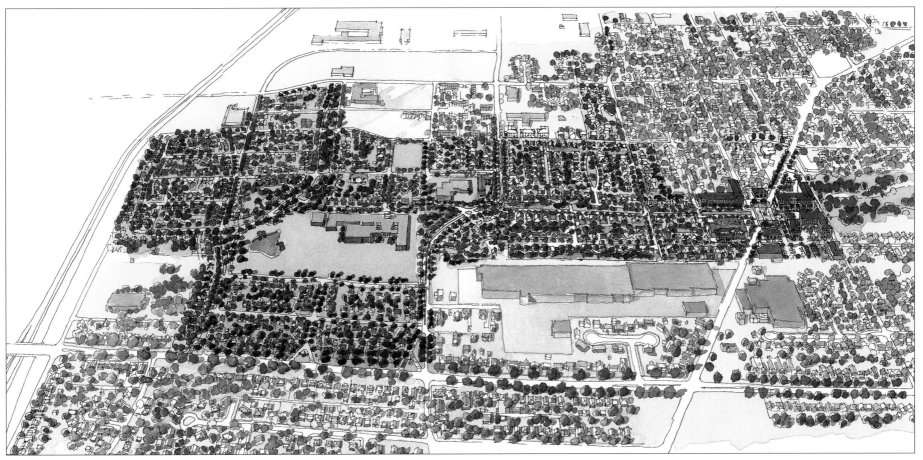

The master plan sought to reshape the derelict site into a vibrant new mixed-income community that was safe, attractive, marketable, and connected to the urban fabric of Louisville. At final buildout, residents will have educational, recreational, retail, and commercial components within walking distance.

156

Right: Among the mix of 1,008 housing units are 613 owned and rented multifamily dwellings. Apartment buildings designed to look like large single-family homes blend easily with for-sale homes. From left to right: triplex, fourplex, and sixplex rental configurations.

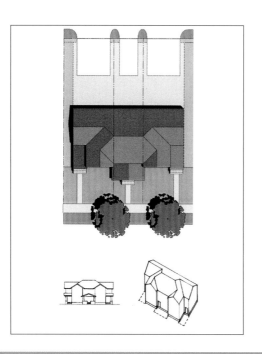
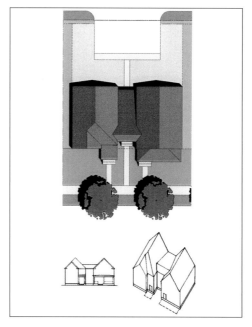
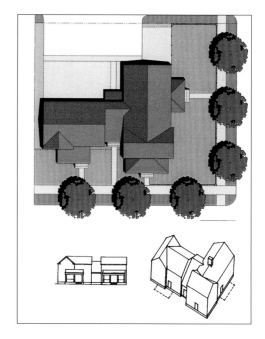

Above: To accommodate a mixed-income program, various residential products were developed. All were designed as houses, not buildings, to create the look and feel of a traditional neighborhood. A duplex (left) and triplex (right) are pictured.

Louisville Craftsman

This style evolved during the 1920s as the Craftsman style gained popularity in California and became a national style in house design, available both in pattern book housing for builders and as custom design offered by architects. The craftsman style was thus adapted to more modest housing as well as the high end of urban markets at the time. The style often displays deep eaves, grouped windows and handsome trim on windows, doors and porches. The interiors were often distinguished by attractive built-in cabinetry, paneled doors and walls, interior columns and room dividers and the feel of the house as a piece of furniture.

In Louisville, many of the traditional Colonial Revival house bodies were reworked with Craftsman detailing.

Essential Characteristics

1. Deep eaves, often with exposed, molded rafter ends and ornamental brackets
2. Grouped windows in pairs or in threes with upper sashes or divided light patterns
3. Deep porches with ornamental half-timbering, wood columns that are often tapered or on brick piers, and solid railing
4. Simple, straightforward volume with low slope gabled or hipped roof
5. Continuous horizontal trim band or belt course, at the second floor window line

PARK DUVALLE PATTERN BOOK

ARCHITECTURAL PATTERNS — 33 — Louisville Craftsman   Elements of Style

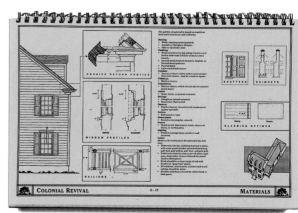

COLONIAL REVIVAL   MATERIALS

157

The development and adoption of the Park DuValle Pattern Book helped to ensure that buildings would have the look and feel of a traditional Louisville neighborhood. Community patterns, architectural patterns, and landscape patterns are addressed in the book's three sections, which combine text, drawings, and photographs.

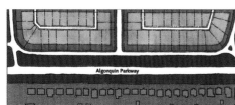

Partial Plan of Algonquin Parkway

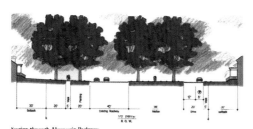

Section through Algonquin Parkway

view of Algonquin Parkway looking west

Algonquin Parkway

The strengths of the Parkway as an address — the wide tree lawn and grandeur of its trees — will be preserved and reinforced through the creation of a traditional service drive. The boulevard-like effect of Algonquin Parkway between 39th Street and the new Park Drive will provide grand and dramatic front door for the community.

The elegantly designed houses along Algonquin Parkway will present the table of contents for the architectural styles in the neighborhood and set the stage for the collection of smaller scale streets, each with its own character but using the same pool of style types.

The front yard setback is 30 feet along Algonquin Parkway. Front driveways accessed from the service drive are permitted. The use of planting strips in front driveways is encouraged.

PARK DUVALLE PATTERN BOOK

COMMUNITY PATTERNS   — 15 —   Addresses   Algonquin Parkway

158   Top: The physical character of the houses is local in origin. Three Louisville architectural styles—Victorian, Colonial Revival, and Craftsman—served as prototypes. Street-oriented front porches encourage social interaction, while utilitarian needs are met via rear service alleys.

Bottom: New single-family and attached houses are mixed-income rental development, 75 percent of which are subsidized for low-income residents, and 25 percent of which are market rate.

doors, composition, and porches for three architectural styles—Old Louisville Victorian, Colonial Revival, and Louisville Craftsman; and Landscape Patterns, which describes landscape elements within the community. Although only three architectural styles were permitted in Park DuValle, the wide range of details, colors, and materials illustrated in the UDA Pattern Book for each style gives homebuilders considerable flexibility, as can be seen in the variety of homes actually built. As a result, the new community feels very much like such classic Louisville neighborhoods as Cherokee Triangle and Old Louisville.

Adding to the neighborhood's distinction is the fact that all of the rental units have been designed as a collection of houses, rather than as conventional blocks of apartments. Rental units are built in duplexes, triplexes, fourplexes, and sixplexes—many look like large single-family houses—and are interspersed with the for-sale homes. All entrances to attached units and apartments have porches to reinforce the sense of identity for each family.

Park DuValle's block sizes are designed to the scale of blocks in adjacent historic neighborhoods as well, replacing the barracks-like layout of conventional public housing. Streets and new parkways are lined with closely spaced houses with front doors, porches, and large windows facing the street. Alley lanes provide access to parking. The size of the blocks easily accommodates a variety of housing types, from single-family detached to townhouses to apartments, giving the developer maximum flexibility as the market changes over time, and also permitting a mix of housing types within any one block.

Waiting for Retail

Park DuValle has proved to be attractive to a broad cross section of residents in the Louisville market; both rentals and sales have far exceeded expectations, and apartments are renting faster than they can be built. The first 50 lots designated for homeownership units sold a year ahead of schedule, with a waiting list of 250 for the next phase.

The biggest remaining challenge for Park DuValle, according to the developers, is to identify and attract neighborhood-scale retail. Five years after the first phase of construction was begun, neither a developer nor the financing has materialized for a 25,000-square-foot (2,323-square-meter) neighborhood retail center included in the master plan. Nevertheless, the new Park DuValle has by almost any standard achieved its goal of transforming a run-down inner-city neighborhood into a vibrant mixed-income neighborhood.

Top: The new parkway system crosses Wilson Avenue, a main thoroughfare, and leads to Algonquin Park. The intersection is designed as a town square surrounded by a variety of uses.

Above: Rental and owned units are mixed throughout the community on a street-by-street basis. No architectural distinction is made between subsidized and market-rate rental units.

POUNDBURY

DORCHESTER, DORSET, UNITED KINGDOM

One of the first traditional neighborhood developments (TNDs) in Great Britain, Poundbury is a high-profile expression of the public backlash against modernism in architecture and housing planning. By the mid 1980s, economic recession and five years of Prime Minister Thatcher's administration had combined to end 30 years of post-War government sponsorship of vast public housing schemes in Britain. To the public, economic unrest, intensifying social problems, and the hard-edged geometries of modernist housing and urban design all seemed indistinguishable from one another. It was Prince Charles who, at the 150th birthday party of the Royal Institute of British Architects in 1984, surprised his hosts by declaring, "For too long, planners and architects have consistently ignored the feelings and wishes of ordinary people."

Prince Charles's Ten Principles

The Prince's provocative sentiments rang true with the public as well as mainstream and avant-garde architects and planners throughout much of Europe and North America. Most notably, the Luxembourg-born architect, Léon Krier (whom the Poundbury development commissioned in 1988 to master plan the community), had been championing the cause of the new urbanism. Prince Charles and Krier formed an alliance, out of which came Prince Charles's book, *A Vision of Britain* (1989), in which he proposed that architecture and planning should follow ten principles: (1) PLACE: New buildings should blend with the landscape; (2) HIERARCHY: The size and site of buildings should relate to their importance, with a clear distinction between different elements within a building; (3) SCALE: New buildings should relate to human proportions and respect the scale of buildings around them; (4) HARMONY: Each building should be in tune with its neighbor; (5) ENCLOSURE: Buildings should form enclosures; (6) MATERIALS: Revival of the use of local materials and traditional craftsmen would protect the character of each area and in time engender a locally based economic revival; (7) DECORATION: Architecture should be reinstated "as the mistress of the arts and crafts," with a revival of the use of ornament; (8) ART: Art should be an integral part of all new buildings; (9) SIGNS and LIGHTS: Signs, street lighting, and standardized designs for storefronts of chain stores need to be controlled; and, (10) COMMUNITY: People should be involved from the start in the improvement of their own surroundings, to encourage pride.

Poundbury reifies these principles so thoroughly that were it not for the automobiles, it would look like a setting for one of Dorset-born Thomas Hardy's Wessex novels. Indeed, visitors have stopped residents to ask if "it's open," as if Poundbury were a theme park. When the plan for Poundbury was first unveiled, critics saw it as a pet project of a prince lost in idealism and out of touch with the realities of real estate development. Today, when taxi drivers call it Charlieville, it is with cheeky, but deserved respect.

Building a Sense of Place

The duchy of Cornwall, created in 1337 to provide an income for the heir apparent to the throne, owns real estate properties in 22 counties totaling 126,000 acres (50,990 hectares). Some of its land holdings are in Dorchester, an unincorporated town of 15,000 people in Dorset county, southwest of London, midway along the English Channel coast of England. In 1987, the local planning authority selected 400 acres (162 hectares) of land on Dorchester's western edge as a place for future expansion. It was centered on Poundbury Farm, owned by the duchy.

The first phase of development at Poundbury covers 18.5 acres (7.5 hectares) of the eventual 400 acres (162 hectares). Construction began in 1993, and was completed in 2000. This phase includes both rental and for-sale homes, offices, and light-industrial and retail facilities. At buildout, which the duchy estimates will take 20 to 25 years, Poundbury will comprise 250 acres (101 hectares) of mixed-use buildings and 150 acres (61 hectares) of open space and landscaping, and will add 5,000 people to Dorchester's population.

Guiding the planning process were the ten principles expounded in Prince Charles's book. Privately owned and publicly assisted housing would be intermingled and designed to be indistinguishable from each other. Rather than a rigid, geometric street pattern setting the framework for the development, streets were designed around the houses to create urban spaces with

Opening page: Architectural authenticity is one of Poundbury's most distinctive qualities. While the most prevalent facing material is stone, variety is achieved not only by the off-the-grid articulation of similar forms, but also by the occasional use of unexpected forms and materials, such as this cedar-shake conical roof over a private gazebo.

Right: The master plan for Poundbury's 18.5-acre (7.5-hectare) first phase is a high-density development with a public space, Pummery Square, at its center. Concentrated here are retail, commercial, and light-industrial uses, surrounded by residential blocks of mixed multifamily and single-family housing.

Opposite, clockwise from left: This aerial view shows Poundbury's first phase still under construction. Two completed nonresidential buildings are Middlemarch Alternative Therapies Clinic (above, right), and Market Hall on Pummery Square (below).

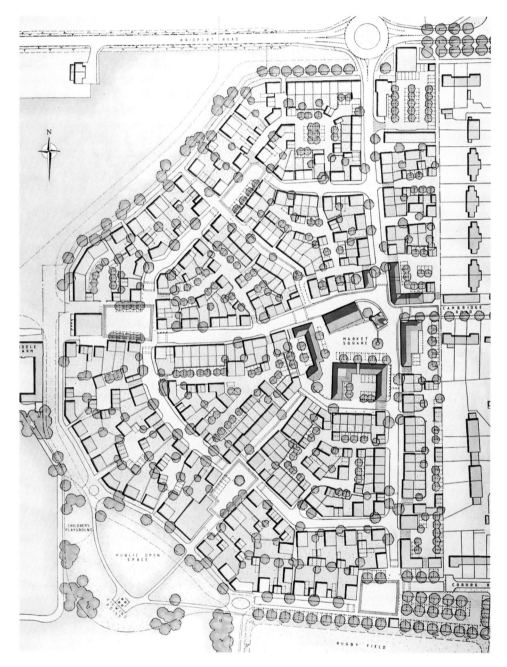

visual interest and a natural tendency to control the flow of automobile traffic. The roads at Poundbury are narrow and on-street parking is widespread, further calming the traffic and favoring pedestrians over cars. Alleyways are paved with fine gravel and connect the roads with courtyard parking areas. The overarching vision for Poundbury was to create an integrated mixed-use development that would be an extension of urban Dorchester, rather than a suburban appendage.

The architecture draws on the centuries-old vernacular design and indigenous building materials of Dorsetshire. Close attention was paid to providing clear signage and attractive landscaping. Active steps have been taken to minimize its impact on the environment. In addition to devoting one-third of the site to landscaped parks and play areas, guidelines called for incorporating readily available energy-efficient technologies. All buildings feature double-glazed windows and higher levels of insulation than required by codes. Homes feature gray water recycling systems to conserve water. To ensure a high aesthetic value, all utility connections at Poundbury are below grade and satellite dishes are not allowed.

One of Poundbury's most important features, however, is its character. It strives to create a sense of place—one that is connected to the traditions and context of the surrounding area. "Far from being 'old fashioned,'" said Prince Charles in February 1999, "Poundbury has merely tried to revisit those timeless principles that are best able to create a real sense of community."

Intermingled Types and Functions

Poundbury was intentionally built with a variety of housing types and styles. Twenty percent of the dwelling units are reserved for low-income families, whose units look like and are intermingled with market-rate units. Poundbury offers homes in detached, semidetached, rowhouse, and multi-family configurations. There also is a 29-unit apartment building reserved for seniors.

Since the duchy of Cornwall was not allowed to actually build anything at Poundbury, several private homebuilders became involved to produce and sell the homes there. Land designated for housing was tendered at market value, while parcels designated for commercial uses were negotiated individually. With the sale of land came a development agreement that compelled the builders to follow the plans for Poundbury. Builders obtained financing for construction in the private market, and all have received acceptable returns on their investment.

Residential densities are approximately 16 units per acre (39 units per hectare), about twice as high as those found in typical housing schemes in Britain. This level of density has been achieved through a combination of narrow streets, small yards, building houses to the front property line, and through the careful arrangement of off-street parking. These densities also help to keep "eyes on the street," perhaps helping to account for the fact that there has not been a single serious crime at Poundbury since it was opened.

164

Right, top and bottom: In accordance with Prince Charles's ten planning principles outlined in his book, *A Vision of Britain,* the size and siting of buildings at Poundbury relate to their importance and function. Civic buildings occupy prominent corner spaces and are taller than their residential neighbors. Likewise, retail buildings at Pummery Square have clearly delineated storefronts and face directly onto public space.

Far right, center: Even without knowing its function, this building declares itself a landmark, with its playfully proportioned square and porthole windows, symmetrically placed dormer windows, and square-pyramidal roof topped with a weathervane as a finial.

Opposite, top: Buildings at Poundbury are intended to harmonize with neighboring buildings, even if differing uses coexist side by side. Here, retail space occupies the ground floor, with residential space above.

Opposite, bottom: Light-industrial buildings at Poundbury establish a small job base where none previously existed.

Right, top and bottom: Streets at Poundbury are considered public spaces and were designed as if they grew organically from the settlement patterns established by the houses. Zero-lot-line houses form continuous street edges with no front gardens. Streets are purposely narrow to calm the traffic; on-street parking and frequent road bends further encourage orderly passage. Streets and alleys favor pedestrians.

Opposite: Off-street parking is dispersed in attractively landscaped courtyards, and even at 2.4 spaces per dwelling unit, parking areas do not dominate the environment.

166   Commercial spaces for offices, workshops, and light-industrial uses, ranging from 450 to 28,000 square feet (42 to 260 square meters), are intermingled with Poundbury's residential uses. Early occupants include a chocolate factory, an advertising and media company, and a manufacturer of optical instruments for the medical profession. Roughly 220 people are employed at facilities like these in Poundbury.

Getting these businesses to come to Poundbury was somewhat difficult, considering that there is little in the way of industry in Dorset to begin with. Nevertheless, these firms were attracted by the facilities at Poundbury, the quality of life available, and the presence of a local workforce.

Slow and Steady

Given the small size of the Dorset housing market, units at Poundbury have been absorbed at a reasonable pace, although somewhat slower than initially expected. Buyers, some drawn by the project's association with Prince Charles, have come from all over Britain and even abroad. Prices carry a premium of 5 to 10 percent over comparable homes elsewhere in the local market, and home values have appreciated substantially since they first came on the market.

The original master plan for Poundbury called for extensive retail facilities. The goal was to provide for most of the needs of the development's residents without compelling them to get in their cars. With time, it became clear that Poundbury simply could not support the number of retailers that the plan envisioned. This was especially true in light of the relatively slow pace of development there, due in part to Poundbury's coming on the market during a national recession, in a locale with an already weak real estate market. Today, shopping opportunities at the development are limited, in part to avoid competing with the traditional shopping areas in Dorchester. The hope is that as additional phases are built and occupied, the threshold number of potential customers will be reached, creating opportunities for more shops.

Opposite: Though all homes share a common palette of materials, each is different and of distinct period style. Diversity is achieved by varying spatial forms, and by the use of materials in combination and in contrast. Classical details, such as balustrades and rusticated ground floors, are interspersed with the vernacular.

Above, left and right: Social (subsidized) housing is designed to be indistinguishable from private (market-rate) housing, whether detached or multifamily.
Left: Backs of houses are as dissimilar from one another as the streetfronts, and each house is identifiable as a discrete residential unit.

RANCHO SANTA MARGARITA

RANCHO SANTA MARGARITA, CALIFORNIA

Rancho Santa Margarita turned a remote, rural enclave into the highest-density master-planned suburban community in the nation—with over half of its units being attached housing types. A balanced and self-sustaining new town that has gone from ground breaking to a self-governed city of over 40,000 in just 15 years, Rancho Santa Margarita pioneered concepts of jobs-housing balance, town center design, governance, and soft infrastructure.

The Santa Margarita Company (SMC) was formed by the O'Neill family, owners of Rancho Mission Viejo in Orange County, California, as a joint venture with Copley Real Estate Advisors for the purpose of master developing Rancho Santa Margarita. Its CEO, Anthony Moiso, a descendant of the original purchaser of the ranch, Richard O'Neill, had been previously involved in the development of Mission Viejo, the sprawling 10,000-acre (4,047-hectare) new community which was subsequently sold to Phillip Morris and is now operated by Shea Homes. In forming the Santa Margarita Company, Moiso recruited from the most seasoned master developers and builders in the region to build an experienced, forward-thinking organization. In the mid 1990s, a period of financial repositioning in the region, operating management of Rancho Santa Margarita was transferred to Benchmark Development, a subsidiary of Metropolitan Life, for the last phases of buildout.

Build It and They Will Come

Rancho Mission Viejo, the land on which Rancho Santa Margarita was developed, was originally a gigantic Spanish land grant ranch that has been in the O'Neill family for over a century. The 40,000 acres (16,187 hectares) of land remaining in the early eighties was increasingly in the path of Southern California's urban expansion. The adjacent development of Mission Viejo had extended roadways up to the ranch's boundaries, especially the northern, relatively flat 4,995 acres (2,023 hectares) known as the Plano Trabuco. Although relatively easy to develop topographically, the site presented a marketing challenge with its inaccessible location at the base of the Santa Ana Mountains and its lack of visibility and presence in the market.

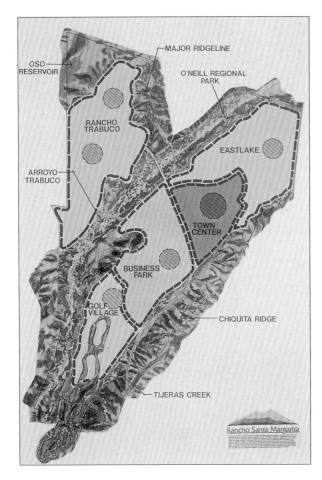

OSO RESERVOIR

MAJOR RIDGELINE

O'NEILL REGIONAL PARK

RANCHO TRABUCO

EASTLAKE

ARROYO TRABUCO

TOWN CENTER

BUSINESS PARK

GOLF VILLAGE

CHIQUITA RIDGE

TIJERAS CREEK

Rancho Santa Margarita

Opening pages: Lake Park, the primary planned recreational component of Rancho Santa Margarita, the first amenity to create a sense of place.

Above: Planners initially conceived five separate villages surrounded by open space that would offer a variety of residential products and lifestyle options.

Right: The illustrative plan depicts the density and scale of the 5,000-acre (2,023-hectare) community, which integrates 14,000+ dwelling units with a town center, business park, recreational facilities, and significant open space.

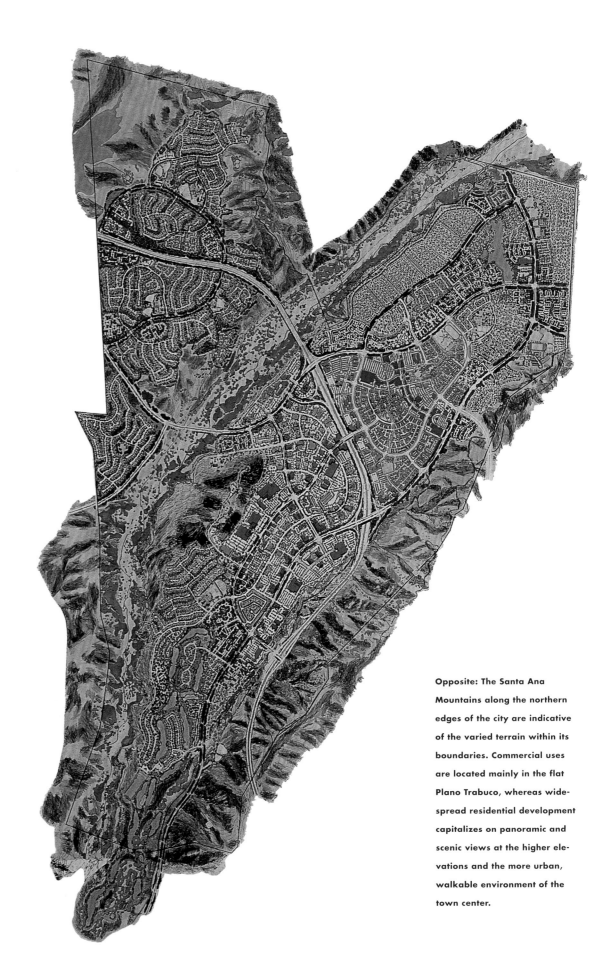

Opposite: The Santa Ana Mountains along the northern edges of the city are indicative of the varied terrain within its boundaries. Commercial uses are located mainly in the flat Plano Trabuco, whereas widespread residential development capitalizes on panoramic and scenic views at the higher elevations and the more urban, walkable environment of the town center.

Although it lay ready for extensions of the regional road network, the site still required a sewer and water infrastructure capable of supporting an entire new town. Thomas Blum, senior vice president, established the Santa Margarita Water District, a quasi-public agency with the ability to sell bonds, fund construction, and acquire water rights for the community. A major sewage treatment plant, large enough not only for Rancho Santa Margarita but also for future portions of the ranch, was initiated and major trunk lines constructed. Under California's Mello Roos legislation, a series of Community Facility District bonds were sold, funding both heavy infrastructure and school construction.

Although locating the first phase at the far north end of the site required long infrastructure extensions, it preserved the more central portions of the site for the future town center, a key component for the creation of a downtown and economic base for the community. The development of the 23-acre (nine-hectare) Lake Park in the first phase, although a major up-front cost, was thought essential to creating visibility and an initial sense of

place, since the amenities envisioned for the town center would not be supportable for a number of years.

Another important market strategy for the project was its focus on affordable housing in an area that has, and still, suffers from a chronically low percentage of households qualifying for a median-priced home. Over half of Rancho Santa Margarita's sales qualify as affordable housing.

Building Density Builds Opportunity

Providing large quantities of housing at affordable prices would require average densities greater than Orange County, the local agency, would normally approve. Richard Reese, vice president for predevelopment, suggested the concept of an "urban village in an open space setting," which would preserve half of the site's 4,995 acres (2,021 hectares) as permanent open space and transfer density to the remaining area. This approach would not only preserve sensitive natural resources, but would allow sufficient density to achieve lower price points and maintain acceptable land value.

A wide mix of housing and lifestyle choice was key not only in attaining population diversity, but in maximizing sales. Optimal market breadth was achieved at two levels. First, a wide array of housing types was available, ranging from three-to-the-acre (one-to-the-hectare) single-family homes up to 27-to-the-acre (11-to-the-hectare) stacked condominiums. At times as many as 14 product lines were offered with as many as half being attached, most of them meeting county low-moderate and moderate affordability criteria. A second layer of diversity and choice was achieved by organizing the community into "lifestyle villages," from the family-oriented lake and hillside villages, to the recreational golf village and more urbane town center village. In order to maintain a singular community identity, "village" concepts were not emphasized in advertising but discovered in the wide variety of choice a consumer encountered in the Home Finding Center.

The pursuit of attainable housing through higher density product forms raises challenging questions: how is an overall perception of quality maintained with a high percentage of attached housing, and how is open space

Opposite, top and bottom: Providing a high-quality and amenity-rich outdoor environment was a crucial program element in the master plan. Fifty percent of the site is allocated for preserved open space, parks, recreational amenities, and trails to offset the confinement of dense residential development.

Above: Flanked by residential and commercial development, Lake Santa Margarita is the community's recreational centerpiece.

A comprehensive system of trails, parks, and open space links the neighborhoods and creates one of the community's most significant amenities. Lake Park features a one-mile (two-kilometer) paved trail that is a community favorite for walking, jogging, and in-line skating.

relief provided when many homes are limited in their private yard size? Reese found the answer to these questions in the historic towns of Europe, where high density and compactness are the norm and where emphasis is placed on public rather than private open space. The result is that all public and quasi-public facilities in Rancho Santa Margarita incorporate plazas, courtyards, and urban space of a style consistent with the Spanish colonial tradition. These gathering places are enhanced with fountains, seating, and rich paving, and are easily identified by their campanile towers with authentic cast bells, which regularly ring out.

Hard *and* Soft Infrastructure

If a truly sustainable new town is to be achieved, an internal jobs-housing balance must be attempted. A 450-acre (182-hectare) business park was scaled to supplement other internal job creation, for an overall 1.7 jobs per household. The business park was placed in a mixed-use urban activity zone to permit the conversion of employment to residential uses if the scale of the park proved untenable as the market matured. It was also important to avoid linking employment phasing with residential phasing, so that each could respond to market demand independently.

Prior to developing the million square feet (92,930 square meters) of retail and entertainment in the town center, retail was carefully phased into the community as homes were occupied. It was considered important to provide services quickly due to the site's perception of remoteness. A small multitenant project was immediately initiated that could provide retail, food, medical, and legal services for first residents. By year four, a ten-acre (four-hectare) neighborhood-scale shopping center was developed in the

Above: Ranging from single-family detached to townhouses, condominiums, apartments, and senior living, numerous housing options were provided in order to increase population diversity as well as meet the county's affordable housing goals. Dwellings reflect the Spanish architectural style prevalent throughout Southern California.

Opposite, top: Small parks provide gathering spaces in high-density housing areas.
Opposite, bottom: An 18-hole Ted Robinson public fee golf course created a market for residential development in a location otherwise considered too remote for high-density housing.

lake village and positioned as a harbinger of things to come in the ultimate town center. A lakefront location, waterfront dining, trail linkages, and a central plaza for special events reflected this concept.

Critical to the success of any community are its schools, and a state-of-the-art educational system was initiated in Rancho Santa Margarita. SMC further supplemented state funds so that schools could adopt the architectural theme of other community facilities by incorporating their characteristic plazas and bell towers.

Notably, the park system was based not on the local park code, but on in-depth analysis of what a town of 40,000 actually needs to meet its recreational demands. This resulted in a fully improved and programmed park and trail system that substantially exceeded local agency requirements, including a wide array of amenities, such as the Lake Park, beach club, and trail system.

From his experience on the Irvine Ranch, Don Moe, vice president of marketing, had learned that value could also be added to a community by "seeding" civic, cultural, and recreational programs and encouraging participation by new residents. The concept—soft infrastructure—has become a household word in development circles, but at the time this was an imaginative approach. First, it would create a positive and upbeat form of community activism, avoiding focus on negative issues that could ultimately interfere with buildout. Second, it would lead to good word of mouth, which would generate personal referrals and additional sales at a low marketing cost. From the outset, fairs, picnics, Fourth of July fireworks, concerts in the park, annual rodeos, and other events brought residents together and ultimately formed one of the most cohesive communities in Southern California. This strategy culminated in the incorporation of the community as a city on January 1, 2000, as the last parcels of land were entering final design for development.

SANTA MARGARITA CENTER

Above and right: The town center incorporates retail, entertainment, restaurants, public facilities, a park, and high-density residential neighborhoods. El Paseo, the main street, links retail areas with a series of plazas where special events take place year-round.

Opposite: Taking advantage of the Southern California climate, outdoor cafés and public plazas are featured prominently throughout the town center. The Spanish Colonial–style architecture reflects the area's historical precedents.

Santa Margarita Center

Rancho Santa Margarita further enhanced its walkable downtown by including 1,800 homes in its town center village. Residents can walk to community shopping, restaurants, a regional library, Central Park, and a cinema within a 250-acre (101-hectare) pedestrian precinct. By providing the option of a quasi-urban lifestyle in a market over-imbued with sprawling, low-density bedroom communities, it was believed overall absorption of land and housing could be further accelerated.

The Santa Margarita Center master plan consisted of two primary axes: the north-south, auto-free pedestrian Promenade linking a series of higher density residential neighborhoods; and an east-west traditional main street, El Paseo, with community and neighborhood retail shopping centers functioning as respective anchors on each end. The Promenade and El Paseo meet at the Central Plaza, which is planned as a hub of restaurants, a cinema, and civic uses. A nine-acre (four-hectare) Central Park functions as a communal space for special events, concerts, and festivals.

In developing Santa Margarita Center, timing was everything. Substantial carrying costs built up and burdened the land so that development was initiated prior to market demand reaching its full potential. This led to lower than optimal densities and a mix of tenants that was further compromised by competition from an adjacent community, which was better located relative to conventional retail outlets. Economic pressures from the deep recession of the early 1990s also forced value engineering that limited the amenity and hardscape development a rich, urban environment requires. Despite these setbacks, Santa Margarita Center still plays a central role in the daily life of the community and is a focus of town activity.

Rancho Santa Margarita's market strategies, combined with a strong economy coming out of the early-1980s recession, fueled annual absorption of over 1,700 closings a year and placed it in the top three master-planned communities nationwide through the late eighties and into the nineties.

RESTON

RESTON, VIRGINIA

At Reston's inception in 1962, when it was the largest new town in the nation, the 7,400-acre (2,995-hectare) community revolutionized community planning in the United States. It was the brainchild of Robert E. Simon, who envisioned the town as a "serious experiment in urban planning undertaken on a citywide scale, and an attempt to discover what could be done to create a quality environment."

Simon, the original developer, purchased the land, developed the concept and plan, and initiated development. The first homes were sold and occupied in autumn 1964. In 1967 a tight money market forced Simon to surrender control to the principal investor, Gulf Oil, who in 1978 sold the primary undeveloped portions to Mobil Corporation. Terrabrook now manages Reston; its primary goal is to complete the town center.

Located 22 miles (35 kilometers) west of Washington, D.C., along the Dulles Airport Toll Road, Reston is the primary office, retail, and residential center of western Fairfax County, Virginia. Early on, two developments contributed to the success of Reston. First, Dulles International Airport opened nearby in 1962. Second, in that same year, Fairfax County adopted the Planned Residential Community (PRC) zoning ordinance that was conceived specifically for Reston through the initiative of Simon and his planning team. At Simon's behest, the planning and design process engaged representatives from all parts of the community.

The planning and development of Reston has been guided since the beginning by Simon's seven goals for the project: (1) That the widest choice of opportunities be made available for the full use of leisure time. This means that the new town should provide a wide range of recreational and cultural facilities as well as an environment for privacy. (2) That it be possible for anyone to remain in a single neighborhood throughout his life, uprooting being neither inevitable nor always desirable. By providing the fullest range of housing styles and prices, housing needs can be met at a variety of income levels, and at different stages of family life. (3) That the importance and dignity of each individual be the focal point for all planning and take precedence over large-scale concepts. (4) That people may be able to live and work in the same community. (5) That commercial, cultural, and recreational facilities be made available to the residents from the outset of the development—not years later. (6) That beauty—structural and natural—is a necessity of the good life and should be fostered. (7) That Reston be a financial success.

Simon's principles have had a far-reaching effect. Today, many of the best new communities still strive to meet similar objectives.

Implementing the Vision: A Place in Which to Live, Work, and Play

The program for Reston was based on a then-groundbreaking mixed-use plan that included the full range of residential types, for all ages and incomes, as well as employment and shopping centers. Community facilities included schools, libraries, churches, daycare centers, health care facilities, fire and police services, recreational and cultural opportunities, public transit, and open space. Sites for corporate headquarters, commercial offices, institutions, and government facilities were identified. Today, Reston has achieved an employment-housing balance of over 40,000 jobs and 63,000 residents, a self-sustaining mix of uses, infrastructure, community facilities, and amenities.

Conceived from the start as a place in which to live, work, and play, Reston has a reputation for environmentally sensitive development with extensive natural preserves that buffer neighborhoods from collector roads. Clusters of houses are often barely visible through the heavy tree cover.

The Reston Homeowners Association cares for the land and facilities in common ownership: open spaces, parking areas, pathways, streets, and other public properties that occupy more than one-third of the entire tract. Recreational facilities include two golf courses (one daily fee and one private), 17 outdoor swimming pools, numerous tennis courts, a community center complex, and a series of lakes and parks, for a total of over 1,100 acres (445 hectares) of open space. Over 55 miles (89 kilometers) of trails and pathways, including footbridges that are separated from vehicular ways and cross-stream valleys, link the village centers and neighborhoods to the open space. The community's aesthetic quality was mandated by protective covenants which established the Design Review Board for

RESTON

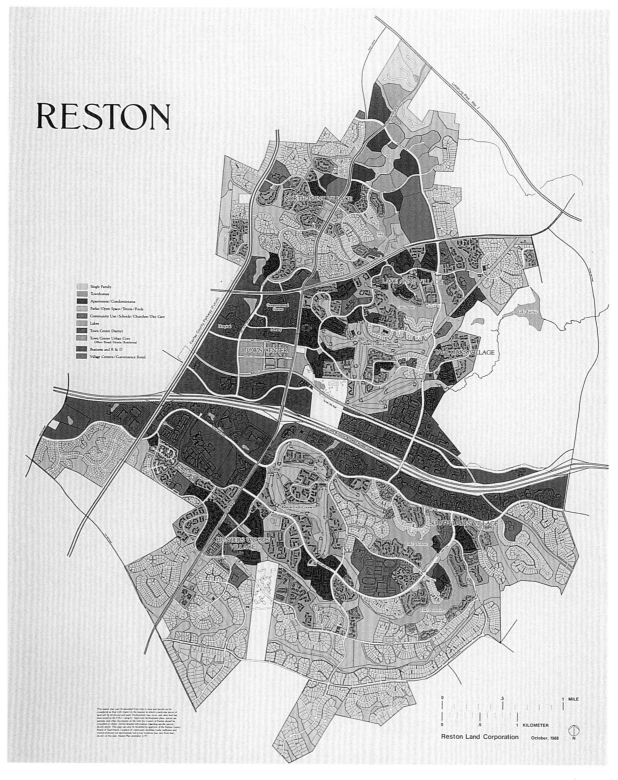

Reston Land Corporation   October, 1988

Previous page: Reston's five manmade lakes provide idyllic settings for residential development and leisure activities. Above: The master plan that has guided Reston's development for over 40 years has withstood the test of time and given rise to much emulation for its pioneering concepts in new town design. Nearing completion, this "place in which to live, work, and play" supports 63,000 residents and 40,000 jobs.

Opposite: For the original village of Lake Anne, Robert E. Simon wanted to mix many elements of the cityscape—high-rise apartments above stores and a plaza where people could gather. Though Lake Anne Plaza was in the vanguard of the trend toward mixed-use developments, it has only been a partial success as a people magnet and shopping center. The original townhouse clusters of Lake Anne Village have stood the test of time.

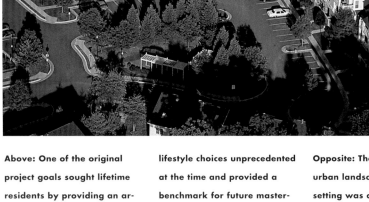

Above: One of the original project goals sought lifetime residents by providing an array of housing products and amenities. This inspired approach created a variety of lifestyle choices unprecedented at the time and provided a benchmark for future master-planned communities.

Opposite: The concept of an urban landscape in a rural setting was achieved by linking the site's commonly held and managed open space, including active and passive recreation, with 55 miles (89 kilometers) of trails and extensive nature preserves.

residential properties and the Architectural Board of Review for commercial properties. The covenants also established that utilities would be placed underground.

A Pioneer in Housing Variety

Reston pioneered the concept of incorporating multiple housing types so that a household could grow, mature, and age without having to leave the community. It was developed as a series of five villages—Lake Anne, Hunters Woods, Tall Oaks, South Lakes, and North Point—each focused around a mixed-use village center.

Lake Anne Village, the first, was developed around Lake Anne Village Center and one of five built lakes. Noted residential architects were hired to design the contemporary-style townhouses of the first village, which were unheard of in suburban settings of the time. Best known for its waterfront plaza lined with ground-level shops and residences above, Lake Anne Village Center embodied Simon's vision for Reston based on pedestrian-oriented European precedents.

While the village's ambience has attracted residents and visitors, Lake Anne has not been successful in maintaining a retail center. Weak retail performance may stem from at least two limiting factors. First, cars and pedestrians are completely separated, requiring people to get out of their cars and walk into the center before they see the retail storefronts. Second, Lake Anne's retail space was conceived as a finite entity without room for expansion, making the center unattractive to today's larger retailers.

With Hunters Woods, at the southern end of Reston, Simon sought to temper the market risk by developing a more conventional suburban enclave of single-family houses on lots ranging from a quarter acre (one-tenth hectare) to about two acres (one hectare). Like the other villages, it offers shopping centers, schools, and recreational facilities. The remaining villages developed their residential mix in response to market conditions at the time of their development. Architectural styles evolved as well, moving from the contemporary cedar-and-glass structures of the 1960s to more traditional styling and materials by the 1980s.

South Lakes Village includes single-family houses, townhouses, and patio homes nestled around two connecting built lakes and a campus with an elementary school, middle school, and high school. North Point, the last village to be developed, includes luxury lakefront houses that cater to the strong demand for the Reston lifestyle. In all of the villages, many of the best lots have lake frontage or views, and clusters of development are buffered by woods, maintaining a sense of pastoral beauty and privacy despite relatively high densities.

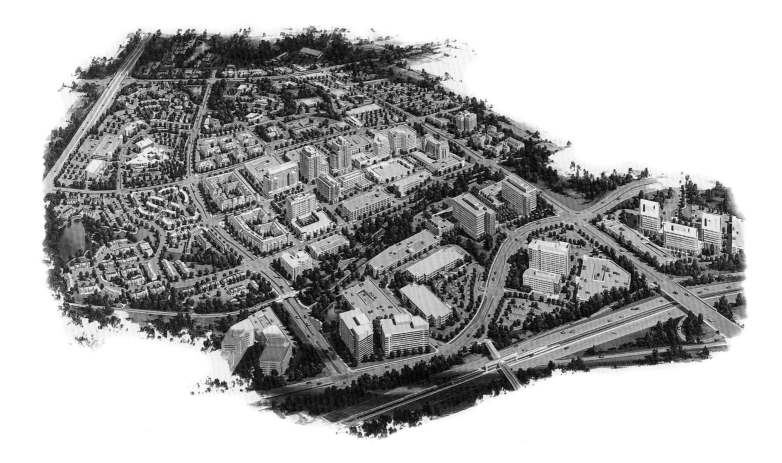

Reston Town Center

In the early 1980s, the PRC zoning that provided for the initial development of Reston was amended to add a town center zoning category, providing the mechanism to develop concentrated higher density mixed-use centers. To date, Reston Town Center is the county's only project developed under this zoning category.

Reston's population was over 43,000 by the time of the town center's groundbreaking in 1988, providing a solid economic base for the community's "downtown." Located on the north side of the Dulles Toll Road, the 12-block town center is organized along a pedestrian-oriented main street. Its distinctive skyline has become a landmark visible to commuters on the Toll Road, and residents from the entire metropolitan region are drawn to its offices, shops, restaurants, and weekend activities.

From the outset, Terrabrook's intention was for Reston Town Center to feel like it evolved over time like a traditional downtown, rather than as a single project. The town center is subsequently being developed in phases and is being designed by a number of different architects. Phase one includes 530,000 square feet (49,239 square meters) of commercial and retail space in buildings ranging from five to 11 stories. The plan is centered on Fountain Square and the 514-room Hyatt Regency Hotel. The second phase, known as Freedom Square, is west of Fountain Square. More dense and taller than originally conceived—owing to the success of Fountain Square and a strong commercial office market—Freedom Square I and II

contain a total of 820,000 square feet (76,181 square meters) in buildings of 16 and 18 stories.

Stratford House, part of a luxury mid-rise and high-rise condominium development at the east end of the town center, introduced the first residential component to the commercial area. Other urban-style townhouses, condominiums, and rental apartments followed. Residents of these developments are just a short walk from the shops, restaurants, and offices.

Coming of Age

Reston currently is home to approximately 63,000 residents living in 21,000 residential units, ranging from single-family houses to high-rise apartments. The community is planned to contain 23,000 residences upon completion.

A sign of Reston's coming of age is the replacement of 1960s-era one- and two-story office buildings with more substantial buildings tenanted by prestigious nationally recognized companies. In conjunction with these developments, the associated surface parking lots have been redeveloped as parking garages.

Simon's seven goals for the development of Reston have guided every phase of the project for 40 years. In reaction to the change in developers, however, and fearing that Simon's principles would be abandoned, residents formed the Reston Community Association to serve as a watchdog over future phases.

At age 87, Robert Simon still lives in Reston.

Opposite: Reston Town Center will encompass a 12-block area when phased development is complete. Designed by different architects, this mixed-use district is a regional employment, residential, and entertainment destination and serves as a model for town center development.

Left, top: Main Street is the organizing element around which Town Center grew. A Hyatt Regency and a 13-screen cineplex anchor opposing ends.

Left, center: One of the 16 eateries amidst retail and entertainment venues luring residents and visitors to Town Center.

Left, bottom: Urban residential development in Town Center is more compact and dense than in other parts of Reston.

Below: The focus of Reston Town Center is Fountain Square, where people, art, and water converge in a sophisticated urban space.

SUMMERLIN

LAS VEGAS, NEVADA

Las Vegas has been one of America's fastest growing metropolitan areas since the 1970s. During the year 2000, between 6,000 and 7,000 people moved to Las Vegas every month. Strong new home sales in the region continue to be driven by the expanding hospitality industry, a diversifying economic base, a pro-business environment, and the city's attractiveness to vacationers and retirees.

For the last decade, Summerlin has been the most successful master-planned community in the nation. In a city not regarded for its livability or quality of life prior to the late 1980s, Summerlin has redefined the concept of community and set the standard regionally for solid, family-oriented, amenity-driven planned community development.

The Howard Hughes Corporation (THHC) was the original developer of Summerlin. In 1996, the Rouse Company merged with Hughes. In addition to Summerlin, the Rouse Company owns and operates more than 200 retail, office, mixed-use, and industrial properties throughout the United States.

In the early 1950s, Howard Hughes acquired a sprawling 25,000-acre (10,117-hectare) parcel of land located along the western rim of the Las Vegas Valley, well outside the Las Vegas City limits. Five miles across and over eight miles long, it still ranks as one of the largest properties adjacent to a major metropolitan area under single ownership.

Unfolding along the western rim of the Las Vegas Valley, in the shadow of the Spring Mountain Range and Red Rock Canyon National Conservation Area, Summerlin's topography ranges from steep along the western mountains to gently sloping along the eastern boundary. It can be characterized as a Mojave Desert landscape with sparse vegetation and arroyos (drainage channels) of various sizes crossing the site.

Prior to Summerlin's development, the site had limited access and was considered remote by many Las Vegans. To ensure Summerlin's early marketability and viability, it was essential to build an attractively landscaped and efficient roadway to the community's front door. Funding for the construction of utilities and roads, including the Summerlin Parkway and Nevada's first trilevel interchange, came from several Special Improvement Districts created from bonds issued by the city of Las Vegas and Clark County. The dramatic landscape treatment of the parkway serves as an impressive entry for residents and potential purchasers.

The Village Concept

In 1988, after three years of preparation, a master plan consisting of 30 villages, village centers, business parks, resorts, and a town center was unveiled. In 1996, the plan was redefined and clarified. The plan, heavily influenced by master planning for Irvine Ranch in California and the Woodlands in Texas, consists of distinct villages grouped around mixed-use village centers, business centers, and the town center. The village concept allows a relative degree of intimacy, variety, and individuality in what would otherwise be a community of overwhelming size and scale.

Three types of villages make up Summerlin: *primary*, with a full range of housing product and a village focus area consisting of a park, school, and/or worship site; *amenity*, with mostly high-end housing and at least one public or private golf course; and *low-density*, having modest to high-end housing, some with golf courses and a resort and/or hotel. Sixteen villages have been completed or are in some stage of development. They range in size from 360 to 1,300 acres (146 to 526 hectares).

Each village has its own character and form and is differentiated by size, population, housing types, street plan and streetscape design, price range, and amenity concept. Topography, landform, view corridors, and open space vary widely from village to village and tend to define their size and character. A core of community services, including schools, parks, daycare centers, houses of worship, and recreation centers, becomes the focal point of each village. Villages are connected to surrounding neighborhoods by a richly landscaped trail system.

Within each village, a variety of neighborhoods, based on single-builder product lines, are arranged around the open space, trail, and amenity framework. Since 1996, each neighborhood has a pocket park around 10,000 square feet (929 square meters) in size. In the current town center villages, curb-separated, tree-lined sidewalks are included, with curb neck-

NORTHERN AREA

SOUTHERN AREA

192

PRIMARY VILLAGE
AMENITY VILLAGE
LOW DENSITY VILLAGE
AGE QUALIFIED VILLAGE
VILLAGE CENTER
SUMMERLIN CENTRE CORE
BUSINESS PARK
MIXED USE
OPEN SPACE / WASH
RESORT HOTEL WITH GAMING
NEVADA POWER CO. SUBSTATION
VILLAGE FOCUS
GOLF COURSE CLUB HOUSE
REGIONAL TRAIL
VILLAGE TRAIL (NOT ALL SHOWN)
NATURAL TRAIL
NATURAL TRAIL

Opening page: Streetside, village, regional, and natural trails are the four components of the 160-mile (258-kilometer) trail system planned for Summerlin. It will eventually connect with Clark County's regional trail.

Above: Split into three distinct geographic areas, the 22,460-acre (9,089-hectare) site master plan is based on a hierarchy of planning elements: villages, neighborhoods, and village centers. It defines the nature and character of the 30 villages as well as the location of other major land uses and road alignments.

Opposite, left: Roundabouts are used abundantly to maintain traffic flow, increase road safety, reduce pollution from idling cars, and visually enhance the community's streetscapes.

Opposite, top right and bottom right: The Red Rock Canyon National Conservation Area is located adjacent to Summerlin.

downs to calm traffic. Each neighborhood's street design, grading, landscape, and architecture go through a rigorous design review process guided by village-specific design guidelines.

Several of Summerlin's villages pursue niche and specialty markets, such as the two seniors-oriented villages of Del Webb's Sun City, which encompasses 2,500 acres (1,012 hectares), three golf courses, and Sunrise Colony Company's Siena, a guard-gated community encompassing 665 acres (269 hectares).

An amenity village is the Ridges, a 795-acre (322-hectare) luxury golf course village featuring Jack Nicklaus's first Bear's Best Golf course, which incorporates replications of signature Nicklaus holes from the Southwest United States and Mexico. Red Rock Country Club, an upscale golf-course community situated on 738 acres (299 hectares), is being developed by Sunrise Colony Company and features two Arnold Palmer–designed golf courses, more than 1,000 luxury homes, and a 40,000-square-foot (3,716-square-meter) tennis, swimming, and health club.

A Village Center

The system of villages is organized around three geographically distributed village centers, Summerlin Centre, the centrally located town center, and several business parks. Hills Village Center, the first village-level commercial center, is planned in a radial street pattern with the 38,500-square-foot (3,577-square-meter) Summerlin Library and Performing Arts Center at its center. The Plaza at Summerlin, a class-A multitenant office complex, the 36,000-square-foot (3,345-square-meter) Donald W. Reynolds Cultural Center, and the future gas station, health club, retail center, and business center are models for the other two future village centers.

The Crossing Business Center, Summerlin's first major business employment center, debuted in 1994 on a 115-acre (47-hectare) site in the Crossing Village. Central to the community along Town Center Drive, the Center draws its architecture from regional materials and colors, blending in with its Red Rock Canyon National Conservation Area backdrop.

Ensuring Protection of the Land

Because Summerlin is located at an elevation higher than the rest of the Las Vegas Valley, careful consideration was given to building homes and facilities that maximize the glittering views of the Las Vegas Strip and the expansive valley to the east. Wherever possible, the natural topography has been preserved and incorporated into the landscape, including natural wash arroyos throughout the community's many linear parks and two Tournament Players Club golf courses. Much of Summerlin's trail system is built

In addition to being one of the community's top active recreational amenities, its eight golf courses are flanked by premium residential development. Natural drainage and arroyos are preserved throughout these courses, often serving a dual purpose as walking trails and paseo parks.

within natural drainage areas landscaped with native vegetation.

In 1987, THHC executed perhaps the most important act of preparation for its community—the exchange of more than 5,000 acres (2,023 hectares) of land with the Bureau of Land Management. This exchange, facilitated by the nonprofit Nature Conservancy, resulted in the creation of the Red Rock Canyon National Conservation Area. It also preserves and protects the beauty of the rugged Red Rock mountains that provide the striking backdrop for Summerlin. The community's edges along these natural areas are characterized by less dense and obtrusive design and architecture.

The striking treatment of community-level landscaping helped significantly improve the image and popularize the use of desert landscaping throughout the entire Las Vegas Valley at a time when it was considered unimaginative and unattractive. Arterial and collector streets are designed and planted in a manner that seeks a careful balance between desert authenticity, visual richness, and the creation of a pleasant pedestrian setting. Colorful, drought-tolerant, and low-water-use landscapes were created in abundance in Summerlin and have since become the standard for landscaping throughout the valley.

Summerlin Centre

The 1,300-acre (526-hectare) Summerlin Centre is envisioned as the "downtown" for the western Las Vegas Valley. A framework of thematic streets, boulevards, and parks will structure its residential, commercial, institutional, and cultural uses. In a region where walkable urban space is rare, Summerlin Centre is planned as a closely-knit pedestrian precinct of multistory office buildings; regional-serving retail outlets; gaming; cultural, hotel, and conference facilities; parks; and a variety of housing options.

The plan for the center consists of closely organized and overlapping districts, each with a primary function, character, and urban design goal. Park Center Drive, a broad, park-lined street reminiscent of boulevards in traditional northeastern cities, links the Central Park to a district of high-density residential neighborhoods. Pavilion Center Drive, a walkable, high-visibility street, is the backbone of an office and retail district. A regional shopping center will be a primary anchor for the village, but in a form adapted to reinforce street life and connectivity to adjacent districts.

The village is planned to provide a unique lifestyle for the Las Vegas Valley: the opportunity to live, work, shop, and play within a cohesive village setting with minimal use of the automobile—a truly rare way of life for this region.

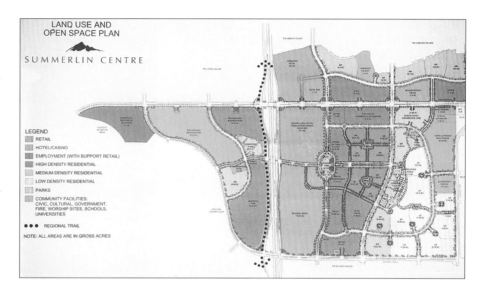

LAND USE AND OPEN SPACE PLAN

SUMMERLIN CENTRE

LEGEND
- RETAIL
- HOTEL/CASINO
- EMPLOYMENT (WITH SUPPORT RETAIL)
- HIGH DENSITY RESIDENTIAL
- MEDIUM DENSITY RESIDENTIAL
- LOW DENSITY RESIDENTIAL
- PARKS
- COMMUNITY FACILITIES: CIVIC, CULTURAL, GOVERNMENT, FIRE, WORSHIP SITES, SCHOOLS, UNIVERSITIES
- ●●● REGIONAL TRAIL

NOTE: ALL AREAS ARE IN GROSS ACRES

195

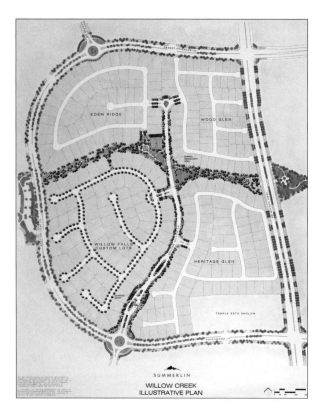

Above: The master plan is based on a village concept. Each of the villages, which encompass 12 to 15 neighborhoods, incorporates community design standards while forging a unique identity.

Right, top: Each village has its own distinctive style of architecture and design, evident in streetscapes, landscaping, and village walls. For the gatehouse at Willow Creek Village, stone and building forms echo the dramatic topography.

Right, bottom: The village of Willow Creek features 80 large-lot homesites.

The Willows Village

The Willows, at 731 acres (296 hectares), illustrates the typical components that make up a non-golf-oriented village in Summerlin. Surrounded by housing types ranging from custom single-family homes to apartments, its core consists of the the Willows Community Center, a pool complex, and two community parks.

The village's central organizing feature is the Willows Paseo Park, a 13-acre (five-hectare) linear park linking the east and west portions of the village with community parks, a daycare center, and an elementary school. Large sculptures of Aesop's Fables characters—the Tortoise and the Hare, and the Lion and the Mouse, with attendant stories told on concrete tablets—are unique landscape features. The village was organized to allow prospective homebuyers to find all model homes on an amenitized loop street within the village, the sales center being the first stop along this loop. The first phase of the village combined all builders' models into one centrally located model complex called "the Homewalk," which allowed one-stop shopping.

In response to competition within the regional luxury home market, a gated mini-village was developed in the center of the village that includes three luxury neighborhoods and one custom neighborhood, all sharing private amenities: a six-acre (two-hectare) park, tennis courts, basketball court, and picnic pavilion.

The Canyons Village

The Canyons Village is one of the multiuse villages in Summerlin that feature not only residential but also retail, office, golf, and resort uses. Positioned directly adjacent to Summerlin Parkway, the 541-room JW Marriott Las Vegas anchors the village with two hotel towers, the JW Marriott Grand Palms and the JW Marriott Grand Spa.

The village is organized around the Tournament Players Club at the Canyons, a daily-fee golf course managed by the PGA Tour. The course is carefully sited along natural drainage arroyos and washes, which enhance both the golf course and the overall park and trail system. The residential mix is high-end in this village, with single-family and multifamily neighborhoods, custom-home neighborhoods, and a luxury apartment complex that shares its mixed-use setting with the 200,000-square-foot (18,581-square-meter) Canyons Center office complex and Covington Cross Service Center.

The Canyons is the first village to feature an architectural theme that was not defined by an existing style, i.e., Pueblo or Southwestern, but instead by a concept of desert elegance. Roof forms, building materials, and building colors were more clearly dictated, as was a desert palette of richly colored landscape materials.

Above: The village of Willows Creek features a community center for active and passive recreation.
Left: In Willows Paseo Park, paseos balance low-water desert landscape materials with the needs of a family-oriented population.

The Canyons combines a mix of high-end custom, single-, and multifamily homes and apartments with a Tournament Players Club golf course and a major hotel complex. Nevada's only two TPC golf courses are at Summerlin.

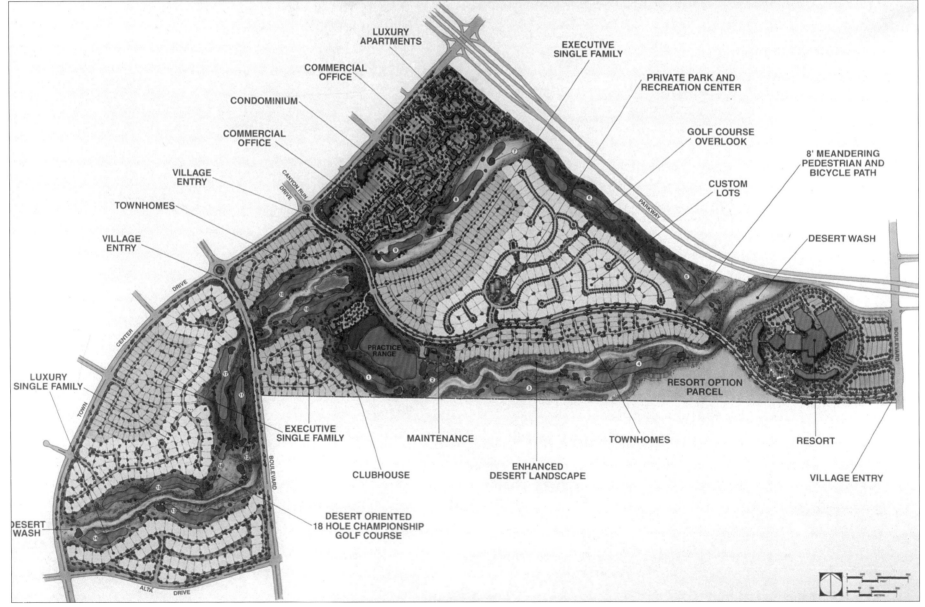

Left, top: Executive homes distinguish the Palisades neighborhood of the Canyons. Drought-tolerant, low-water-use landscapes appropriate to the Mojave Desert setting are promoted throughout Summerlin.

Left, bottom: At the Canyon Villas apartment homes, water is used sparingly but wisely, providing a refreshing change of scenery in the arid climate.

Above: Commercial uses are organized into three village centers equidistant to the town center. In addition to office and retail, they contain cultural and service facilities as well as multifamily housing. Pictured above is Covington Cross Center, located in the Canyons Business Center.

THE WOODLANDS

200 Nestled in 27,000 acres (10,927 hectares) of forest, 31 miles (50 kilometers) north of Houston, the Woodlands is one of the nation's first master-planned communities. From its inception in 1974, the Woodlands has pioneered the blending of nature with modern development practices, creating a benchmark in balance and quality of community development. The Woodlands has ranked as number one in Texas and number four in the nation in terms of new home sales.

The development was founded by developer George Mitchell, president of Mitchell Energy Company, as a response to the problems that he felt were besetting many urban areas in the 1960s and early 1970s. In 1964, Mitchell acquired 3,000 acres (1,214 hectares) that were to become part of the Woodlands. It took him another 11 years and 300 transactions to assemble the 19,000 acres (7,689 hectares) that made up the Woodlands site in 1975.

The site, characterized by flat to gently sloping terrain covered by dense oak and pine forest, was not a pristine wilderness when Mitchell acquired it. The timber industry had been active in the area from 1880 into the 1930s. Repeated harvesting of the more mature pines and hardwoods had degraded the forest structure. Nonetheless, all members of the planning team quickly recognized the forest as a major amenity, in part because it contrasted with the short-grass prairie so common in the Houston area. The community is named the Woodlands to acknowledge the special nature of the forested setting.

Ecological Planning

In the late 1950s, Mitchell, concerned about the economic and environmental problems associated with the flight of middle- and upper-class families to the suburbs, sought an alternative. He became interested in the new town concept that was guiding the development of the Irvine Ranch in California, Columbia in Maryland, and Reston in Virginia. That concept called for housing in virtually all price ranges, jobs within the new town, and a complete balance of public facilities such as schools, parks, shopping, libraries, and health services. Mitchell decided that the Houston metro-

politan area, with its continuing growth, needed such a community.

The master plan of the Woodlands is a seven-village concept, separated by several major commercial and institutional districts and an extensive open space network. Six villages (Grogan's Mill, Panther Creek, Cochran's Crossing, Indian Springs, Alden Bridge, and Sterling Ridge) are completed or under construction. Each offers a variety of housing types, complemented by schools, recreational facilities, shopping, houses of worship, and community services.

The villages are divided into smaller neighborhoods, each with its own identity, where homes are nestled among towering trees on winding cul-de-sac streets. Many neighborhoods include small parks, and are linked by a network of trails that connect to schools, shopping, and recreational amenities.

The plan was based on more than just the notion of a holistic new town. The Woodlands holds the distinction of being the first plan for a new city produced through ecological planning, taking into account the site's natural systems, its processes, and complex interrelationships. During initial site analysis, Ian McHarg, the noted landscape architect credited with first introducing ecology to large-scale planning, discovered that conventional development practices would alter the site's natural rates of groundwater recharge and surface water runoff. It would result in increased downstream flooding and would significantly lower both on- and off-site groundwater levels. McHarg used his system of overlaying environmental constraints in order to identify lands most suitable for development. Building envelopes were based on maximizing groundwater recharge, protecting permeable soils, maintaining the water table, reducing runoff, retarding erosion and siltation, increasing the base flow of streams, and protecting natural vegetation and wildlife habitats. Thus the ecological planning study became the major determinant in preparing the land plan for the community.

Existing stream corridors and other ecologically valuable areas for hydrology, wildlife, and vegetation were identified as conservation zones within the community's open space system. Arterial and collector roads were sited on ridgelines away from drainage areas; development density was

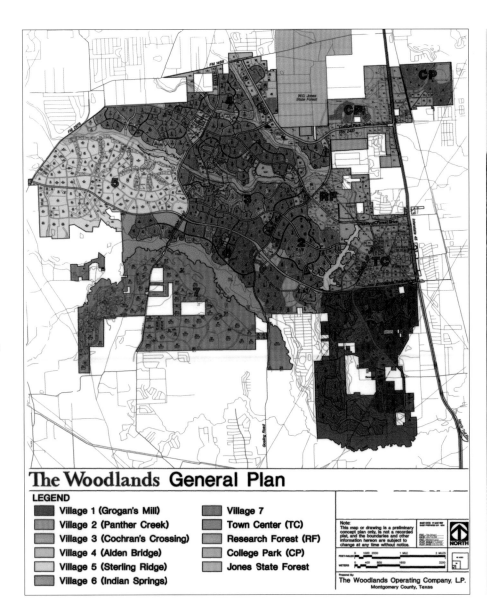

The Woodlands General Plan

LEGEND

- Village 1 (Grogan's Mill)
- Village 2 (Panther Creek)
- Village 3 (Cochran's Crossing)
- Village 4 (Alden Bridge)
- Village 5 (Sterling Ridge)
- Village 6 (Indian Springs)
- Village 7
- Town Center (TC)
- Research Forest (RF)
- College Park (CP)
- Jones State Forest

Note:
This map or drawing is a preliminary concept plan only, is not a recorded plat, and the boundaries and other information herein are subject to change at any time without notice.

NORTH

Prepared by:
The Woodlands Operating Company, L.P.
Montgomery County, Texas

Previous page: A herd of deer sculptures at the entrance to the Woodlands represents the community's agile balancing of nature and humankind.

Above, left: The general plan details the major components of the 27,000-acre (10,027-hectare) development: seven villages and three main commercial areas. What it does not give a sense of is the vast amount of recreational and open space that constitute 25 percent of the site.

Above: A retention pond as scenic water feature.

Opposite, top: *The Rise of the Midgard Serpent* is part of a public artwork program funded by commercial property owners.

Opposite, bottom: PGA Tournament Players Course, one of six 18-hole courses planned for the Woodlands.

generally most intense near major roads and intersections and decreased near sensitive areas. Intensive development was located on areas of impermeable soils. Minor residential streets were designed as berms perpendicular to the slope of the site to impede flow over excessively permeable soils.

Similar to Bonita Bay (see page 41), the master plan for the Woodlands does not have a strong geometric pattern, axial, loop, grid, or other formal structure. Rather, the plan is based on the natural systems of the site with the resulting development pattern reflecting the complexity of the underlying natural systems.

Building a Balanced Community

Once the physical structure was delineated, Mitchell could focus on the components of a balanced, family-oriented new town. Education was identified as an essential component and resulted in an exemplary public and private school system. Higher education opportunities were developed at the Montgomery College and the University Center, an innovative partnership between the North Harris Montgomery Community College District and six major Texas universities.

The plan provides for a wide selection of new homes and includes single-family houses on a variety of lot sizes, townhouses, apartments, a range of senior living options, and short-term corporate housing. For-sale home prices range from the low $100,000s to over $1 million, with an average home price of $250,000. Some of the Woodlands's newer sections include Cottage Green, a modified new urbanist neighborhood in the village of Alden Bridge, which includes homes with rear lanes for garages, and more suburban-style homes with garages at the front. The Woodlands's first controlled-access gated community, tucked away on the westernmost side of the development, opened in 2001.

Market research is leading the Woodlands to create more communities specifically designed for older adults. Ashley Greens, a 68-unit adult community, opened in 1998. A second 450-unit adult community, Windsor Hills, opened in 1999. A draw for Windsor Hills is its location next to Montgomery College, which is developing continuing education programs for these active adult residents.

Fulfilling founder George Mitchell's vision of a self-sufficient new town, the Woodlands has it all: residential variety, recreational facilities, cultural amenities, entertainment venues, and retail, commercial, and public buildings.
Top: Cynthia Woods Mitchell Pavilion, an outdoor performing arts venue located in the Woodlands Town Center that draws visitors from the entire region.

Above: Windsor Clubhouse, the Windsor neighborhood's activity center designed for active adults.
Above, center: Each village has its own commercial center, which features grocery and convenience stores and professional services. Alden Bridge, with its *Big Barbara* sculpture, is pictured.

Economic Self-Sufficiency

Within the fabric of the community, convenient village shopping centers offer a range of stores and services that are easy to reach on foot or a short drive from any neighborhood. Each village contains a selection of restaurants.

The Woodlands is planned and phased to be economically self-sufficient. The current ratio of one job per household is planned to ultimately achieve one and one-half jobs per household, the natural jobs-housing ratio in the region. Employment centers now hold nearly 1,000 companies and employ approximately 25,000 people. Companies credit the ability to recruit and retain top people to the community's appealing lifestyle and quality of recreational opportunities.

Mitchell also realized that conferences and hotel nights were a good means of marketing the community to the outside world. The Woodlands Resort and Conference Center was developed with a blend of accommodations, meeting and conference space, and resort-style recreation, including a 65,000-square-foot (6,039-square-meter) conference facility and learning center. The facility has won several awards and for over 25 years has been

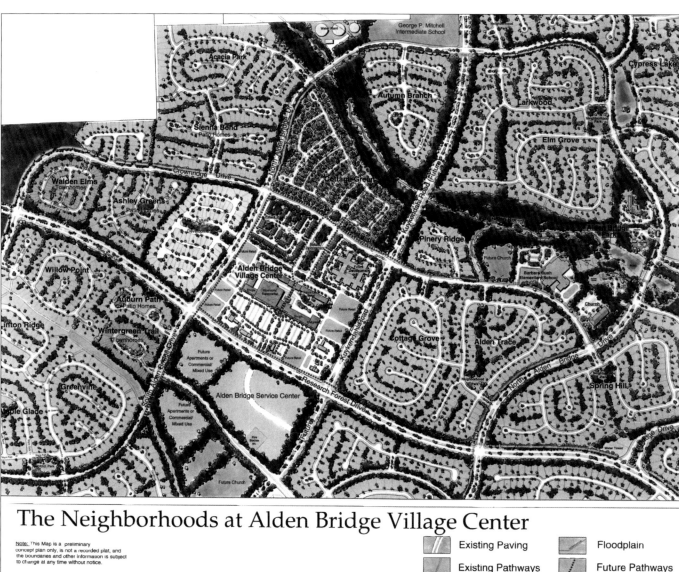

The Neighborhoods at Alden Bridge Village Center

Note: This Map is a preliminary concept plan only, is not a recorded plat, and the boundaries and other information is subject to change at any time without notice.

Existing Paving   Floodplain

Existing Pathways   Future Pathways

named one of Texas's finest. The community also has its own open-air performing arts pavilion and a hospital.

The Woodlands Town Center has, since the original planning concepts, been envisioned as a mixed-use core of retail, restaurants, entertainment, and community activity. Early phases include the Woodlands regional mall, anchored by several major department stores. A mixed-use central waterway is currently under development, which will provide a central pedestrian spine of commercial and civic uses, tying together future town center districts. As more retail space, restaurants, and office buildings open along the central waterway, loft-style apartments are being built, along with five-story urban-style apartment buildings, to meet the increasing demand for downtown housing.

Living with Sustainability

The Woodlands's early adherence to ecological planning gives it milestone status in the history of master-planned communities. From the beginning, attention has been paid to the ecology of the site, with an emphasis on preserving natural vegetation. The seven goals of land use organization were to

Above: Seven villages of approximately 2,000 acres (809 hectares) each will fan out from their respective village centers at project completion. Housing types are mixed, but product stays consistent within a neighborhood. Curvilinear residential streets with culs-de-sac are typical.

When the final buyer goes to settlement, there will be 45,400 dwelling units at the Woodlands, 75 percent being single-family detached. Housing types include condominiums, townhouses, duplexes, patio and courtyard homes, active adult housing options, plus many choices in the size and style of single-family homes available.

208

The Woodlands Town Center has always been envisioned as a mixed-use core of retail, restaurants, entertainment, and community activity. Early phases include the Woodlands regional mall (above, right), which is slated for expansion to tie into a mixed-use central waterway, currently under development.

High-density apartment buildings will be built along the new waterway to meet the increasing demand for downtown housing (above). Fronting the new waterway district, this two-building Class A office complex (right) leased quickly at premium rates.

minimally disrupt the surface and subsurface hydrological regimen; preserve woodlands; establish a natural drainage system; preserve vegetation; provide wildlife habitats and movement corridors; minimize the cost of development; and avoid hazards to life or health.

Approximately 25 percent of the community's land area will ultimately be retained in forest preserves, parks, golf courses, lakes, and other types of open space. Stringent design controls encourage the preservation and restoration of native vegetation along drainage courses, major roadways, and in all residential and commercial areas.

Planning for the first phase of development, the village of Grogan's Mill, allowed for the refinement of the concept of a natural drainage system. Instead of using curbs, storm drains, pipes, and concrete channels to carry storm runoff quickly from roofs and roadways into streams, a system of grassed and planted trenches, swales, and berms was proposed to collect runoff and encourage its percolation into the ground. Designs for impoundment, settlement ponds, golf courses, and roadways were adapted to meet the demands of this natural drainage system.

The new Woodlands Waterway will be the centerpiece of the town center and marks its latest phase of development. When complete, the town center will include 18 million square feet (1.7 million square meters) and commercial space supporting 40,000 employees, thus making the Woodlands one of the few master-planned communities to achieve a 1:1 housing-to-jobs balance.

Market studies, however, found that most homebuyers simply did not like the rustic appearance of natural drainage improvements and were willing to pay a premium for conventional engineering techniques. To improve marketability, the Woodlands modified the natural drainage system over time by combining the best elements of natural drainage (i.e., natural stream channel preservation, retention reservoirs, vegetation preserves, and greenbelts) with more conventional engineering practices.

Maintaining the integrity of the forested environment continues to be a challenge, both during development and after residents move in. New homebuyers from outside the community often require some education to prevent them from removing the preserved forest understory in their yards to create more expansive lawns and other high-maintenance landscapes.

The legacy of the Woodlands is that of a master-planned community that has incorporated environmentally responsible features and is an important resource for further study and analysis. Lessons learned from the Woodlands's experience can help increase collective knowledge about how to design with nature in a way that is both environmentally responsible and profitable.

Opposite: A public-private partnership is responsible for development of the Waterway. The corridor will link commercial, residential, and entertainment facilities in the Town Center via three primary modes of transportation that exclude automobiles: pedestrian, trolley, and water taxi.

Above: The planned Waterway Marriott Hotel and Convention Center will offer 70,000 square feet (6,503 square meters) of meeting space, 345 hotel rooms, restaurants, and retail. It is intended as the first step in positioning the Woodlands as a tourist destination.

Left: Residents living along the Waterway will have an abundant choice of amenities ranging from views, recreational open space, and walking paths along the canal to restaurants, specialty shops, entertainment venues, and transportation links.

NEW VISIONS

CIVANO

TUCSON, ARIZONA

Sponsored by the American Community Fund of Fannie Mae, Civano is a master-planned community long in development and even longer in its view of how to build sustainably in the Sonoran Desert. The original proposal for a "Solar Village," where Civano is now rising, was initiated in the 1970s by advocacy groups and the local government in response to that decade's energy crisis. The project's focus on passive energy technologies proved too narrow to attract much interest, but it did lay the groundwork for Civano, an 880-acre (356-hectare) environmentally conscious project set in motion in 1996, with urban design by Moule & Polyzoides, Duany Plater-Zyberk & Company, and Wayne Moody.

Civano aims, say the designers, to merge the standards and initiatives of the new urbanism with "as advanced an environmental protocol as ever proposed for an urbanist project in the United States." Environmental impact goals, known collectively as the Civano Standard, are: buildings will use 50 percent less energy than specified in the 1995 Model Energy Code; buildings will consume 65 percent less potable water than Tucson's baseline 1990 residential average; construction activity will generate 30 percent less solid waste and 40 percent fewer trip miles than the local average; and one on-site job will be created for every two residences built, with 20 percent of the housing being "affordable."

Making Fabric

The long-term vision for Civano calls for four neighborhoods and a town center, with 1,500 households and a substantial amount of office, retail, and institutional space, all conforming to established standards of open space and building types. The immediate goal, however, is to complete Neighborhood One, a 600-dwelling district set on 380 acres (154 hectares). The master plan for the first neighborhood will be realized in two phases. Designed by Moule & Polyzoides, the plan is based on the Transect, a concept developed by proponents of the new urbanism that establishes a system of classification deploying the conceptual range of 'more rural–more urban' to arrange in useful order the typical elements of urbanism. The idea focuses on a design continuum in which, to use an example provided by the design team,

"a street is more urban than a road, a curb more urban than a swale, and an allee of trees more urban than a tree cluster."

The concept also serves as a design tool. "The correlation of various design elements within a common 'rural-urban range' of architectural form" explain the designers, "is the basis for deciding the location and particular architecture for the various housing and public space types that define the character of Civano." While the big picture for Civano is based on the interrelatedness of building, neighborhood, and region, the internal structure of Neighborhood One is defined by three conditions of location and form: center, general, and edge. The center zone is dense, multifunctional, and public. The general zone is principally residential with limited additional uses, its character derived from the adjacency of diverse housing types, parks, and greens. The edge zone, in direct contrast to the center, is low-density residential.

An Agenda for Community Building

The look and feel of Neighborhood One is shaped by four fundamental concepts: encouraging community, connection with the land, respect for climate and place, and regeneration. The first concept is a basic building block for the development of a cohesive community; following the principles of the new urbanism, the plan calls for a diversity of building types and uses, street design that elevates the pedestrian above the vehicle, and a public realm that supports social activities. The second concept, connection with the land, places stewardship of the land high on the community agenda, respecting indigenous patterns of natural growth, drainage, and erosion; local history and culture; and the native flora and fauna.

Hoping to minimize an already compromised geography, where decades of uncontrolled development throughout much of the Southwest has damaged the aquifer and the desert landscape, the developers and designers of Civano are determined to respect climate and place, their third governing concept. Recurring patterns of sun, wind, and the seasons are expressed through the overall form, materials palette, and orientation of buildings and gardens. Finally, strategies for conservation, restoration of native riparian habitats,

Previous page: Long in the making, the desert community of Civano exemplifies the union of new urbanist and environmentalist design principles.

Above: Civano's streets are designed to be walked as well as driven. Generous use of native plants adds visual interest and shade.

Right: The master plan for Civano envisions four neighborhoods and a town center district.

Opposite: The regulating plan for Neighborhood One illustrates the layout of its three zones, which manifest four fundamental concepts: encouraging community, connection with the land, respect for climate and place, and regeneration. The plan is based on the new urbanist concept of the Transect, a categorization system that organizes an environment on a scale from urban to rural.

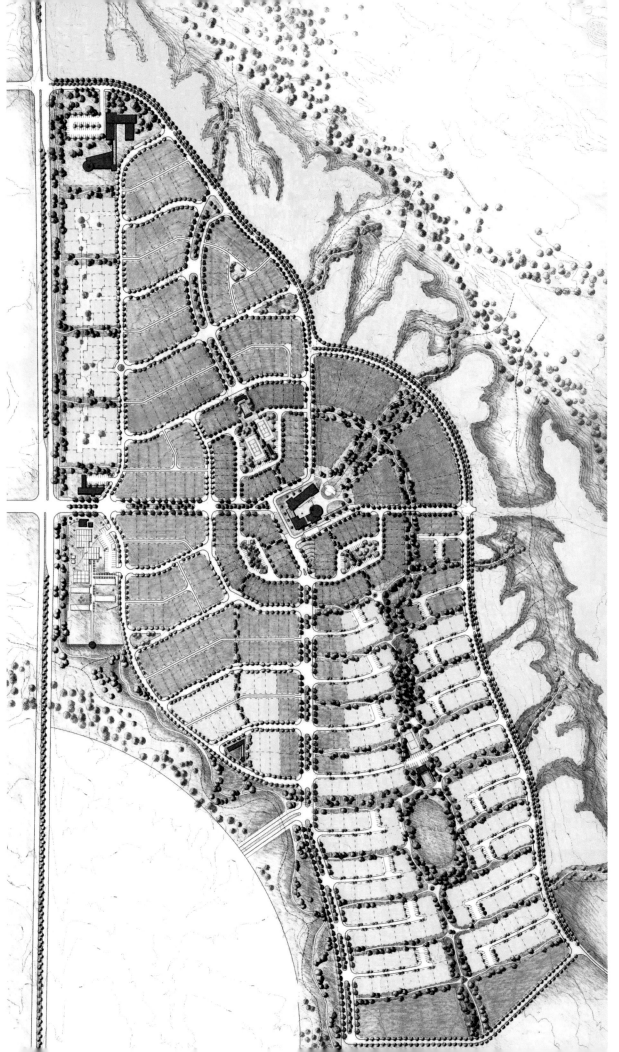

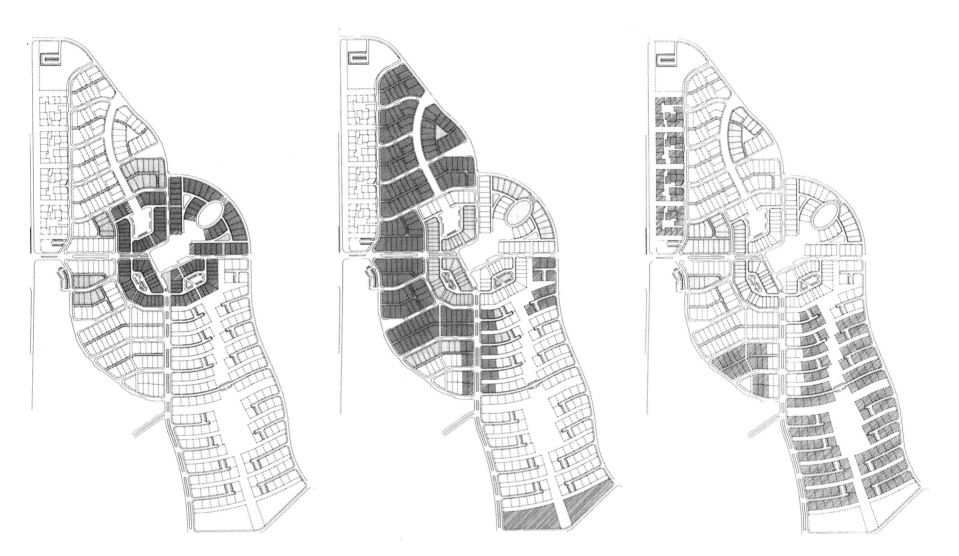

Center Zone: As the neighborhood social condenser, this zone is dense, multifunctional, and centrally located. Streetscapes are urban, with open space occurring as plazas and squares.

General Zone: The largest area of the neighborhood, this zone is primarily residential, but still relatively urban in character. Medium-density housing is interspersed with small parks and greens.

Edge Zone: Development is strictly low-density residential in this zone. Streetscapes are rural and open space is likely to take shape as parks with a proximate greenbelt.

In its 15-year evolution from a conceptual solar village to a model for sustainable growth, Civano is planned for 2,500 homes and over 6,000 residents. Active and passive energy and natural resource conservation are at the forefront of design for every housing type. Methods include building massing and orientation, minimized windows, shading devices, color palette, solar water heaters, photovoltaic panels, reclaimed water, plumbing line heaters, and lumber substitutes.
Above: Courtyard housing.
Opposite, left: Site plan for compound housing.
Opposite, right: Patio homes.

and the stewardship of natural resources are deeply rooted in the concept of regeneration, the fourth concept for place making.

An Anti-Monoculture

Diversity, interdependency, and walkability are to coalesce in Neighborhood One with the aid of design principles that focus on public space orientation, pedestrian dominance, and diversity of building types. Designed as "a holistic network" of various open spaces, the first neighborhood includes streets, parks, and squares—all typical components of the new urbanism—and landscaped zones derived from existing natural patterns of the site, directing the flow of water run-off into areas that support vegetation and wildlife. A regenerative agricultural model employs community and organic home gardens, the development of a comprehensive waste treatment facility for recycling and waste water using decomposing and sericulture, organic landscape management, and the reclamation of lands damaged by overgrazing.

The long-term health of the land is seen as a benefit of pedestrian-oriented planning. The center of Neighborhood One holds a mixture of retail, commercial, and residential programs. The edges of the center are located within a quarter-mile of the neighborhood matrix to discourage car use. Blocks throughout the neighborhood are relatively compact for pedestrian-friendly access. A catalog of rights-of-way, part of the design guidelines for Civano, illustrates the calibration of many street types in an effort to support pedestrian use and define distinctive neighborhood character.

Residential products in Neighborhood One are variations on eight housing types: town, courtyard, patio, university, cottage, desert village, and compound. Through variation in size, configuration, style, and price, these types encourage many spatial dispositions, a range of densities, and broad market appeal.
Top and opposite, top: Townhouses.
Right: University homes.

Above, left: Fifty university homes comprise a small percentage of Neighborhood One's 600-home total. This housing type is inspired by early-20th-century detached homes near the University of Arizona's Tucson campus. Each unit has its own front, side, or rear yard, defined by a wall and a detached garage.

Above, center and right: Civano's townhouses are located in the mixed-use, dense center zone. For architectural variety, four alternative two-story designs were developed. All units have private street entrances. In response to the neighborhood grid, four sets of townhouses face four different cardinal points.

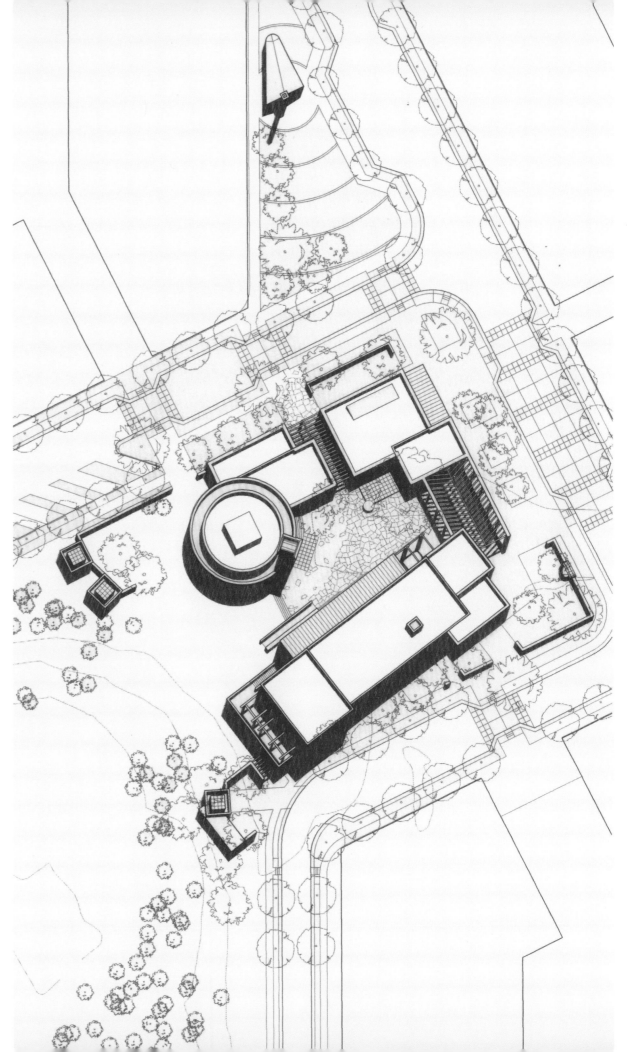

Opposite, right: The neighborhood center, shown in plan, embodies Civano's social and environmental ideals. The modern structures of this commercial and civic hub incorporate such traditional Southwestern forms as the kiva, dating back thousands of years. An enclosed courtyard provides a casual meeting place.

Left: Sidewalks and open space border a café and retail stores, emphasizing the center's connection with surrounding residential blocks. Buildings here were planned, designed, and constructed to overcome the negative aspects of sun and heat in an environmentally sustainable manner. Opposite, far left: Respect for the Sonoran Desert landscape inspired Civano's ecologically attuned development.

Green Acres

Like the streets and public spaces, there is great diversity in housing types in Neighborhood One. Size, configuration, style, and price in a range of densities offer an opportunity for socioeconomic variety. In the center zone, there are townhouses, courtyard housing, detached patio houses, and villas. The general zone holds university homes and cottages, while the edge zone comprises desert country homes and compound housing. Most homes, designed in an architectural language that "reinterprets" regional Southwestern living traditions, are designed to have a solar water heater and the capacity to accept photovoltaic panels.

Summer heat gain is minimized through building massing and orientation. Additional passive solar techniques include small openings on west-facing facades, shading devices on south facades, and the use of light, non-absorbent exterior color finishes on solar-exposed building surfaces. Building setbacks, height restrictions, and the appropriate location of deciduous and evergreen trees are also outlined in the Neighborhood One residential design principles.

Environmental and social agendas are synthesized in the design of the neighborhood center. The building is the focal point of Civano's first development phase, located within walking distance of all 600 households. Its mix of uses includes offices, a café, an art gallery, retail shops, and a meeting hall. Built with adobe, RASTRA block, wood frame, and straw bales, the community building is meant as a model of sustainable construction in a desert environment. The courtyard-style complex, with its trellised entrance and patio, arcades, and its cooling tower embodies the ideals of Civano, setting an example of sustainability for both residents and the region.

Even with such successes, the designers believe that Civano suffers from some disparities and lack of coherence in its building fabric. They cite the fact that the project never adopted an urban code that was developed to guide both visual compatibility among building types and desired thermal building performance in terms of shading, daylighting, ventilation, and insulation. The code addressed urban, thoroughfare, architectural, environmental, landscape, and use standards, and included a regulating plan.

COFFEE CREEK CENTER

CHESTERTON, INDIANA

Environmental sustainability is the genus loci of Coffee Creek Center. From site preparation to building materials, from wetlands restoration to efficient energy systems, the 675-acre (272-hectare) master-planned community 45 miles (72 kilometers) southeast of Chicago seeks to integrate the natural and the built into a seamless whole. The concept for Coffee Creek, developed by Lake Erie Land Company on property purchased in 1995, is a direct response to the national debate over urban sprawl and its incompatibility with the health of natural systems. The master plan calls for a series of compact, mixed-use, pedestrian-oriented neighborhoods, where homes, workplaces, and retail centers sit lightly on the land.

The developers of Coffee Creek believe that the diverse needs of daily life can be met within the scale of the neighborhood; the production-curbing, fuel-consuming, hour-long commute need not be the only way to link home and office. The implementation of traditional town planning principles, they argue, can ensure that commercial and retail needs are brought within walking distance of a diverse residential community.

With approximately 4 million square feet (371,612 square meters) of commercial and retail space, 3,000 residential units of varying size and typology, civic and public facilities on 20 acres (eight hectares), and 225 acres (91 hectares) of open and recreational space, the development intends to meet its goal of self-contained economic and ecological sustainability over a five-phase buildout scheduled for completion by 2015.

Principled Design

Coffee Creek Center, an extension of Chesterton in northwestern Indiana near the intersection of three major highways, is shaped by a team of planners, including William McDonough + Partners, an architecture and planning firm long known for its innovative approach to sustainable design, as well as Looney Ricks Kiss and Gibbs Planning Group. The master plan brief was to create an environmentally sensitive community defined by urban-like densities and walkable destinations. Unlike the sprawling bedroom communities that often displace vast ecosystems with low-density development and car-dependent services, Coffee Creek is designed as a compact,

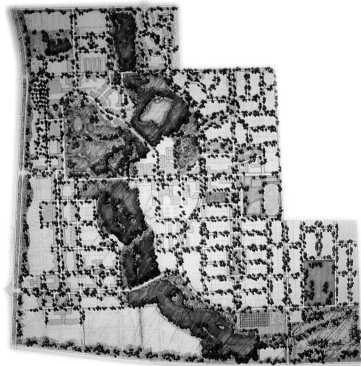

Opening pages: The larger of Coffee Creek Center's first two neighborhoods, Village Green, features a restored prairie park and lake.

Above: Coffee Creek Center is an extension of the Chesterton community, with pedestrian-oriented mixed-use areas intermingled with public open space. Meandering through the center of the site is the Coffee Creek Conservancy District, a broad preserve encompassing the creek, its banks, and adjacent land.

Right: Village Green shares a boundary, views, and access with the Conservancy District. This neighborhood features medium-density housing on second floors or higher in mixed-use buildings. The maximum height for all building types is four stories.

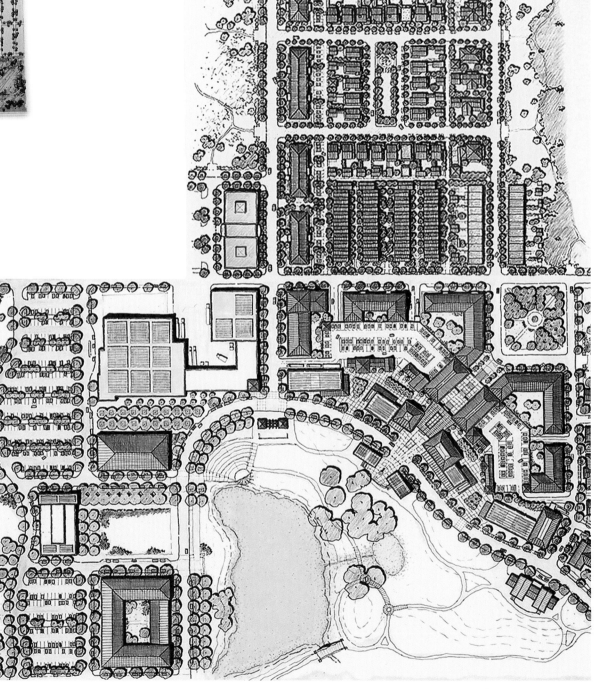

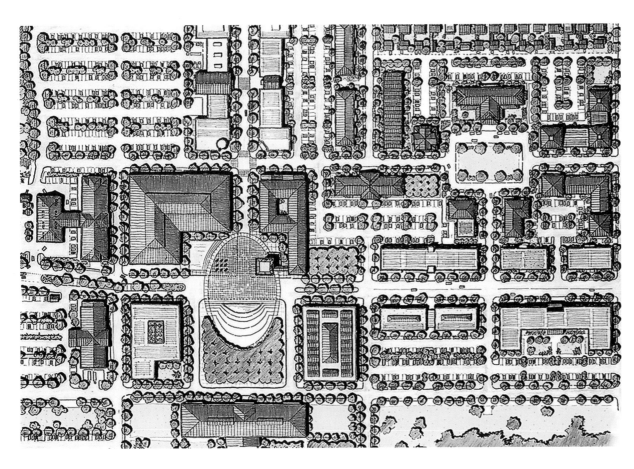

A range of commercial facilities at Coffee Creek provides residents with a base for both employment and services. Commercial areas are laid out on a grid and have a main street orientation, with park- ing tucked behind buildings. All are within walking distance of residential neighborhoods and open space areas.

pedestrian-oriented community with extensive bicycle paths, advanced energy systems, restored native ecosystems and habitats, and advanced data and communications technology. Streets are made for walking and bicycle routes are an integral part of the landscape.

Buildings, be they residential or commercial, will be oriented to take advantage of solar resources for daylighting and energy production; photovoltaic and wind power are among the renewable energy sources tapped at Coffee Creek. Buildings will employ sustainable materials selected to enhance indoor environmental quality. A 167-acre (68-hectare) Coffee Creek Watershed Conservancy is the centerpiece of the community's open space preservation program.

The first two neighborhoods underway at Coffee Creek are the 87-acre (35-hectare) Morgan's Corner and the 112-acre (45-hectare) Village Green. The former is a mixed-use residential neighborhood, with 59,843 square feet (5,560 square meters) of commercial office space and 1,795,653 square feet (166,822 square meters) of residential space, organized along a main intersection at Sidewalk and Dickinson Roads. To the north, there are apartments, townhouses, civic spaces, and a grocery store. To the south of the intersection are a variety of residential building types, including live-work units, townhouses, and attached and detached homes, as well as public parks.

The Village Green, with 600,000 square feet (55,742 square meters) of office and retail space and 325 residential units, is built around a 40-acre (16-hectare) park on restored prairie land. Here, a 400-seat amphitheater, brick-paved walking trails, overlooks, boardwalks, and an open-air pavilion with two fireplaces establish an outdoor framework for community and individual activities. The village includes medium-density housing (on second and/or third floors) in mixed-use buildings, offices, and retail directed at the needs of both residents and area employees. Shops and after-hours entertainment venues are located in this neighborhood.

A major downtown district is the centerpiece of the second phase of Coffee Creek Center. Due to its location directly adjacent to two major regional arteries—the Indiana Toll Road and Indiana State Route 49— private developers in this mixed-use district are permitted to build commercial structures with up to eight stories. The districtwide plan can accommodate 1.9 million square feet (176,516 square meters) of commercial, retail, and office space on 45 acres (18 hectares); 750 residential units (apartments above retail, multifamily, and single-family detached) on nearly 11 acres (four hectares); and set aside 54 acres (22 hectares) for open space. Significantly, the downtown area is within walking distance of both the Morgan's Creek and Village Green neighborhoods.

228 The downtown district planned for the next phase of development combines open space, 750 residential units, and nearly 2 million square feet (185,807 square meters) of commercial, retail, and office development on 110 acres (44 hectares). The residential component includes single- and multifamily housing.

Nurturing Nature

While the Coffee Creek Center site contains only 17 acres (seven hectares) of nonbuildable areas and wetlands, nearly one-third of the development is retained in preserved green space, parks, and constructed wetlands. Early in the planning process a natural inventory was taken that identified 14 soil types within a landscape of prairie, savannah, marshes, fens, and riparian forest, as well as Coffee Creek, its banks and flood plains. The natural ecosystem that existed prior to the settlement and row-crop agricultural development of the region in the 1830s featured prairie, wetlands, wet prairie, and other ecosystems. Through these systems, water flowed naturally into Coffee Creek through the vertical infiltration of storm water into the dense root systems of diverse native plants, and subsequently flowed into the creek, reducing the effects of drought and flood conditions.

Nearly two centuries later, there is evidence of highly advanced erosion to the stream beds, which wipes out plant and animal habitat and contributes to downstream flooding. To reverse such environmental degradation, the Coffee Creek watershed is being restored to its presettlement condition. Further, deep-rooted native plants are being reestablished in prairies, savannahs, and open woodlands. A storm water system has been installed

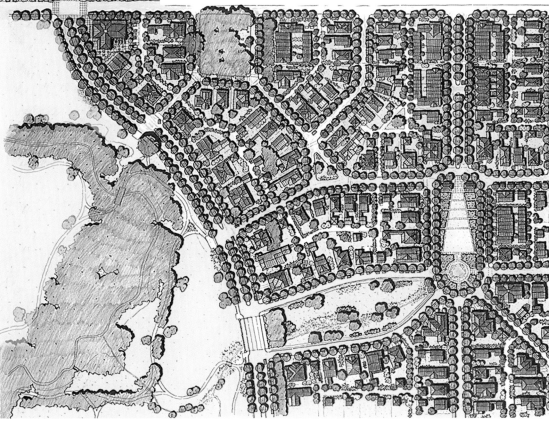

Morgan's Corner is a mixed-use neighborhood with 315 attached and 179 detached residential units. The Coffee Creek Declaration of Principles governs physical maintenance as well as social infrastructure throughout the community.

230 Streetscapes that promote walking and bike routes are an integral part of the plan. Undeveloped areas have been restored to presettlement condition to create a healthier environment for soil, plants, and wildlife. Storm water systems were modeled after the natural ecology by minimizing impervious surfaces and using native plant systems to clean, filter, and absorb water.

to take advantage of the ability of native ecosystems to absorb and retain rainwater. Waste water will be treated on site using natural biological processes in a system of constructed wetlands. The designation and development of an ambitious eco-industrial district at Coffee Creek is in a very early conceptual stage.

Building Community

The physical building blocks of the Coffee Creek community—be they reconstructed wetlands or civic buildings—are shored up in other ways, social and economic initiatives among them. Strong neighborhoods are characterized by a network of connections—to jobs, civic places, and retail; between individuals sharing common goals as well as citizens on opposite ends of the spectrum. Housing options and job opportunities are wide-ranging at Coffee Creek. Indeed, the Coffee Creek Center Declaration of Principles—a communitywide set of governing documents that address construction, maintenance, environmental, and social issues—mandates that at least 10 percent of all homes should qualify as affordable housing according to the Indiana Housing Finance Authority.

Above, left: Homes in Coffee Creek Center favor human scale and relate to the architectural traditions of northwestern Indiana. Despite its rural overtones, advanced communications and data and energy systems power the entire community.

Above, right: Townhouses are one of the many housing options that reflects the community's commitment to affordability as set forth in the Declaration of Principles.

JINJI LAKE

SUZHOU, CHINA

Free trade is the engine driving plans for a new large-scale development just east of Suzhou, a 2,500-year-old city known as the Venice of China, where canals and ancient walled gardens draw tourists from around the world. It is also a locale where old and new ways of life merge into one: named one of 14 open economic zones in 1985, the Suzhou metropolitan area is the location of the Suzhou Industrial Park (SIP), an ambitious initiative where foreign investment is allowed to a far greater degree than in other parts of the country. The developer, a joint venture between the governments of Singapore and China, believes that the design and implementation of one of the first major master-planned communities in China will encourage international investment in the SIP. With the capacity for 600,000 residents and the promise of 360,000 new jobs, all by the year 2020, the project is attracting high-profile corporations, including Western product manufacturers.

The 27-square-mile (70-square-kilometer) SIP is an integrated development of industrial, commercial, residential, cultural, entertainment, and recreational programs, all linked by a vast system of new infrastructure. The master plan is defined by both a grid system of urban blocks—an effort to establish a cosmopolitan environment—and a series of canals—an effort to reflect the traditional landscape of Suzhou's historic core. The central portion of the site is residential, interspersed with neighborhood-scale retail for convenient, walkable access to local goods and services. To the north and east of the residential areas are parcels designated for use by industrial and technology companies. The most prominent natural element of the SIP is Jinji Lake, which is also the site of the first of several distinct districts slated for development.

The 1,273-acre (515-hectare) Jinji Lake Waterfront District, planned by EDAW, Inc., includes residential, recreational, and commercial programs arrayed around the lake. To date, 1,200 residential units have been built. Office space has reached 53,820 square feet (5,000 square meters) out of a total of 274,480 square feet (25,500 square meters) planned for the project. Retail space is to top out at 215,278 square feet (20,000 square meters). Proposed transportation systems include buses, a light rail, water taxis, and a trolley. A continuous pedestrian pathway system including a bike trail

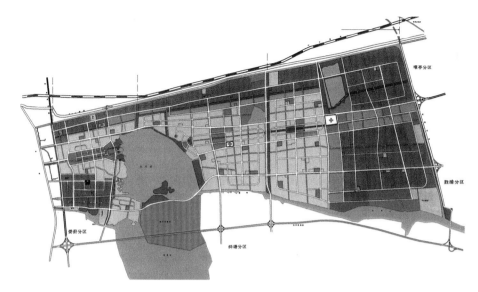

Previous pages: Jinji Lake, one of the largest inland freshwater lakes in eastern China, is the centerpiece for development of the massive Suzhou Industrial Park.

Top: Encompassing 27 square miles (70 square kilometers), the master plan for Suzhou Industrial Park combines complex urban design and environmental solutions to create a new community for 600,000 residents and multinational corporations.

Above: Canals that reference the historic waterways of the ancient section of Suzhou overlay the street grid. The contemporary versions are designed as amenities rather than as thoroughfares for commercial boat traffic.

and promenade wraps around the lake; forests, wetlands, a golf course, tennis courts, a marina, and yachting clubs are among the many amenities in the district.

Principles of the Plan

With such a large tract of land, the adherence to a set of planning principles—inspired by successful waterfront communities from Boston's Back Bay to Sydney's Darling Harbor—was critical to the establishment of a framework for the Jinji Lake Waterfront District. EDAW developed eight principles, among them: create a broad hierarchy of open space and waterfront features, allowing for different uses, elements, and functions to attract a wide variety of users; integrate open space and building forms to create animated plazas, courtyards, promenades, and a variety of waterfront environments; incorporate active commercial and civic uses into key open spaces; form a unique identity for each neighborhood while creating a coherent visual and physical public connection to the lake; and orient local streets toward the lake.

Company Town

A natural asset of great importance to this growing community, Jinji Lake is being developed as part of an open space system that serves as a recreational destination for the whole Suzhou region. In fact, the developer and planners determined early in the design process that the success of this amenity hinged on the character, organization, and synergy of land uses that surround the lake. A series of zones and districts were developed to guide the project.

The master plan for the Jinji Lake Waterfront District proposes the creation of two primary zones organized along an axis that runs northeast to southwest. Public-oriented spaces and amenities are assigned to land on the upper half of the lake. This public zone is characterized by lakeside promenades to bring locals and workers into direct contact with the water's edge. Waterfront parks are adjacent to shopping, entertainment, and cultural destinations. The southeast portion of the lakefront is designed for more passive recreational and private uses. Here, a restricted-use study and educational area called Reflection Point Park is meant to communicate the importance of environmental stewardship. The remainder of the southeast zone includes a residential neighborhood, natural canals, waterways, and trails.

The lake district is to be divided into eight areas, each defined by the water's edge: Cityside Harbor, Grand Promenade, and Marina Cove to the west; Reflection Point to the south; Reflection Gardens to the east; and Mirror's Crossing, Discovered Island, and the Arts and Entertainment Village to the north.

Residential development is found lakeside and in easily accessible adjacent areas. Modeled after the Singapore system, housing is within walking distance of neighborhood centers, a new planning concept for China, according to EDAW. Here, residents can find supermarkets, schools, shopping complexes, parks, a cinema, skating rink, bowling alley, restaurants, cafés, a medical center, and a library. A variety of housing types have been built, including upscale detached homes, bungalows, townhouses, and luxury high rises of 12 to

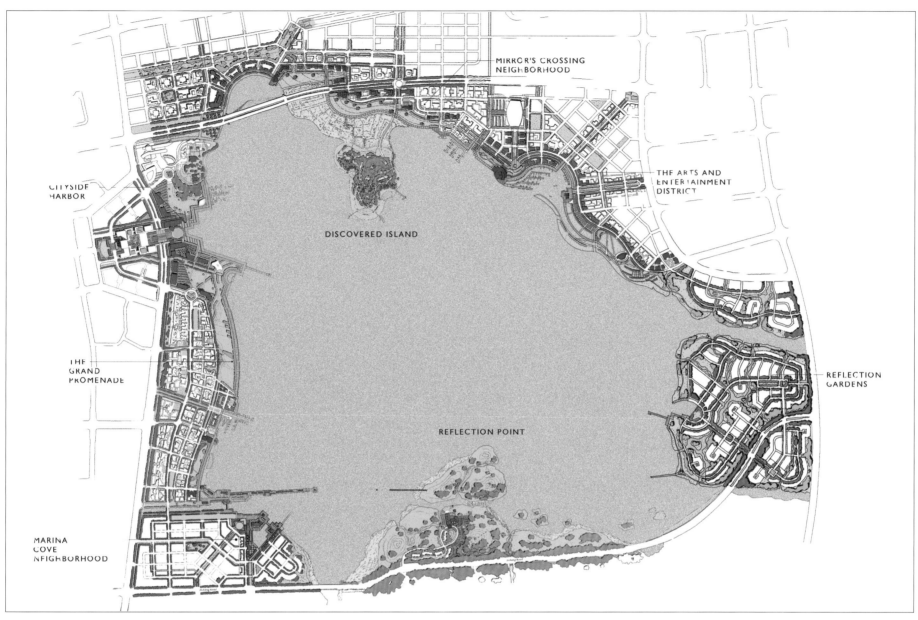

MIRROR'S CROSSING NEIGHBORHOOD

CITYSIDE HARBOR

THE ARTS AND ENTERTAINMENT DISTRICT

DISCOVERED ISLAND

THE GRAND PROMENADE

REFLECTION GARDENS

REFLECTION POINT

MARINA COVE NEIGHBORHOOD

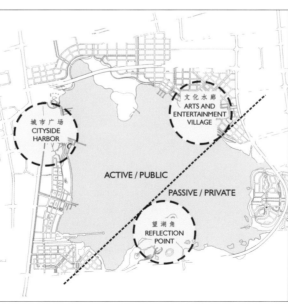

文化水郷
ARTS AND ENTERTAINMENT VILLAGE

城市广场
CITYSIDE HARBOR

ACTIVE / PUBLIC

PASSIVE / PRIVATE

望湖角
REFLECTION POINT

Above: With the creation of a world-class, environmentally responsible waterfront development as the main goal, the Jinji Lake master plan addresses land use, water quality, and the design of public open space and eight different districts.

Far left: The concept of duality was widely explored in Jinji Lake's landscape, which takes historic elements and puts them into a modern context.

Left: Bisected by a central axis, lakefront development has a north-south orientation. Active recreation and entertainment venues are in the north and more passive ones are located in the south.

Below, top and bottom: The Cityside Harbor district features an extensive linear park system designed to attract residents, workers, and tourists to the lakefront. Natural and manmade elements, including public art, are combined to encourage a variety of uses.

Opposite, top: A ceremonial plaza for large gatherings at Cityside Harbor terminates with a lake view. Although there is automobile access, the emphasis is on pedestrian circulation. There will also be substantial parking spaces for bicycles, China's main mode of transportation.

Opposite, bottom, first three from left: The Dusk Clock in Millennium Park creates a narrative landscape where seasonal plantings and dramatic day/night landscapes emphasize the passage of time in ever-changing Suzhou.

Opposite, bottom, far right: The paving pattern in one of Cityside Harbor's many plazas captures the "One Mirror, Two Reflections" project concept as depicted in the Jinji Lake waterfront district logo.

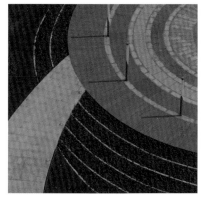 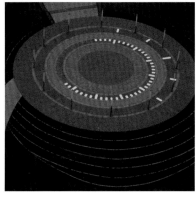 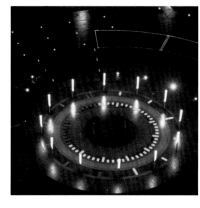 

20 stories on the shore of Jinji Lake. There are also five- and six-story walk-up apartment buildings with ground-floor retail in the neighborhood center.

The image and identity of Jinji Lake is designed to reflect the concept of duality, in which the traditions of historic Suzhou are respected while the requirements of a contemporary community are met. The physical icon for the waterfront district is a bridge that crosses the water in the northwest corner of the lake. The bridge symbolically connects old and new Suzhou, linking the past to the future, art to architecture, land to water, city to village, and Suzhou to the international community.

Free Trade

A large commercial core is intended to serve in the future as the central business district of Suzhou proper. Already in place is a public park—replete with large expanses of green space, an open-air cultural plaza, children's playground, and social facilities. Currently under development is an arts and entertainment district, which will include major museums and performing arts facilities, restaurants, and a Canal Expo where commercial investors in the SIP will be invited to display innovative new technologies and products. A range of hotels and resort properties will coexist with new upscale residential neighborhoods as well. Other projects planned for the commercial core include a wholesale marketplace, an education cluster, resorts, a major medical center, and a convention and exhibition center.

Strong promotional efforts and the infrastructure to support a very large workforce have resulted in commitments to the SIP from a number of multinational companies in electronics, chemicals, pharmaceuticals, health care, precision engineering, food, and other support industries. Companies that have taken residence at the SIP include Glaxo Smith Kline, Revlon, Nokia, Nabisco Food, Olin Chemical, Delphi Delco, Black and Decker, Allied Signal, Advanced Micro Devices, Hitachi, and Fujitsu.

Opposite: Mirror's Crossing is planned as a vibrant residential community with an active waterfront promenade. A signature bridge will symbolically and literally connect the new development to its cultural and spiritual antecedent, old Suzhou.

Left, top and bottom: Understanding the local culture was crucial to programming neighborhoods as well as the open space that comprised nearly 20 percent of the site. "Open space" itself was a new concept, a vast departure from traditional Chinese gardens, yet the past and present were successfully interwoven. The Zig Zag Path (top) and the Camphor Forest Trail (bottom) illustrate how Jinji Lake's flower gardens and themed forests draw upon China's rich cultural heritage.

Opposite, top: The passive
recreation zone along the
southeastern edge of the lake
uses an interpretive landscape
to convey the importance of
environmental stewardship.
Improvement of water quality
and future protection of the

aquatic environment were key
project objectives.
Opposite, bottom: Discovered
Island, a manmade island at
the north end of the lake, features resort and water recreation uses.

Above: Open space and building forms were carefully integrated to create interesting
plazas, courtyards, gardens,
and promenades, and provide
a memorable waterfront experience. In the arts and entertainment district, themed

gardens sponsored by corporate tenants in Suzhou Industrial Park provide a colorful
diversion.

PLAYA VISTA

LOS ANGELES, CALIFORNIA

Playa Vista is one of the largest and most significant new urban infill communities in the country. Its developer, Playa Capital Company, is proposing a dramatic counterpoint to urban sprawl: a series of compact neighborhoods, organized into districts based on the Ahwahnee Principles—23 guidelines for integrated, sustainable, and environmentally based community design established in 1991 by a group of nationally known architects, planners, and designers. The project targets the region's nontraditional households with fast-paced lifestyles and urban cultural values.

Playa Vista is the last major developable property in urban Los Angeles. Located on the Westside of Los Angeles between the bluffs of Westchester and Marina del Rey, it is close enough to the Pacific Ocean to enjoy a year-round temperate climate. Situated in an area with 5,400,000 fewer homes than jobs, it is surrounded by multiple major urban commercial centers.

The 1,087-acre (440-hectare) site was home to Hughes Aircraft. Following the 1976 death of its founder, the Hughes empire reorganized and embarked on a decade-long study to create a plan for the property. In 1985 the plan received initial approval from the city, although it was unpopular with local residents. In 1989, when Maguire Thomas Partners took over management, the plan was revised with extensive input from the community and was approved by the city in 1993.

Urban Lifestyle

The vision for Playa Vista redefines a new type of urban living, reflecting the site's infill location, broadly based market opportunities, and the lack of urban, pedestrian-oriented neighborhood options in the Los Angeles market. The community comprises a series of neighborhoods organized into districts defined by their squares and parks. Public spaces, which range from less than one acre to several acres (one-half hectare to several hectares), are designed to draw in people at all hours of the day. Each park serves a variety of social and recreational functions, as well as the needs of the surrounding housing types. Restaurants and cafés will border selected parks to encourage activity, as will carts, markets, and special events.

244 Opening pages: The community plan for Playa Vista, the
country's largest urban infill and urban wetland reclamation project, shows its
relationship to the city of Los
Angeles and the Pacific
Ocean. The Ballona Wetlands
constitute the entire western
portion of the site.

Right, top: A deceptively typical Southern California–style
entrance belies the fact that
Playa Vista is the first new
community of this scale in the
region to incorporate new
urbanist principles.

Right, bottom: Approximately
half of the Playa Vista site
will be devoted to parks and
open space. Each of the 40
parks will have its own identity, such as Crescent Park
(right), an expansive outdoor
event venue. Local streets
facilitate open access to
parks, and residential buildings around them create an
urban edge.

245

Above: The CenterPointe Club, Playa Vista's first activity and social center, will have a gym and fitness facilities, swimming pools, activity rooms, a business center, meeting rooms, and space for social events.

Left: A mosaic tile fountain depicts the history of the site and is the namesake of Fountain Park.

Playa Vista's neighborhoods are interconnected by a street grid designed to make pedestrians a top priority. Walking distance to public services and activities is minimized and multiple stops and crossings, roundabouts, reduced lane widths, and chokers at intersections collectively slow traffic.

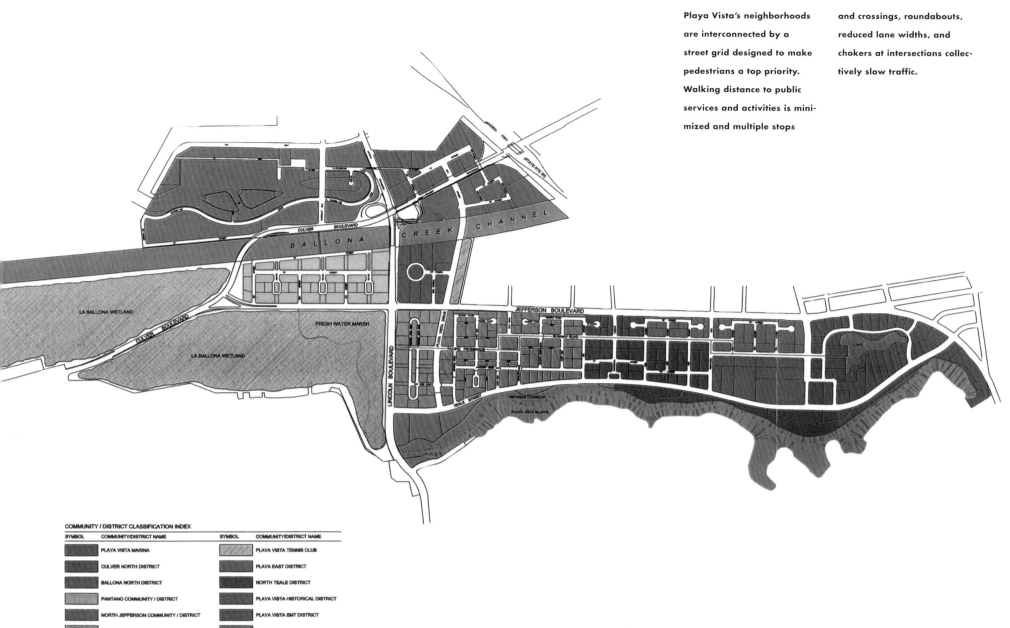

COMMUNITY / DISTRICT CLASSIFICATION INDEX

SYMBOL	COMMUNITY/DISTRICT NAME	SYMBOL	COMMUNITY/DISTRICT NAME
	PLAYA VISTA MARINA		PLAYA VISTA TENNIS CLUB
	CULVER NORTH DISTRICT		PLAYA EAST DISTRICT
	BALLONA NORTH DISTRICT		NORTH TEALE DISTRICT
	PANTANO COMMUNITY / DISTRICT		PLAYA VISTA HISTORICAL DISTRICT
	NORTH JEFFERSON COMMUNITY / DISTRICT		PLAYA VISTA EMT DISTRICT
	LINCOLN BAY DISTRICT		WATER
	GARDEN DISTRICT		FRESH WATER MARSH & WETLANDS
	CENTINELLA DISTRICT		PLAYA VISTA BLUFFS
	PLAYA VISTA COMMUNITY CENTER		PLAYA VISTA PROMENADE
	PLAYA VISTA TOWN CENTER		

Streets are pedestrian-oriented in scale and building orientation. A grid pattern has been laid out to create walkable, accessible districts that optimize traffic flow. Street trees are planted at 25- to 30-foot (7.5- to nine-meter) intervals, with amenities including benches, trash receptacles, and pedestrian-scale lighting. Buildings face the streets in an orderly manner, with careful attention to scale and treatment of transitional areas. High-speed traffic is discouraged through multiple stops, crossings, district squares, and narrower lanes. Transit will be an integral part of the community, with most public uses located within walking distance of transit stops. Population densities will support an effective transit system, which will be routed along major streets.

Rather than locating uses in large, single-purpose districts, they are arranged in a finer-grained, small-parcel pattern. Storefront retail space will be interspersed throughout the neighborhoods, and completed districts will offer shops and amenities that appeal to target resident groups. In true "Main Street" style there will be residences above the shops. Playa Vista

Fifteen different housing types provide myriad choices including condominiums, townhouses, single-family detached, and rental apartments. Artistic renderings of condominiums from top to bottom: The Metro, which lends an art deco flavor to the northern edge of Crescent Park; Villa d'Este's mansion-inspired design conceals interior courtyards with fountains, tiled arches, and gardens; Crescent Walk entry-level condominiums are conveniently located between Crescent Park and the Center-Pointe Club.

248 With 13,000 units at buildout, architectural variety was a must. Conceptually designed by leading architects and fully realized by the project's builders, residential products reflect styles prevalent in the Los Angeles area, including art deco, Spanish, Mediterranean, Italianate, postmodern, and mansion. Neighborhood design emphasizes street orientation of buildings, pedestrian walkways, lush landscaping, and subterranean parking.

Right, top: Located across from Longwood Park, The Tapestry—two- and three-level townhouses clustered around motor courts—take their cue from urban brownstones.

Right, bottom: The Paraiso—garden-level townhouses with loft penthouse units—are inspired by the architecture of Frank Lloyd Wright.

Opposite: Capri Court villas have individual garages clustered around private drive courts.

Village Center, expected to be the focus of the community, will combine commercial, civic, cultural, entertainment, and recreational uses. Its location will be at the center of the community, accessible to the Campus at Playa Vista, an entertainment and media business district, as well as the residential districts of Playa Vista. It will focus on a town green, providing opportunities for socializing, gathering, relaxing, and special events.

Something for Everyone

Based on consumer research, a contemporary mix of housing types and plans was developed, ranging from luxury to affordable. Condominiums, townhouses, cluster, and detached homes will be offered for sale from less than $200,000 to over $1 million. Buyers will have more than 60 house plans within 15 different product forms to choose from, with each district including a variety of types. Rental apartments will also be available in a range of types and price categories.

The overriding characteristic of the residential program is the promotion of urban densities ranging from ten to 80 dwellings per acre (four to 32 dwellings per hectare), for an average net density of about 43 units per acre (17 units per hectare). A full 15 percent of the first phase will be "affordable housing" based on city of Los Angeles standards. An additional 10 percent of the homes will be priced for moderate-income residents. By West Los Angeles standards "entry-level-priced" product is $250,000.

Architectural Guidelines Redefined

Playa Vista has gone beyond the usual architectural design guidelines, instead gathering the leading architects to establish concept designs for the homes, as well as their composition into city blocks. Builders are then recruited to implement the predetermined prototypes. This process has allowed a more literal interpretation of the master developer's vision. All local streets, parkways, and public landscapes are designed and installed by the master developer.

Diverse building materials will be used, with an emphasis on light colors and forms that celebrate the golden years of Southern California. Each neighborhood will have a different mix of architectural styles reminiscent of the best architecture in Los Angeles—art deco, Spanish, Mediterranean, Italianate, postmodern, and the bright white mansions of Beverly Hills. The villas of early-1900s Los Angeles, with courtyards and towers, provide the inspiration for condominium designs, some with circular master bedroom suites overlooking garden courts. Townhouses are designed with parking half a flight down from street level. Almost all parking for the project is underground, minimizing the presence of vehicles from the street scene.

Above: The Visitors Center was the first project completed at Playa Vista. Its interactive displays and multimedia presentation provide information on housing options, commercial development, and environmental attributes.

Opposite: Artistic renderings of a lively arts and entertainment district with water feature (top) and landscaped courtyard (bottom).

Wetlands

The site has been highly degraded, used as it was by Hughes for manufacturing, testing, and developing aircraft, as well as for farming, oil and gas mining, and later for aerospace and defense. As a result, remaining natural features are only remnants of their original state.

The Ballona Wetlands are a major landmark, one of the largest natural restoration projects undertaken in U.S. history. Playa Vista's plans include reclamation of the existing, severely compromised saltwater wetlands. Once restored, the wetlands will include 190 acres (77 hectares) of saltwater marsh, a 26-acre (11-hectare) freshwater marsh system, a 25-acre (ten-hectare) riparian corridor, and nearly 100 acres (40 hectares) of dunes and upland habitat, creating one of the largest native habitats in any major city.

At buildout, Playa Vista will be a balanced community, with 13,000 residential units, 5 to 6 million square feet (464,515 to 557,418 square meters) of office/studio space, 600,000 square feet (55,742 square meters) of retail, and 750 hotel rooms. Over 560,000 square feet (52,026 square meters) will be dedicated to services, including police and fire stations, schools, childcare centers, a library, theaters, museums, and places of worship.

STAPLETON

DENVER, COLORADO

Faced with the closings of military bases, industrial parks, and corporate campuses, communities across the country have been debating the merits of various redevelopment proposals for very large parcels of rural, suburban, and urban land. One of the largest of these sites is the former home of Colorado's Stapleton International Airport. Just outside downtown Denver, the defunct airport will be remade as a master-planned urban infill development of the new urbanism variety, boasting an ambitious sustainable design agenda.

Combating sprawl, preserving green space, and protecting existing ecosystems while providing job growth and housing at a range of income levels are among the goals set by local citizens, developers, and planners of the adaptive use of the airport grounds. Toward this end, Stapleton's Work Force Housing Program ensures the long-term availability of housing that is affordable to households whose incomes are below 80 percent of the area median family income.

Located ten minutes east of downtown Denver and 20 minutes from the new Denver International Airport, which was completed in 1994, Stapleton will be home to approximately 30,000 residents and 35,000 workers when completed over the next 20 years. Conceived through a public-private initiative, the 4,700-acre (1,902-hectare) project is intended to produce an economically and socially diverse community with: 3 million square feet (278,709 square meters) of regional and neighborhood-based retail space; 10 million square feet (929,030 square meters) of office, research and development, and industrial space; a full spectrum of housing types, for renters and homebuyers alike, totaling 12,000 units; and over 1,100 acres (445 hectares) of regional parks and open space. A proposed commuter rail service would link downtown Denver, Stapleton, and the new Denver International Airport.

A Public Planning Process

Stapleton International Airport served as Denver's municipal airport from 1929 to 1995. The decision to move the airport to the present Denver International Airport site in 1989 instigated a citizen-led planning process to find new uses for the old airport site. Thirty-five local residents initiated a planning exercise known as Stapleton Tomorrow. Their concept plan, completed in 1991, emphasized economic development, neighborhood revitalization, environmental quality, high standards of urban design, and the generation of public revenues. Two years later, the city of Denver entered into a partnership with the Stapleton Development Foundation, a nonprofit formed to ensure that the site was developed for maximum public benefit. At the same time, the city appointed a citizens advisory board to oversee the creation of a detailed redevelopment plan.

In 1995, after hundreds of community meetings and thousands of volunteer hours, the foundation produced the Stapleton Development Plan, also known as the Green Book, which sets out the principles that will guide the buildout of the community over the next 20 years. Emphasizing four areas (economic opportunity, environmental responsibility, social equity, and physical design), the Green Book declared the community's commitment "to link economic and social objectives with development, to integrate nature and wildlife with the urban environment on a permanent basis, and to implement a more sustainable pattern of development that consumes fewer natural resources and creates fewer impacts on the natural environment."

Also in 1995, the Stapleton Development Corporation (SDC), a private nonprofit, was established as a vehicle to lease and sell property on the site. By 1997, the Denver Urban Renewal Authority made a finding of blight on the airport property, allowing the site to qualify for tax increment financing. A national real estate company, Forest City Development, through a competitive selection process, became the private development partner of the SDC. The first 270 acres (109 hectares) of Stapleton property were purchased by Forest City in 2001 and work on the site soon followed.

Extending Historic Denver

The concept for the master plan of Stapleton was informed by the street patterns and neighborhood fabric of historic Denver. Long-established neighborhoods—Washington Park, Park Hill, Cherry Creek, and Congress Park among them—are characterized by front porches, modest lots, small parks, and streets lined with sidewalks and mature trees, along with shops

and restaurants within walking distance. The homes and streets of Stapleton will echo these themes and design elements. Streets are punctuated by small urban parks. The design of parks, boulevards, and parkways reflects those found in historic Denver, with shade trees and a formal, ceremonial orientation of surrounding buildings. To reduce the expansive pavement created by utility easements, the developer has worked with local utility companies to produce "skinny streets," reducing widths to reduce the stature of the car in the community.

Residential properties in the early phases of Stapleton's growth are to be designed following 12 typologies, including six single-family detached home products; two types of rowhouses; apartments; rental units, some of which will be live-work; and four- and sixplex buildings designed to look like Denver mansions. To ensure diversity in design, household income, and family profile, the housing types will be mixed in each neighborhood. Garages, so often dominating the street elevation of development homes, are placed in rear alleyways.

Architectural styles are dictated by the Stapleton Design Book created by EDAW, Inc., and published in autumn 2000. Forest City worked with home-builders to produce designs that are aesthetically reflective of Denver's historic residential vocabulary, while respectful of the realities of mass production necessary to provide affordable and market-rate housing. The four primary styles approved in the design book are Victorian, Craftsman, Colonial Revival, and Denver Foursquare, the latter more accurately described as a classic plan-form, not a specific style. Two secondary styles also approved are English Revival and Mediterranean Revival.

254

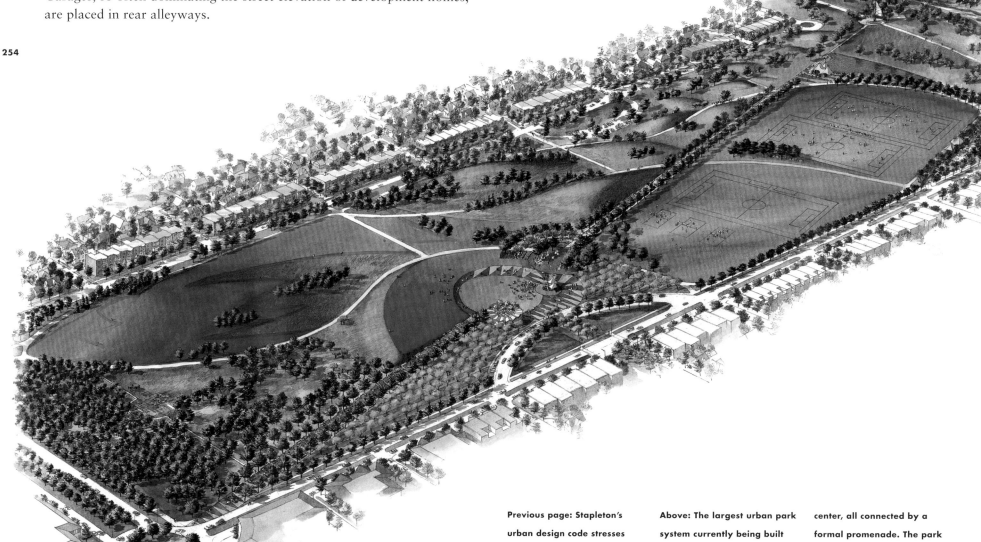

Previous page: Stapleton's urban design code stresses architectural variety and quality in residential design and construction to vitalize the streetscape. Architectural styles reflect those in Denver's historic neighborhoods.

Above: The largest urban park system currently being built in the United States, Stapleton's 80-acre (32-hectare) Central Park will include, among other things, an urban forest, multiuse trails, a public gathering place, and recreation

center, all connected by a formal promenade. The park is designed to preserve mountain and skyline views. Ultimately, this park will reflect its history as a high prairie landscape.

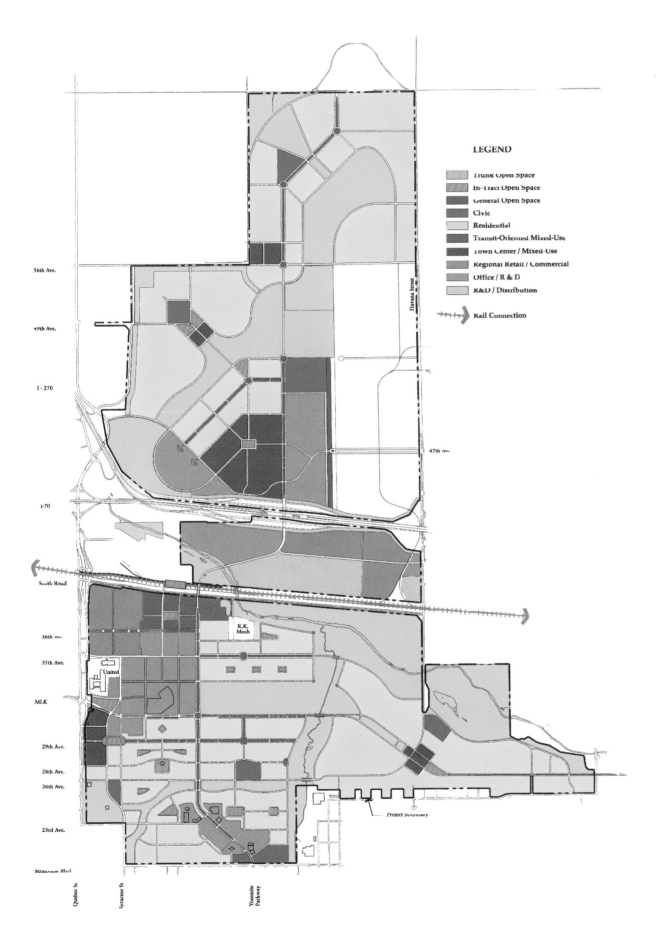

Left: The 4,500-acre (1,902-hectare) site—five miles from downtown Denver and bordered on the north by the Rocky Mountain Arsenal National Wildlife Refuge— will serve as a canvas for ten different land uses. The plan allocates equal space to residential development and open space.

Above: Regional connectivity is integral to the master plan concept for Stapleton, where a grid system based on Denver's traditional forms and patterns becomes the backbone for all modes of transportation. On a more intimate scale, individual neighborhoods incorporate parks and various other community facilities.

LEGEND

Trunk Open Space
In-Tract Open Space
General Open Space
Civic
Residential
Transit-Oriented Mixed-Use
Town Center / Mixed-Use
Regional Retail / Commercial
Office / R & D
R&D / Distribution

Rail Connection

The public gathering place planned for the middle of Central Park will include a performance amphitheater, café, and play area, and will hold 1,500 people. The park's edge will be defined by high-density housing.

Organizing Devices: Zones, Centers, and Open Spaces

The master plan calls for seven planning zones and five mixed-use town centers. Each planning zone covers roughly 500 acres (202 hectares), which will be further divided into 100-acre (40-hectare) neighborhoods. The plan also calls for a 1,116-acre (452-hectare) open space system, which will be maintained by the city and county of Denver, and will traverse the site in a north-south orientation. Connecting with existing and proposed local and regional open space systems, Stapleton's preserved space will be part of the "emerald necklace" that will eventually loop around the Denver metropolitan area.

Similarly, Stapleton's bike paths will connect to Denver's Regional Bikeway and flow into the 27,000-acre (10,927-hectare) Rocky Mountain Wildlife Preserve on the former airport's northern border. Pocket parks, town greens, and parkways account for the balance of Stapleton's open space total. Community residents will also benefit from adjacency to the existing 123-acre (50-hectare) Bluff Lake area and the Sand Creek regional greenway.

Pedestrian Priorities

Large-scale office complexes, contained in two designated districts, will be within walking distance of residential neighborhoods, parks, retail shops, and restaurants. The first district to be developed will be home to the 3 million-square-foot (278,709-square-meter) One Tower Center, among other projects. The Tower Center, the first building planned for this location, gets its name from the airport's former control tower, which will be retained and remade possibly as a public observation deck.

Like many a workplace at Stapleton, mixed-use town centers are also within walking distance of residential neighborhoods. A main street lined with two- and three-story buildings is the main feature of each town center. Retail spaces and offices will occupy ground-floor spaces, while residential lofts and offices will be provided on the upper levels. Stapleton's first town center is scheduled to open in early 2003. In addition to the intimate scale of main street stores and a low-rise streetscape, Stapleton will have regional retail centers for big-box stores. The first to be built is a 75-acre (30-hectare), 750,000-square-foot (69,677-square-meter) complex with three national superstore chains as anchor tenants.

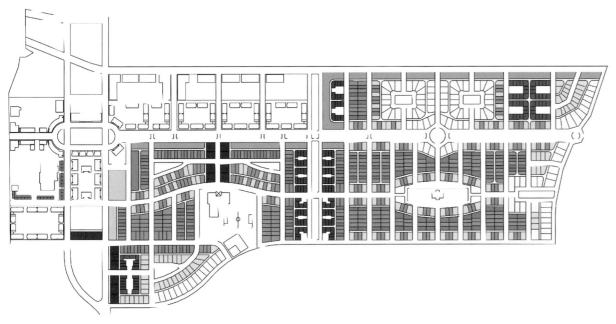

Left: Lot and product diversity is paramount at Stapleton. This diagram from the neighborhood design chapter of the Stapleton Design Book indicates the assortment of lot sizes and product types that will comprise the first phase of development.

Below: Drawing on Denver's urban design traditions, parkways are an elegant component of Stapleton's street system. These will be flanked by larger homes, with smaller homes located on side streets.

Top: Planners sought to infuse Stapleton's neighborhoods with a sense of place and context by designing within the framework of the existing urban pattern. This sketch envisions a garage-less townhouse streetscape.

Above: Streetscapes will borrow from historic Denver by incorporating wide tree lawns and sidewalks. Front porches give this new neighborhood a nostalgic feeling.

Making Way for Nature

The developer, Forest City Development, and EDAW worked closely with Denver's city forester to select landscape materials that support the biodiversity of the site. Natural filtration, constructed wetlands, and gray water reuse are among the cost-effective and environmentally beneficial methods of water management at Stapleton. Restoration of natural systems will benefit indigenous flora and fauna, with native plants used in both the on-site storm water detention and the water quality systems. The recycled aggregate from more than 6 million tons of concrete runways demolished on site will be reused for Stapleton construction projects as well as a number of large projects in the region.

Returns on Long-Term Vision

In the works since 1989, the reinvention of the former Stapleton airport site, all seven and one-half square miles (19 square kilometers) of it, is still a long way from critical mass. In terms of economic feasibility, environmental responsibility, and social diversity, this urban master-planned community could set a national example for a public-private enterprise of nearly unparalleled size and scale. The project, for example, has been recognized as a national demonstration site by the Partnership for Advancing Technology in housing, which brings substantial state and federal resources to Stapleton. Stapleton is also located in Denver's Urban Enterprise Zone, which means that businesses that choose to locate at the development will benefit from significant tax incentives.

Left: Stapleton's five centers, each within a ten-minute walk of most residents, will encompass more than 1 million square feet (92,903 square meters). Following the traditional main street model, the town centers will feature two- and three-story buildings with retail shops and restaurants on the ground floor and residential lofts and offices above.

Above: The development team collaborated with utility companies to preserve the residential character of neighborhoods by relocating unsightly service structures and reducing the amount of paving caused by utility easements.

Victorian

Craftsman

Colonial Revival

Foursquare

English Revival

Mediterranean Revival

Above: The architectural style chapter of the Stapleton Design Book provides guidelines that reflect the diversity of buildings found in Denver's early neighborhoods. The goal is to recreate their memorable character, identity, and appeal within the constraints of current production and market factors.

260

Below: At buildout, Stapleton will have 12,000 housing units. Three types—single-family attached, single-family detached, and apartments—with 12 variations will be offered. Products will be mixed within each neighborhood, thus assuring diversity in appearance, household income, and demographics. Pictured below are single-family detached "green court" homes.

Top: The four- and sixplex buildings shown here are designed to look like single-family estate homes.

Above: A Craftsman house represents one of the six architectural styles to be built at Stapleton. Other styles include Victorian, Colonial Revival, Denver Foursquare, English Revival, and Mediterranean Revival.

VERRADO

BUCKEYE, ARIZONA

One of the few remaining large development sites in the Greater Phoenix area, the 8,800-acre (3,561-hectare) master-planned community of Verrado aims to raise the quality, character, and value of the West Phoenix Valley, an area traditionally perceived as a market less desirable than other sub-regions like north Scottsdale. Verrado will bring traditional town planning elements to the Phoenix area on a scale not seen before, according to its developer, DMB. It will also remediate a stretch of land formerly used to test heavy industrial machinery.

Twenty-five miles west of Phoenix, Verrado sits at the foothills of the 4,000-foot-high (1,219 meter-high) White Tank Mountains, along the Interstate 10 corridor. With the near buildout of the amenity-rich luxury resort communities of Scottsdale and the Southeast Valley, the West Phoenix Valley is emerging as an alternative, with recent improvements to public infrastructure and recreational facilities. On 5,000 developable acres (2,023 hectares), the Verrado site is amenable to town planning principles with its generally flat geography. Keen to create a distinctive sense of place, the developer hopes to attract a diverse population—a mix of residents, incomes, and lifestyles—to set a more heterogeneous tone in the Phoenix market. The target market is wide-ranging and includes singles, young families, mature families, empty-nesters, and second-home buyers.

The development envelope is defined by a complex array of natural elements, including primary washes, landforms, mountain edges, and view corridors. To gain the full benefit from these assets, much needs to be done to restore the site's natural landscape and its ecosystems to good health. For 25 years, the site served as the testing and proving grounds for Caterpillar, the tractor and heavy equipment company. Millions of cubic yards of earth were moved, roads built, and holes dug and filled, resulting in a highly disturbed site with visual scarring and disrupted drainage patterns. Working closely with the Army Corps of Engineers and other public agencies, DMB has developed a redemption plan that includes landform reconstruction, the reestablishment of historic drainage patterns, and restoration of wildlife habitat.

Patterns of Pre-War Town Building

Seeking to avoid the solutions typical of large developments—many winding up as a loosely associated collection of lifestyle villages or sub-communities—the developers and their architects and planners opted for a unified whole, a "One Town" concept, as DMB calls it. Their master plan is based on traditional town planning principles drawn from Southwestern towns and neighborhoods built before World War II.

The planners, EDAW, Inc., have taken their cues from the strong geometry of the downtown Phoenix grid, the more relaxed street patterns of Encanto and Palmcroft, and the curvilinear suburban forms of Scottsdale. In Old Phoenix, the urban design, formal architectural vocabulary, lot size, and blending with the natural landscape varied widely in response to the individual needs of builders and residents. The intention is to differentiate Verrado from the single-product subdivisions for a more diverse pattern of land use. The master plan is organized around a dense, mixed-use town center surrounded by tightly knit urban neighborhoods that gradually soften into more organic patterns at the edges of the development, ending in a more rural setting.

The practice of selling parcels to builders for single-product subdivisions will be replaced with a different model: smaller groupings of lots organized around small parks will be sold to several builders, for a less homogenous neighborhood morphology. Street patterns are preplanned, not left to the whim of individual builders, in order to ensure direct connections between residential neighborhoods and common amenities. In this way, residents will be able to reach parks, shopping, dining, schools, and other services without driving on arterial roadways; walking and bicycling are strongly encouraged.

Community Making, Desert Style

Neighborhood Design Guidelines are meant to inform builders of the small-town character envisioned for Verrado. Consumer preferences, gathered in surveys, give greatest importance to diversity of architectural style, front porches, smaller groupings of single housing types, and small and numerous parks. The developers believe that these unconventional elements (uncon-

BIRD'S EYE VIEW OF PHŒNIX MARICOPA CO. ARIZONA

Previous page: Inspiration for Verrado's form was derived in part from studying older sections of Phoenix and emulating those that had retained their character and value over time.

Right: Saguaro cacti stand sentinel in the foothills, plains, and washes that characterize the rugged Sonoran Desert landscape of Buckeye, where Verrado is taking shape.
Far right: Evidence of early native inhabitants, such as these petroglyphs, is being preserved for educational and interpretive programs.

264

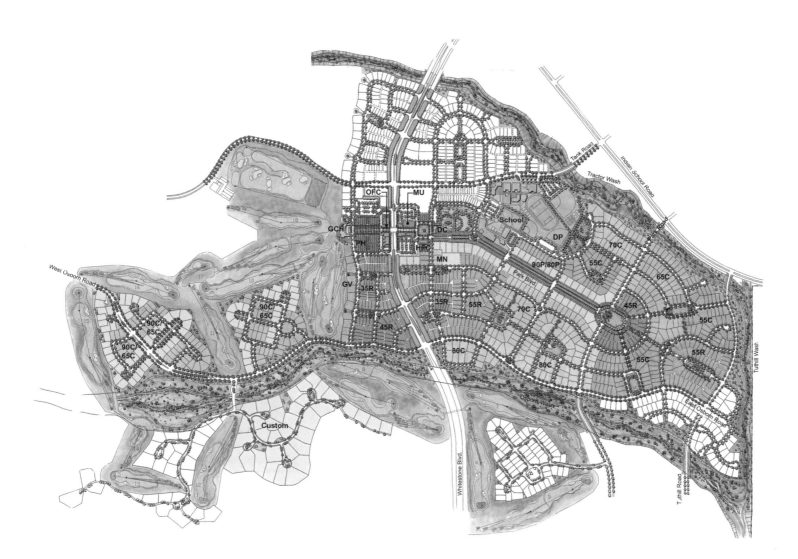

Left: The master plan for Verrado, which encompasses 8,800 acres (3,561 hectares), features residential, recreational, and open space wrapped around a central business core. Density is highest in the core and plains, becoming sparser toward the foothills.

Opposite: Neighborhoods in the golf district are somewhat unusual in that they maintain the lifestyle amenities of the setting but retain the urban character of the neighborhoods found elsewhere in the community. As in the other three Phase One districts— core, park, and foothills— these neighborhoods are organized around a small park so that interior lots are also exposed to open space.

ventional in Phoenix, at least) would create added value for both home-builders and homeowners. Nine carefully detailed architectural styles and 14 housing types will characterize the first phase of development.

When built out, Verrado will have its own downtown, along with several smaller mixed-use commercial districts. There will also be golf courses, custom lots, shopping centers, a variety of housing types, and an interconnected system of open spaces. Located in the heart of the community is the town center, a pedestrian hub for employment, shopping, dining, entertainment, potential resort uses, and educational campuses, as well as some housing.

Adjacent to Interstate 10, the mixed-use district will provide Verrado with a base for commercial employment and services at a regional scale. It will be more automobile-dependent than the town center, but will offer services more typically found at a regional transportation corridor. Along with the town center, Verrado will eventually have a total of 4 million square feet (371,612 square meters) of commercial space.

The long-term goal for Verrado's residential component is to have over 10,000 housing units on 2,700 acres (1,093 hectares). Dwelling options vary, from high-density live-work spaces; apartments in the town center and mixed-use district cores; and medium- and low-density houses; to single-family detached houses in traditional neighborhoods and on golf "islands"; and large custom-built homes in the foothill areas.

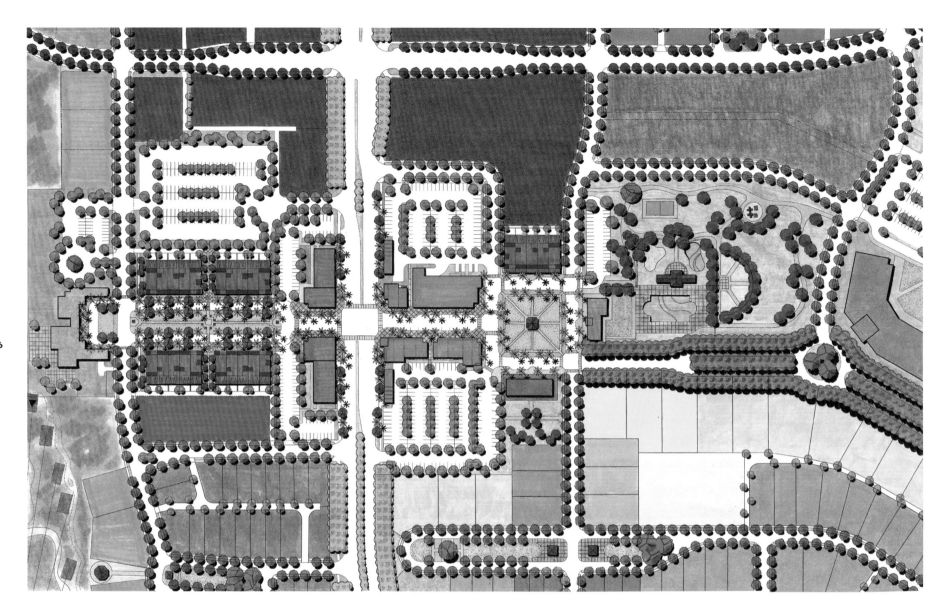

Above: The Phase One core district consists of high-density housing organized around a cluster of stores, restaurants, and offices on Main Street. Live-work rental units are planned above stores. Most of the housing in this district is alley-loaded, unique to the Phoenix housing market.

Nearly half of the site—3,900 acres (1,578 hectares)—is given over to open space. Environmental preservation and recreational use are key amenities, including a large section within the White Tank Mountains and several natural washes that incorporate trail and day-use areas. Biking, hiking, and equestrian trails are on- and off-street, and 325 acres (132 hectares) of parkland are set aside for a major sports park, village greens, and a series of small-scale neighborhood parks, among other types of open spaces. A few remnants of early native habitation are still visible on the site and will be preserved for interpretive and educational programs.

First Things First

Phase one of the development will be realized on 1,100 acres (445 hectares) and have 1,800 dwellings with all the amenities and support services of a balanced residential community. Its diverse, interconnected neighborhoods are arrayed around a walkable, mixed-use core. An 18-hole golf course is also in the offing, as are open space washes.

Below: Framing the golf clubhouse, Clubhouse Commons anchors Main Street on one end. At the opposite end are the district square, community center, and sales center.

Bottom: Natural drainage courses provide the basis for an open space corridor and trail network on the site, which was formerly occupied by Caterpillar, the tractor and heavy equipment company. Used as their testing and proving ground for years, the site was adversely impacted. A comprehensive plan to restore environmental systems, land features, and habitat has been initiated by the developer.

Right: At the eastern portion of the site, the park district contains low- and medium-density housing integrated with neighborhood and community parks, schools, and open space. Communitywide street patterns are designed to create direct connections between homes and surrounding amenities.

The first phase is organized into four districts—core, park, golf, and foothills—with each responding to its own unique landforms and proximity to the town center. The core consists of high-density housing types, shops, offices, dining, and recreation around a traditional small-town main street. Based on early Phoenix neighborhoods, the street pattern is a grid, with much of the housing alley-loaded. A district club for community meetings and other activities will be integrated into the golf clubhouse. The park district, with its low- and medium-density housing, focuses on a traditional family lifestyle and is within easy walking distance of elementary and

middle schools. Its bent-grid street pattern is reminiscent of historic neighborhoods like Encanto and Palmcroft in old Phoenix. Neighborhoods in the golf district, with all the amenities typical of such a setting, are organized around small parks. The foothills district, located at the base of a mountain ridge, is characterized by custom lots on one or more acres. Curvilinear streets and organic plan forms are hallmarks of the foothills neighborhoods, where the natural topography of the land and mountain vistas set the tone.

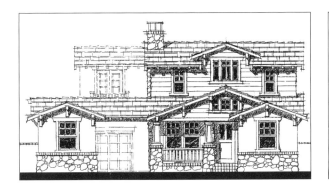

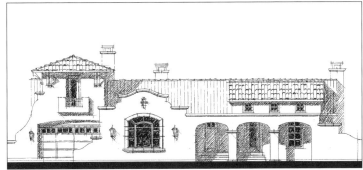

Above and left: In a multiple builder environment, neighborhood design guidelines were developed to safeguard the developer's vision for Verrado. Phase One will feature 14 different types of housing and as many as nine different architectural styles, the goal being broad appeal

Below: Technical diagrams augment the design guidelines and help communicate specific neighborhood treatments and conditions to the builders. Design criteria for the park district are shown.

Park District

Sensitive Edges Along Park Boulevard

Landscape Feature Around 70C Product

Neighborhood Park 1

Neighborhood Park 3

Sensitive Edges Along Wash

Landscape Feature Around 80C Product

Park Boulevard

Sensitive Edges Along Wash

Neighborhood Park 6

Neighborhood Park 5

Neighborhood Park 2

Landscape Feature Around 55C Product

Neighborhood Park 7

Neighborhood Park 4

Legend

- Corner Lots - Primary and Secondary Treatment
- Signature Lots Treatment Required
- Special Criteria Areas
- Sensitive Edges Along Park Boulevard
- Sensitive Edges Along Primary Washes

WATERCOLOR

SEAGROVE BEACH, FLORIDA

The developer, Arvida, and planners, Cooper, Robertson & Partners, of this 499-acre (202-hectare) village and resort on the Emerald Coast of north-west Florida aim to create a community with a thoroughly Southern flavor. Its siting and scale are shaped by the principles of small-town planning and characterized by vernacular architecture, walkable neighborhoods with overlapping residential and commercial components, public spaces of varying size and topography, and respect for existing natural systems. The site, which borders the Grayton Beach State Recreation Area, is endowed with white-sand beaches on the Gulf of Mexico and a freshwater coastal dune lake bordered by marshes, creeks, and wood uplands.

Physically linked to two existing communities—Seaside and Seagrove—WaterColor will initially serve the area's still-growing vacation home market, but is intended to evolve into a year-round locale. Like Seaside, WaterColor is conceived as a return to a simple lifestyle, where neighbors know each other, big-box stores are nowhere to be found, and the beauty of the landscape is respected. The planners worked to create a "character of place" with a pattern of streets, blocks, and open spaces of varying size and design to complement, not compete with, the existing contours of the land.

The long-term vision for buildout includes four neighborhoods with a total of 1,140 residential units on 207 acres (84 hectares), 100,000 square feet (9,290 square meters) of retail and office space, a 60-room inn and conference center, a beach club, a boathouse and marina, a tennis club, smaller recreational centers, sites for potential schools and community centers, 248 acres (100 hectares) of parks and open space, and a villagewide system of pedestrian and bicycle trails. Phase one is currently underway on 102 acres (41 hectares); it includes 350 residences and 40,000 square feet (3,716 square meters) of retail space, as well as the boathouse, beach club, and tennis club.

Connecting People and Places

The phased development of WaterColor, spread out over a decade, works outward from the town center. A scenic coastal highway that connects several nearby communities, including Seaside, bisects the town center, dividing the village into a beachfront portion to the south and a lakefront portion to the north. The town center is organized along what the designers refer to as a "water axis," a landscaped view corridor between the gulf and the lake. The view corridor, called Cerulean Park, is 200 feet (61 meters) wide and 600 feet (183 meters) long, and is bordered by large single- and multifamily residences.

A crossroads, so typical of Southern downtowns, is formed by the intersection of the coastal highway and the main entry road, which forms part of the water axis, into WaterColor. It is an arrangement that links the village to the larger community of the Emerald Coast, working toward the economic viability of the town center and avoiding the exclusive posture of gated developments. The southern end of the axis is anchored by the beach club, which acts as the main portal to the gulf for village residents. North of the commercial area is the park, which leads to a series of demonstration and cutting gardens. A path from the flower beds continues north to the lake—and the end of the view corridor—where the boathouse (complete with swimming pool and restaurant) and marina are available for village residents.

Nature's Plan

The plan of the coastal village respects and celebrates the existing flora and fauna and wetlands systems. Distinct, identifiable neighborhoods within the village are inscribed by surrounding natural features and existing regional roads that traverse the site. Each neighborhood is contained within a one-quarter-mile (one-half-kilometer) radius, within which are an interconnected network of pedestrian-scaled streets lined with sidewalks, public spaces, and a mix of residential and commercial programs. Connecting three of the four neighborhoods, a conservation area along the full length of the dune lake is dedicated to hiking, cycling, and other nature-oriented activities. Landscaping is restricted to indigenous plant material. Open spaces preserve existing patterns of hydrology.

To reinforce their pedestrian-oriented philosophy of town planning and commitment to an ecologically friendly setting, designers of WaterColor

Previous page: Scenic coastal Highway 30A runs through the mixed-use town center at WaterColor, boosting its commercial viability.

Right, top: WaterColor will wrap around and become a logical extension of the existing Seaside and Seagrove communities, shown in this predevelopment aerial view.

Right, bottom: A mecca for vacation homes and tourists, Florida's best Gulf Coast communities are oriented to the beach and leisure activities. Here, a restaurant and lounge overlook the pool at Water-Color's popular Beach Club.

Opposite, top: Anchoring the southern end of the town center, the Beach Club's views to the Gulf are part of this community's many lifestyle amenities.

Opposite, bottom: When the project is fully built, 50 percent of the 499-acre (202-hectare) site will be open space, with the remainder supporting residential and a mix of commercial, recreational, and civic development. Special features will include a town center, beach club, boathouse and marina, tennis club, inn and conference center, and a villagewide system of pedestrian and bike trails.

Opposite, top: One of five major parks named after vibrant watercolor pigments, Cerulean Park—located at the town center—is at the heart of the community. A linear canal running through the park symbolically connects the waters of the Gulf to the south and Western Lake to the north. Opposite, bottom: Town center building design is rooted in the regional architectural vernacular. Uses are clearly differentiated by facade treatment. Stucco and arcades mark street-level retail, whereas clapboard siding, porches, and balconies express the residential nature of the upper two stories. Left: Artist's rendering of Cerulean Park as viewed from a town center resident's balcony. There are 140 multifamily residential units in the town center.

recognize the necessity of the automobile, but deny it prime real estate. Parking is located along street frontages, at the back of lots accessed by alleys, and in designated lots behind commercial and mixed-use buildings.

Toward a Regional Architecture

Cooper, Robertson & Partners studied the traditional plan-forms, architectural details, materials, and finishes typical of the region's architecture. They considered traditional building methods and how structures were shaped by their natural surroundings. The planners also investigated vernacular precedents of other subtropical environments, blending the best from a variety of cultures and countries with similar climates. To provide both continuity and heterogeneity, they developed a pattern book that guides all private development at WaterColor, addressing building placement and setbacks, materials, formal expression, building heights, and color. A design review process ensures that the code is adhered to by individual builders and architects.

The plan of the town center is influenced by the dense fabric associated with French and Spanish colonies. All mixed-use buildings have stucco bases with deep arcades sheltering ground-floor spaces from the hot Florida sun. The upper facades are clapboard-sided and have porches and balconies overlooking the street. Deep-set windows, shutters, screens, blinds, and deep eaves provide protection from the harsh coastal climate and improve efficiency of heating and cooling. Civic buildings, which are sited at each end of the water axis, are rich in historic iconography, from clock towers and fountains to arcades and loggia.

The architecture and siting of the four residential districts that radiate out from the town center are typical of Southern "crossroad" towns, where clusters of homes in a relatively rural setting were influenced by English planning traditions. All houses are oriented toward the street and fronted by generously proportioned porches, which are meant to convey a sense of community and civic engagement. Low fences and hedges provide a friendly reminder of the division between public and private. A broad range of housing types and price levels are integrated into each neighborhood. Above-garage flats can be built as guest rooms or income-generating rental units. Multifamily buildings and townhouses offer one-, two-, and three-bedroom units.

Environmental Dividends

Taking its goal of Southern hospitality to the land on which it sits in the Florida Panhandle, WaterColor's commitment to sustaining the beauty of the natural environment is reflected in the work of both its resident horticulturalist and its naturalist, the latter being responsible for monitoring and preparing conservation initiatives. The developer's regional impact plan, approved by the state of Florida, addresses the health and stability of ecological systems. One project cited in the impact plan and already complete is the restoration of two breaches to the dunes that had occurred prior to the village's development. The breaches—breaks created by foot traffic across the dunes—were filled with color-matched beach sand, and a variety of native dune plant species were planted to restore the area. To ensure the continued health of the dunes, boardwalks were built to minimize future degradation.

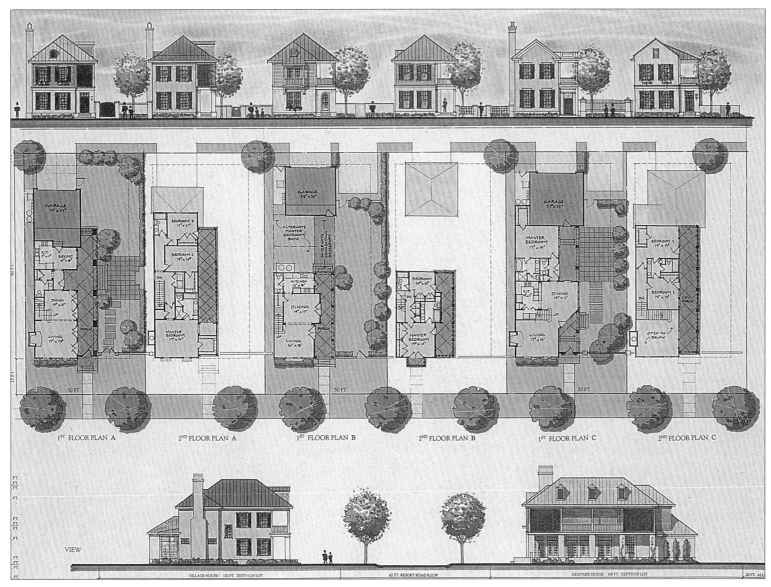

1ST FLOOR PLAN A   2ND FLOOR PLAN A   1ST FLOOR PLAN B   2ND FLOOR PLAN B   1ST FLOOR PLAN C   2ND FLOOR PLAN C

VIEW

VILLAGE HOUSE 100 FT. DEPTH OF LOT   62 FT. RESORT ROAD R.O.W.   SIDEYARD HOUSE 100 FT. DEPTH OF LOT   20 FT. ALL

Opposite: The four neighborhoods of WaterColor will reflect a range of housing types and pricing to satisfy market demand, including single- and multifamily as well as garage flats. Pictured here are the one-and-one-half-story cottages (top) and multifamily housing flanking Cerulean Park (bottom).

Left, top: Study of side-yard housing plans from a pattern book provide guidelines for treatment of common areas, architectural style, and lot siting. Single-family lots allow for a variety of housing types ranging from modest cottages to grand three-story beachfront and lake homes.

Left, bottom: WaterColor's residential character was inspired by these regional precedents.

Notes

278

1 Theodore Tilton, *Independent*, May 26, 1864.

2 Olmsted first visited the site of Riverside about August 20, 1868, printed the "Preliminary Report upon the Proposed Suburban Village of Riverside, Near Chicago," September 1, 1868 (New York, 1868), and prepared plans for Riverside, during Calvert Vaux's trip to Europe, from August 5 to November 16, 1868. (See David Schuyler and Jane Turner Censer, eds., *The Papers of Frederick Law Olmsted*, volume VI (Baltimore: The Johns Hopkins University Press, 1992), p. 289.

3 Riverside Improvement Company, *Riverside in 1871 with Description of Its Improvements Together with Some Engravings of Views and Buildings*, originally printed by D. & C. H. Blakely, Chicago, 1871, and reprinted by the Frederick Law Olmsted Society of Riverside in 1981.

4 Lawrence Halprin, "Revisiting the Idea," *Progressive Architecture*, May 1993, pp. 92–93.

5 For a discussion of federal programs assisting master-planned communities see Alexander Garvin, *The American City: What Works, What Doesn't* (New York: McGraw-Hill, 1996), pp. 343–349.

6 Clarence Stein, "The Nature of Communities" (1943), reprinted in Kermit Carlyle Parsons, ed., *The Writings of Clarence Stein* (Baltimore: The Johns Hopkins University Press, 1998), p. 442.

7 Clarence Stein, *New Towns for America* (originally published in 1950) (Cambridge: MIT Press, 1966), p. 189.

8 Ibid, p. 195.

9 Gregory C. Randall, *America's Original GI Town — Park Forest, Illinois* (Baltimore: The Johns Hopkins University Press, 2000), pp. 78–90.

10 Olmsted, Vaux, & Co., "Preliminary Report upon the Proposed Suburban Village at Riverside, Near Chicago" (New York, 1868), reprinted in David Schuyler and Jane Turner Censer, eds., *The Papers of Frederick Law Olmsted*, volume VI (Baltimore: The Johns Hopkins University Press, 1992), p. 286.

11 William S. Worley, *J.C. Nichols and the Shaping of Kansas City* (Columbia, Mo.: University of Missouri Press, 1990), pp. 63–77.

12 Ibid, p. 103.

13 Ibid, pp. 264–286.

14 Diane Galloway and Kathy Matthews, *The Park Cities* (Dallas: Southern Methodist University Press, 1988), p. 9.

15 Richard Longstreth, *City Center to Regional Mall* (Cambridge: MIT Press, 1997), pp. 159–175.

16 Community Builders' Council, *The Community Builders Handbook* (Washington, D.C.: ULI–the Urban Land Institute, 1947), p. 1.

17 David Schuyler and Jane Turner Censer, eds., *The Papers of Frederick Law Olmsted*, volume VI (Baltimore: The Johns Hopkins University Press, 1992), p. 539.

Project Data

In Order of Appearance

CONTEMPORARY COMMUNITIES

Beacon Cove
Port Melbourne, Victoria, Australia

Development Team
Developer Mirvac, 85 Coventry Street, South Melbourne, Victoria, Australia, 3207, www.mirvac.com.au
Planner/Architect HPA Architects, Planners & Interiors, 85 Coventry Street, South Melbourne, Victoria, Australia 3207, www.mirvac.com.au
Planner The Hassel Group, Level 4, 120 Collins Street, Melbourne, Victoria, Australia 3000

Land Use
Acres (Hectares), Percent of Site
Residential 48 (20), 53.1%
Town Center 3 (1), 3.1%
Open Space 14 (6), 15.0%
Recreation/Amenities 3 (1), 3.0%
Roads/Parking 22 (9), 24.5%
Other 1 (1), 1.3%
Total 91 (38), 100%

Residential Information
Number Units Planned/Number Units Built
Single-Family Detached 127/127
Townhouses 343/343
Apartments 1,047/368
Total Units 1,517/838

Commercial Space Information
Square Feet (Meters) Approved/Square Feet (Meters) Built
Retail 57,588 (5,350)/56,781 (5,275)
Total 57,588 (5,350)/56,781 (5,275)

Total Project Development Cost
Site Acquisition Cost $100 million AUD
Site Improvement Cost $900 million AUD
Total Cost $1 billion AUD

Development Schedule
Site Purchased 1995
Planning Started 1992
Construction Started 1995
Sales Started 1996
Number of Phases 11
Phases Completed 9
Percentage Completed 55%
Estimated Date of Completion 2009

Bonita Bay
Bonita Springs, Florida

Development Team
Developer The Bonita Bay Group, 3451 Bonita Bay Boulevard, Suite 202, Bonita Springs, Florida 34134, T: 941-495-1000, www.bonitabay.com
Planner Wilson Miller, 3200 Bailey Lane, Suite 200, Wilson Professional Center, Naples, Florida 34105, T: 941-649-4040, www.wilsonmiller.com
Other Key Members Robert Charles Lesser & Co.; KC & Associates; Deloitte & Touche; SunTrust; Tom Fazio and Arthur Hills; Dick Dietrich; Hillier & Associates

Land Use
Acres (Hectares), Percent of Site
Residential 1,077 (436), 44%
Commercial 70 (28), 3%
Roads 102 (41), 4%
Open Space 37 (15), 2%
Reserve/Slough 589 (238), 24%
Golf Courses 551 (223), 23%
Total 2,426 (981), 100%

Residential Information
Number Units Planned/Number Units Built
Single-Family Detached 620/620
Villas 641/641
Carriage 1,330/1,330
Multifamily Condominiums 709/219
Total Units 3,300/2,810

Total Project Development Cost
Site Acquisition Cost $17 million
Site Improvement Cost $68 million
Soft Costs $56 million
Total Cost $141 million

Development Schedule
Site Purchased 1979
Planning Started Early 1980s
Construction Started Fall 1983
Sales Started January 1985
Percentage Completed 85–90%
Estimated Date of Completion 2010

Celebration
Celebration, Florida

Development Team
Developer The Celebration Company, 610 Sycamore Street, Suite 310, Celebration, Florida 34747, T: 407-566-2200, www.celebrationfl.com
Planner Robert A.M. Stern Architects, 460 West 34th Street, New York, New York 10001, T: 212-967-5100, www.ramsa.com
Planner Cooper, Robertson & Partners, 311 West 43rd Street, New York, New York 10036, T: 212-247-1717, www.cooperrobertson.com

Land Use
Acres (Hectares), Percent of Site
Residential/Commercial 1,500 (607), 30%
Town Center 30 (12), 1%
Open Space and Wetlands 2,700 (1,093), 55%
Public and Civic Facilities 70 (28), 2%
Recreation/Amenities 200 (81), 4%
Roads/Parking 400 (162), 8%
Total 4,900 (1,983), 100%

Residential Information
Number Units Planned/Number Units Built
Single-Family Detached NA/1,300

Townhouses NA/150
Multifamily Condominiums N/A/99
Apartments NA/1,200
Total Units 5,000-6,000/2,309

Commercial Space Information
Square Feet (Meters) Approved/Square Feet (Meters) Built
Retail 200,000 (18,581)/68,000 (6,317)
Office (Including Hospital) 2,000,000 (185,806)/1,251,000 (116,222)
Total 2,200,000 (204,387)/1,319,000 (122,539)

Development Schedule
Site Purchased Mid-1960s
Planning Started Mid-1980s
Construction Started Spring 1995
Sales Started January 1996
Number of Phases 5–6 major phases
Phases Completed 5 Villages
Percentage Completed 50% of residential
Estimated Date of Completion
Residential 2004–2005
Commercial 2010–2012

DC Ranch
Scottsdale, Arizona

Development Team
Developer DC Ranch LLC, 9255 East Desert Camp Drive, Scottsdale, Arizona 85255, T: 480-502-2725, www.dcranch.com
Land Planner Swaback Partners PLLC, 7550 E. MacDonald Drive, Scottsdale, Arizona 85250, T: 480-367-2100, www.swabackpartners.com

Land Use
Acres (Hectares), Percent of Site
Residential 2,300 (931), 27.8%
Town Center 60 (24), 0.7%
Open Space 760 (308), 9.2%

Public and Civic Facilities 100 (40), 1.2%
Recreation/Amenities 400 (162), 4.8%
Retail/Commercial 30 (12), 0.4%
Resort/Residential 50 (20), 0.6%
Other (Nondevelopable space) 4,581(1,854), 55.3%
Total 8,281 (3,351), 100%

Residential Information
Number Units Planned/Number Units Built
Single-Family Detached NA/1,103
Apartments NA/222
Total Units 5,000/1,315

Commercial Space Information
Square Feet (Meters) Approved
Retail 150,000 (13,935.5)
Office 150,000 (13,935.5)
Total 300,000 (27,871.0)

Development Schedule
Construction Started 1997
Sales Started January 1997
Percentage Completed 26%
Estimated Date of Completion 2010

Fairview Village
Fairview, Oregon

Development Team
Developer/Planner/Architect Holt & Haugh, Inc., 1200 NW Naito Parkway, #620, Portland, Oregon 97209, T: 503-222-5522, www.holtandhaugh.com
Planner Lennertz & Coyle Architects & Town Planners, 321 SW Fourth Avenue, Portland, Oregon 97204, T: 503-228-9240, www.lcaarchitects.com
Architects Group McKenzie; Barry R. Smith, Architect; Myhre Group Architects; Wm. L. Dennis Architecture & Town Design; Gary Rommel Architectural Partnership; Ankrom Moisan Architects; Joseph Griggs & Associates Architects; Sienna Architects & Company

Land Use

Acres (Hectares), Percent of Site

Residential 36 (15), 38%

Town Center 26 (11), 27%

Open Space 5 (2), 5%

Public and Civic Facilities 3 (1), 3%

Recreation/Amenities 5 (2), 5%

Roads/Parking 15 (6), 16%

Other (Misc. Infrastructure) 6 (2), 6%

Total 96 (39), 100%

Residential Information

Number Units Planned/Number Units Built

Single-Family Detached 140/136

Townhouses 14/11

Rowhouses 84/66

Live-Work Rowhouses 12/12

Apartments 232/128

Other (Duplexes) 24/24

Total Units 506/377

Commercial Space Information

Square Feet (Meters) Approved/Square Feet
(Meters) Built

Retail 219,000 (20,346)/135,000
(12,542)

Office 183,000 (17,001)/25,000 (2,323)

*Total 402,000 (37,347)/160,000
(14,865)*

Total Project Development Cost

Site Acquisition Cost $2.8 million

Site Improvement Cost $6.7 million

Soft Costs $1.8 million

Total Cost $11.3 million

Development Schedule

Site Purchased September 1994

Planning Started May 1994

Construction Started March 1995

Sales Started October 1995

Number of Phases 7

Phases Completed 7

Percentage Completed 87%

Estimated Date of Completion
95% by 2003

Harbor Town

Memphis, Tennessee

Development Team

Developer Henry Turley Company,
65 Union Avenue, Suite 1200, Memphis,
Tennessee 38103, T: 901-527-2770,
www.henryturley.com

Master Planner RTKL Associates, Inc.,
Commerce Street, One South Street, Suite
1000, Baltimore, Maryland 21202, T: 410-
528-8600, www.rtkl.com

Town Planner/Architect Looney Ricks
Kiss, 175 Toyota Plaza, Suite 600, Memphis,
Tennessee 38103, T: 901-521-1440,
www.lrk.com

Land Use

Acres (Hectares), Percent of Site

Residential 71 (29), 52%

Town Center 8 (3), 6%

Open Space 27 (11), 20%

Roads/Parking 21 (9), 15%

Other (Flood Plain) 9 (4), 7%

Total 136 (56), 100%

Residential Information

Number Units Planned/Number Units Built

Single-Family Detached 457/392

Townhouses and Condos 122/56

Apartments 421/415

Total Units 1,000/863

Commercial Space Information

Square Feet (Meters) Approved/Square Feet
(Meters) Built

Retail 25,000 (2,323)/15,000 (1,394)

Office 30,000 (2,787)/5,000 (465)

Total 55,000 (5,110)/20,000 (1,859)

Total Project Development Cost

Site Acquisition Cost $2.25 million

Site Improvement Cost $10.5 million

Soft Costs $2.5 million

Total Cost $15.25 million

Development Schedule

Site Purchased 1987

Planning Started 1988

Construction Started 1989

Sales Started 1990

Number of Phases 21

Phases Completed 20

Percentage Completed 95%

Estimated Date of Completion 2003

I'On

Mount Pleasant, South Carolina

Development Team

Developer The I'On Company, 159 Civitas
Street, Mount Pleasant, South Carolina
29464, T: 843-971-1662,
www.ionvillage.com

Planner Duany Plater-Zyberk & Co.,
1023 SW 25th Avenue, Miami, Florida
33135, T: 305-644-1023, www.dpz.com

Planner Dover Kohl and Partners, 5879
Sunset Drive, Suite 1, South Miami, Florida,
T: 305-666-0446, www.doverkohl.com

Planner Seamon-Whiteside and Associ-
ates, 503 Wando Park Blvd., Suite 100,
Mount Pleasant, South Carolina 29464,
T: 843-884-1667, www.swasc.com

Land Use

Acres (Hectares), Percent of Site

Residential 122 (49), 50%

Open Space 60 (29), 25%

Public and Civic Facilities 16 (7), 6%

Roads/Parking 46 (19), 19%

Total 244 (104), 100%

Residential Information

Number Units Planned/Number Units Built

Single-Family Detached 762/250

Total Units 762/250

Commercial Space Information

Square Feet (Meters) Approved/Square Feet
(Meters) Built

Retail 30,000 (2,787)/16,000 (1,486)

Total 30,000 (2,787)/16,000 (1,486)

Total Project Development Cost

Site Acquisition Cost $6.5 million

Site Improvement Cost $13 million

Soft Costs $5.5 million

Total Cost $25 million

Development Schedule

Site Purchased June 1, 1997 (in rolling
take down)

Planning Started 1994–1995

Construction Started August 1997

Sales Started February 1998

Number of Phases 8

Phases Completed 5.5

Percentage Completed 62%

Estimated Date of Completion 2005

The Irvine Ranch

Irvine, California

Development Team

Developer/Planner The Irvine Company,
550 Newport Center Drive, Newport Beach,
California 92658, www.irvineco.com

Land Use

Acres (Hectares), Percent of Site

Residential 20,000 (8,094), 22%

Town Center 8,000 (3,237), 8%

Open Space 50,000 (20,234), 54%

Other (Church, Streets, Easements)
15,100 (6,111), 16%

Total 93,100 (37,676), 100%

Residential Information

Number Units Planned/Number Units Built

Total Units 125,000/88,000

Development Schedule

Planning Started 1960

Percentage Completed 70%

Estimated Date of Completion 2015

Karow Nord

Berlin-Weissensee, Germany

Development Team

Developer ARGE Karow Nord, Groth
Gruppe, Torstrasse 33+35, 10119 Berlin,
T: 030-880 94 106, www.grothgruppe.de

Planner Moore Ruble Yudell Architects &
Planners, 933 Pico Boulevard, Santa Monica, California 90405, T: 310-450-1400,
www.moorerubleyudell.com

Associate Architect Lunetto & Fischer,
Oranienburger Strasse 37, 10117 Berlin,
Germany, T: 011-49-30-231 296 13,
lunetto-fischer@snafu.de

Landscape Architect Luetzowplatz 7
(formerly Mueller Knippschild Wehberg),
10785 Berlin, Germany

Housing Developer Groth Gruppe

(formerly Groth + Graalfs), Torstrasse
33+35, 10119 Berlin, Germany, T: 011-49-
30-88 094 0, www.grothgruppe.com

Housing Developer Gehag, Achilles-
strasse 57, 13125 Berlin, Germany,
T: 011-49-30-47 40 06 10, www.gehag.de

Land Use

Acres (Hectares), Percent of Site

Residential and Town Center 114 (46),
47.0%

Open Space 49 (20), 20.5%

Public and Civic Facilities 25 (10), 9.9%

Recreation/Amenities 15 (6), 6.2%

Roads/Parking 40 (16), 16.4%

Total 243 (98), 100%

Residential Information

Number Units Planned/Number Units Built

Townhouses 400/400

Apartments 4,800/4,800

Total Units 5,200/5,200

Commercial Space Information

Square Feet (Meters) Approved/Square Feet
(Meters) Built

Retail 73,195 (6,800)/73,195 (6,800)

Office 21,528 (2,000)/21,528 (2,000)

Total 94,723 (8,800)/94,723 (8,800)

Total Project Development Cost

Total Cost $1.25 billion (2.5 billion DM)

Development Schedule

Planning Started 1992

Construction Started 1994

Number of Phases 4

Phases Completed 4

Percentage Completed 100%

Estimated Date of Completion 1999

Kentlands

Gaithersburg, Maryland

Development Team

Developer Great Seneca Development
Corporation (post-1991), 7501 Wisconsin
Avenue, Chevy Chase, Maryland 20815,
T: 310-986-6000

Developer Joseph Alfandre & Co., Inc.
(pre-1991), 1355 Piccard Drive, Suite 380,
Rockville, Maryland 20855, T: 301-670-0343

Planner Duany Plater-Zyberk & Co., 1023
SW 25th Avenue, Miami, Florida 33135,
T: 305-644-1023, www.dpz.com

Land Use

Acres (Hectares), Percent of Site

Residential 137 (55), 39%

Town Center 91 (37), 26%

Open Space 56 (23), 16%

Public and Civic Facilities 20 (8), 6%

Roads/Parking 48 (19), 14%

Total 352 (142), 100%

Residential Information

Number Units Planned

Single-Family Detached 522

Townhouses 398

Multifamily Condominiums 443

Apartments 459

Other (Live-Work) 47

Total Units 1,869

Commercial Space Information

Square Feet (Meters) Approved/Square Feet
(Meters) Built

Retail 675,000 (62,710)/650,000
(60,387)

Office 70,000 (6,503)/35,000 (3,252)

*Total 745,000 (69,213)/685,000
(63,639)*

Development Schedule

Site Purchased 1987

Planning Started 1987

Construction Started 1989

Sales Started 1990

Percentage Completed 99%

Estimated Date of Completion 2002

Ladera Ranch

Orange County, California

Development Team

Developer Rancho Mission Viejo Com-
pany, DMB Ladera, 28811 Ortega Highway,
San Juan Capistrano, California 92675,
T: 949-240-3363

Planner EDAW, Inc., 17875 Von Karman
Avenue, Suite 400, Irvine, California 92614,
T: 949-660-8044, www.edaw.com

Architect William Hezmalhalch Architects,
Inc., 17875 Von Karman Avenue, Suite 404,
Irvine, California 92614, T: 949-250-0607,
www.whainc.com

Landscape Architect Land Concern Ltd.,
1750 East Deere Avenue, Santa Ana,
California 92705, T: 949-250-4822,
www.landconcern.com

Land Use

Acres (Hectares), Percent of Site

Residential 1,135 (459), 28%

Town Center 100 (41), 2%

Common Open Space 300 (121), 7%

Public and Civic Facilities 60 (24), 1%

Recreation/Amenities 150 (61), 4%

Roads/Parking 680 (275), 17%

Other (Preserved Open Space) 1,600
(648), 41%

Total 4,025 (1,629), 100%

Residential Information

Number Units Planned/Number Units Built

Single-Family Detached 4,577/1,460

Townhouses 2,188/420

Apartments 1,285/220

Total Units 8,050/2,100

Commercial Space Information

Square Feet (Meters) Approved/Square Feet
(Meters) Built

Retail 550,000 (51,097)/100,000 (9,290)

Office 320,000 (29,729)/0

*Total 870,000 (80,826)/100,000
(9,290)*

Total Project Development Cost
Site Improvement Cost $401 million
Soft Costs $310 million
Total Cost $711 million

Development Schedule
Site Purchased Developer owned
Planning Started 1993
Construction Started 1998
Sales Started 1999
Number of Phases 6
Phases Completed 2
Percentage Completed 30%
Estimated Date of Completion 2005

McKenzie Towne

Calgary, Alberta, Canada

Development Team

Developer Carma Developers Ltd., 7315 8th Street, NE, Calgary, Alberta, Canada T2E 8A2, T: 403-231-8900, www.carma.ca/scripts/index.asp
Planner Stantec Consulting Ltd., 1122 4th Street, SW, Calgary, Alberta, Canada T2R 1M1, T: 403-716-8200, www.stantec.com
Planner Southwell Trapp & Associates Ltd., 520, 1110 Centre Street North, Calgary, Alberta, Canada T2E 2R2, www.southwelltrapp.com
Planner (Initial Concept) Duany Plater-Zyberk & Co., 1023 SW 25th Avenue, Miami, Florida 33135, T: 305-644-1023, www.dpz.com
Architect Gibbs Gage Architects, 505, 237 Eighth Avenue, SE, Calgary, Alberta, Canada T2G 5C3, T: 403-233-2000, www.gibbsgage.com
Engineer Walker Newby Engineering, 200, 1212 First Street, SE, Calgary, Alberta, Canada T2F 2H8, T: 403-263-4595, www.walkernw.com
Landscape Architect Carson McCulloch Associates Landscape Architects, 203, 603 Eleventh Avenue, SW, Calgary, Alberta, Canada T2R 0E1, T: 403-234-8544

Land Use

Acres (Hectares), Percent of Site
Residential 508 (206), 53%
Town Center 46 (19), 5%
Open Space 49 (20), 5%
Public and Civic Facilities 50 (20), 5%
Recreation/Amenities 9 (3), 1%
Roads/Parking 265 (107), 28%
Other 33 (13), 3%
Total 960 (388), 100%

Residential Information

Number Units Planned/Number Units Built
Single-Family Detached 5,000/1,900
Townhouses/Multifamily 1,500/600
Total Units 6,500/2,500

Commercial Space Information

Square Feet (Meters) Approved/
Square Feet (Meters) Built
Total 207,000 (19,231)/107,000 (9,941)

Total Project Development Cost
Site Acquisition Cost $12.3 million CDN
Site Improvement Cost $74.8 million CDN
Soft Costs $4.3 million CDN
Total Cost $91.4 million CDN

Development Schedule
Site Purchased 1988
Planning Started January 1992
Construction Started September 1994
Sales Started October 1995
Number of Phases 60
Phases Completed 25
Percentage Completed 45%
Estimated Date of Completion 2015

Orenco Station

Hillsboro, Oregon

Development Team

Developer PacTrust, 15350 SW Sequoia Parkway, Suite 300, Portland, Oregon 97224, T: 503-624-6300, www.orencostation.com
Architect Fletcher Farr Ayotte Architects, 708 SW Third Street, Suite 200, Portland, Oregon 97204, www.ffadesign.com
Planner Iverson Associates, Inc., 151 Kalmus Drive, C140, Costa Mesa, California 92626, T: 714-549-3479
Engineer Alpha Engineering, Inc., P.O. Box 669, Bear, Delaware 19701, T: 302-834-3344, www.alpha-engineering.com
Landscape Architect Walker Macy Landscape Architects, 111 Southwest Oak, Suite 200, Portland, Oregon 97204, T: 503-228-3122, www.walkermacy.com
Residential Developer Costa Pacific Homes, 8625 SW Cascade Avenue, Suite 606, Beaverton, Oregon 97008, T: 503-646-8888, www.costapacific.com
Hotel Developer Stonebrook International, 6375 South Highland Drive, 2000 East, Salt Lake City, Utah 84121, T: 801-278-1111, www.stonebrook.com
Apartment Developer Fairfield Properties (Fairfield Residential LLC), 2045 N. Highway 360, Grand Prairie, Texas 75050, T: 817-816-9400, www.fairfieldresidential.com
Multifamily Developer Simpson Housing Solutions, 320 Golden Shore, Suite 200, Long Beach, California 90802, T: 562-256-2000, www.simpsonsolutions.com

Land Use

Acres (Hectares), Percent of Site
Open Space 63 (25), 31%
Roads/Parking 76 (32), 36%
Buildings 70 (28), 33%
Total 209 (85), 100%

Residential Information

Number Units Planned/Number Units Built
Single-Family Detached 428/169
Townhouses NA/92
Multifamily Condominiums NA/263
Apartments NA/503
Other (Live-Work) NA/13
Total Units 1,906/1,040

Commercial Space Information

Square Feet (Meters) Approved/Square Feet (Meters) Built
Retail 350,000 (32,516)/218,000 (20,253)
Office 60,000 (5,574)/27,500 (2,555)
Hotel 54,000 (5,017)/64,000 (5,946)
Other (Industrial) 30,000 (2,787)/0
Total 494,000 (45,894)/309,500 (28,754)

Development Schedule
Site Purchased 1986
Planning Started November 1993
Construction Started January 1997
Sales Started September 1997
Estimated Date of Completion 2003

Park DuValle

Louisville, Kentucky

Development Team

Developer The Community Builders, Inc., The Starks Building, 455 South 4th Avenue, Suite 1445, Louisville, Kentucky 40202, T: 502-583-8800, www.tcbinc.com
Planner Urban Design Associates, Gulf Tower, 31st Floor, 707 Grant Street, Pittsburgh, Pennsylvania 15219, www.urbandesignassociates.com
Architect Tucker & Booker, Inc., 10172 Linn Station Road, Louisville, Kentucky 40299, T: 502-426-7452
Engineer Sabak, Wilson, & Lingo, Inc., 315 West Market Street, Louisville, Kentucky 40202, T: 502-548-6271
Engineer ClasSickle, Inc., 4501 Bardstown Road, Louisville, Kentucky 40218, T: 502-493-2722, www.classickle.com

Land Use

Acres (Hectares), Percent of Site
Residential 78 (31), 59%
Town Center 3 (1), 2%
Open Space 5 (2), 4%
Public and Civic Facilities 4 (2), 3%
Roads/Parking 41 (16), 31%
Other 1 (.5), 1%
Total 132 (52.5), 100%

Residential Information

Number Units Planned/Number Units Built
Single-Family Detached 395/128
Apartments 613/421
Total Units 1,008/549

Commercial Space Information

Square Feet (Meters) Approved/Square Feet (Meters) Built
Mixed-Use Town Center 40,000 (3,716)/2,500 (232)
Medical Center 25,000 (2,323)/0
Total 65,000 (6,039)/2,500 (232)

Total Project Development Cost
Site Acquisition Cost $5.9 million
Site Improvement Cost $121.2 million
Soft Costs $18.2 million
Total Cost $145.3 million

Development Schedule
Site Purchased 1997
Planning Started January 1996
Construction Started August 1998
Sales Started December 1999
Number of Phases 4
Phases Completed 3
Percentage Completed 54.46%
Estimated Date of Completion December 2003

Poundbury

Dorchester, Dorset, United Kingdom

Development Team

Developer Duchy of Cornwall, Poundbury, 2 Longmoor Street, Dorchester, Dorset DTI 3GN, United Kingdom, T: 44-1304-250-533
Planner Léon Krier, 8 Rue de Chapeliers, Claviers–VAR, France, 83830, T: 33-494-478-595

Land Use

Acres (Hectares), Percent of Site
Residential 18 (7), 5%
Open Space 150 (61), 37%
Other 232 (94), 58%
Total 400 (162), 100%

Residential Information

Number Units Built
Single-Family 240
Apartments 40
Total Units 280

Commercial Space Information

Square Feet (Meters) Built
Retail 10,000 (929)
Office 30,000 (2,787)
Total 40,000 (3,716)

Development Schedule
Planning Started 1988
Construction Started 1993
Sales Started 1994
Number of Phases 2
Phases Completed 1
Estimated Date of Completion 2010

Rancho Santa Margarita

Rancho Santa Margarita, California

Development Team

Developer Rancho Santa Margarita Joint Venture, 30211 Avenida de las Banderas, Rancho Santa Margarita, California 92688, T: 949-888-6650
Planner EDAW, Inc, 17875 Von Karman Avenue, Suite 400, Irvine, California 92614, T: 949-660-8044, www.edaw.com
Planner PBR, 7 Upper Newport Plaza, Newport Beach, California 92660, T: 949-261-8820
Engineer Huitt Zollars, 15101 Redhill Avenue, Tustin, California 92780, T: 949-259-7900, www.huitt-zollars.com
Landscape Architect Land Concern Ltd., 1750 East Deere Avenue, Santa Ana, California 92705, T: 949-250-4822, www.landconcern.com
Landscape Architect HRP Landesign, 3242 Halladay, Suite 203, Santa Ana, California 92705, T: 714-557-5852, www.hrplandesign.com

Land Use

Acres (Hectares), Percent of Site
Residential 1,733 (701), 35%
Town Center 402 (163), 8%
Open Space 2,203 (891), 44%
Public and Civic Facilities 206 (83), 4%
Recreation/Amenities 209 (85), 4%
Roads/Parking 242 (98), 5%
Total 4,995 (2,021), 100%

Residential Information

Number Units Planned/Number Units Built
Single-Family Detached 5,700/5,572
Townhouses and Condos 5,479/5,479
Apartments 2,574/2,574
Other (Senior Apartments/Beds) 275/275
Total Units 14,028/13,900

Commercial Space Information

Square Feet (Meters) Approved/
Square Feet (Meters) Built
Retail 1,300,000 (120,774)/879,000 (81,662)
Office 1,700,000 (157,935)/1,400,000 (130,064)
Other (Industrial) 1,700,000 (157,935)/1,540,000 (143,071)
Total 4,700,000 (436,644)/3,819,000 (354,797)

Development Schedule
Site Purchased Developer owned, joint venture formed 1983
Planning Started 1980
Construction Started 1985
Sales Started 1986
Number of Phases NA
Percentage Completed 95%
Estimated Date of Completion 2003

Reston

Reston, Virginia

Development Team
Developer Terrabrook, 12010 Sunset Hills Road, Suite 710, Reston, Virginia 20190, T: 703-467-0448, www.terrabrook.com

Land Use
Acres (Hectares), Percent of Site
Residential 3,960 (1,603), 53%
Town Center 1,330 (538), 18%
Open Space 1,100 (445), 15%
Public and Civic Facilities 330 (134), 5%
Roads/Parking 680 (275), 9%
Total 7,400 (2,995), 100%

Residential Information
Number Units Planned/Number Units Built
Total Units 28,000/22,000

Commercial Space Information
Square Feet (Meters) Approved/Square Feet (Meters) Built
Retail 1,700,000 (157,935)/1,200,000 (111,484)
Office (Including Hospital) 20,000,000 (1,858,060)/15,000,000 (1,393,550)
Total 21,700,000 (2,015,995)/16,200,000 (1,505,034)

Development Schedule
Site Purchased 1961
Planning Started 1962
Construction Started 1963
Sales Started Autumn 1964
Number of Phases 6 (5 village centers and 1 town center)
Phases Completed 6
Percentage Completed 99%
Estimated Date of Completion 2005

Summerlin

Las Vegas, Nevada

Development Team
Developer/Planner The Howard Hughes Corporation/The Rouse Company, 10275 Little Patuxent Parkway, Columbia, Maryland 21044, T: 410-992-6000, www.therouse company.com
The Howard Hughes Corporation, 10000 West Charleston, Suite 200, Las Vegas, Nevada 89135, www.howardhughes.com
Architects Arthur Elliott, AIA; Fielden & Partners; G.C. Wallace, Inc.; Holmes Sabatini Associates; JMA Architecture Studios; KGA Architecture; Lucchesi Galati Architects; McLarand, Vasquez & Partners, Inc.; Musil Perkowitz Ruth, Inc.; Purvis Architects; RNL Associates; Tate Snyder Kimsey Architects; Wells-Pugsley Architects; Carrier Johnson; William Hezmalhalch Architects, Inc.; Lee & Sakahara Architects AIA; H&S International; KTGY Architects
Engineers G.C. Wallace, Inc.; The Keith Companies; Pentacore; T.J. Krobe Engineering; VTN; Kimley-Horn and Associates, Inc.

Graphic Design Davies Associates; Habitat
Land Planners David Jensen Associates; Design Workshop; Hyatt, Raines, Vitek; P.B.R.; Land Plan Associates; EDI Architecture; Greey/Pickett; EDAW, Inc.
Landscape Architects Design Workshop; Glanville Associates; IDEA, Inc.; Richard Price & Associates, Inc.; HRP Landesign; Cella Barr Associates; Brandt and Greey; Southwick and Associates; Peridian International, Inc.; The SWA Group
Market Research The Myers Group; Robert Charles Lesser & Co.

Land Use
Acres (Hectares), Percent of Site
Residential 12,800 (5,180), 57%
Retail/Services 400 (162), 2%
Employment 1,760 (712), 7%
Industrial Included in Employment
Town Center Included in Employment
Open Space 6,500 (3,035), 30%
Recreation/Amenities Included in Open Space
Roads/Parking 1,000 (405), 4%
Total 22,460 (9,494), 100%

Residential Information
Number Units Planned/Number Units Built
Single-Family Detached /23,279
Townhouses /1,016
Multifamily Condominiums /1,973
Apartments /1,935
Total Units 64,000/28,203

Commercial Space Information
Square Feet (Meters) Approved/Square Feet (Meters) Built
Retail 3,800,000 (353,032)/560,000 (52,026)
Office 16,000,000 (1,486,463)/1,200,000 (111,484)
Total 19,800,000 (1,839,498)/1,760,000 (163,510)

Total Project Development Cost
Site Acquisition Cost $85 million (by TRC in 1996)
Site Improvement Cost $2.2 billion
Total Cost $2.3 billion

Development Schedule
Site Purchased 1952
Planning Started 1980s
Construction Started 1989
Sales Started 1990
Number of Phases 30
Phases Completed 16
Percentage Completed 40%
Estimated Date of Completion 2015

The Woodlands

The Woodlands, Texas

Development Team
Developer/Planner The Woodlands Operating Company, LP, 2201 Timberloch Place, The Woodlands, Texas 77380, T: 281-719-6100

Planner Phillips, Brandt, Reddick (PBR), 7 Upper Newport Plaza, Newport Beach, California 92660
Planner P & D Consultants, 1100 Town & Country Road, Suite 300, Organce, California 92868, T: 714-835-4447, www.pdconsultants.com
Planner David Jensen Associates, 1451 South Parker Road, Denver, Colorado 80231
Planner EDAW, Inc., 17875 Von Karman Avenue, Suite 400, Irvine, California 92614, T: 949-660-8044, www.edaw.com
Planner RTKL, 1717 Pacific Avenue, Dallas, Texas 75201, T: 214-871-8677, www.rtkl.com
Planner Wallace McHarg, Roberts and Todd (WMRT), 260 South Broad Street, Suite F18, Philadelphia, Pennsylvania 19120, www.wrtdesign.com
Engineering Consultant LGA Engineering, 193 Rockland Street, Hanover, Massachusetts 02339, T: 781-826-8900, www.lgaengineering.com
Engineering Consultant Pate Engineering, 70 Walnut Street, Wellesley, Massachusetts 02181, www.pate.com
Engineering Consultant TC&B Engineering, 5757 Woodway, Houston, Texas 77057, T: 713-780-4100, www.tcandb.com

Land Use
Acres (Hectares), Percent of Site
Residential 10,250 (4,148)/40%
Commercial/Other Salable 4,000 (1,619)/15%
Recreation/Open Space 6,750 (2,732)/25%
Roads 6,000 (2,428)/20%
Total 27,000 (10,927)/100%

Residential Information
Number Units Planned/Number Units Built
Single-Family Detached 32,000/19,900
Townhouses/Condominiums 5,500/1,440
Apartments 7,900/4,200
Total Units 45,400/25,540

Commercial Space Information
Square Feet (Meters) Built
Retail 4,800,000 (445,935)
Office 4,300,000 (399,483)
Total 9,100,000 (845,418)

Development Schedule
Site Purchased 1964
Planning Started 1966
Construction Started 1972
Sales Started 1974
Number of Phases 7 Villages, Town Center, Research Forest, College Park
Phases Completed 5 Villages
Percentage Completed 50%
Estimated Date of Completion 2010

Civano

Tucson, Arizona

Development Team
Developer CDC Partners, LLC, Managers for the Community of Civano, 10501 East Seven Generations Way, Suite 201, Tucson, Arizona 85747, T: 888-224-8266, www.civano.com
Planner Duany Plater-Zyberk & Co., 1023 SW 25th Avenue, Miami, Florida 33135, T: 305-644-1023, www.dpz.com
Planner/Architect Moule & Polyzoides, 180 East California Boulevard, Pasadena, California 91105, www.mparchitects.com

Land Use
Acres (Hectares), Percent of Site
Total 880 (356), 100%

Residential Information
Number Units Planned/Number Units Built
Single-Family Detached 620/180
Townhouses 50/5
Multifamily Condominiums 20/0
Total Units 690/185

Commercial Space Information
Square Feet (Meters) Approved/Square Feet (Meters) Built
Office 35,000 (3,252)/35,000 (3,252)
Retail 15,000 (1,394)/15,000 (1,394)
Total 50,000 (4,646)/50,000 (4,646)

Development Schedule
Site Purchased September 1995
Planning Started September 1996
Construction Started April 1998
Sales Started April 1999
Number of Phases 3
Phases Completed 3
Percentage Completed 100% of site work
Estimated Date of Completion Residential buildout end of 2003

Coffee Creek Center

Chesterton, Indiana

Development Team
Developer Lake Erie Land Company, 1010 Sand Creek Drive South, Chesterton, Indiana 46304, T: 219-935-5300, www.lelcompany.com
Planner William McDonough + Partners, 410 East Water Street, Suite 700, Charlottesville, Virginia 22902, T: 434-979-1111, www.mcdonough.com
Planner Looney Ricks Kiss, 19 Vandeventer Avenue, Princeton, New Jersey 08540, T: 609-683-3600, www.lrk.com
Planner Gibbs Planning Group, 148 Pierce Street, Birmingham, Michigan 48009, T: 248-642-4800, www.gibbsplanning.com

Land Use
Acres (Hectares), Percent of Site
Residential 300 (121), 44.4%
Town Center 50 (20), 7.4%
Open Space/Recreation 225 (91), 33.3%
Public and Civic Facilities 20 (8), 3.0%
Roads/Parking 80 (32), 11.9%
Total 675 (272), 100%

Residential Information
Number Units Planned/Number Units Built
Single-Family Detached 1,300/5 (240+ in development)
Townhouses 200/5
Apartments 1,500/24 (40+ under construction)
Total Units 3,000/34

Commercial Space Information
Square Feet (Meters) Approved/Square Feet (Meters) Built
Retail 1,000,000 (92,903)/80,000 (7,432)
Office 2,000,000 (185,806)/12,000 (1,115)
Other 1,500,000 (139,355)/3,000 (279)
Total 4,500,000 (418,064)/95,000 (8,826)

Development Schedule
Site Purchased 1995
Planning Started 1997
Construction Started 1999
Sales Started 1999
Number of Phases 5
Phases Completed 0
Percentage Completed 10%
Estimated Date of Completion 2015

Jinji Lake

Suzhou, China

Development Team
Developer Suzhou Industrial Park Administrative Committee, 9/F International Building, 2 Suhua Road, Suzhou 215021, China, T: 86-512-2881-680
Planner EDAW, Inc., 753 Davis Street, San Francisco, California 94111, T: 415-433-1484, www.edaw.com

Land Use
Acres (Hectares), Percent of Site
Civic Culture 67 (27), 5%
Retail 91 (37), 7%
Commercial/Office 62 (25), 5%
Institutional 27 (11), 2%
Sports/Recreational 67 (27), 5%
Mixed-Use/Sports 12 (5), 1%
Residential 247 (100), 19.5%
Hotel 67 (27), 5%
Mixed-Use/Transportation 20 (8), 2%
Open Space 247 (100), 19.5%
Other 366 (148), 29%
Total 1,273 (515), 100%

282

Residential Information
Number Units Planned/Number Units Built
Total Units N/A/1,200

Commercial Space Information
Square Feet (Meters) Approved/Square Feet
(Meters) Built
Retail 215,278 (20,000)/0 (0)
Office (Including Hospital) 274,480
(25,500)/53,820 (5,000)
**Total 489,758 (45,000)/53,820
(5,000)**

Playa Vista
Los Angeles, California

Development Team
Developer Playa Capital Company, 1255
West Jefferson Boulevard, Suite 300, Los An-
geles, California 90066, www.playavista.com
Planner Legorretta Arquitectos, Palacio de
Versalles 285 'A,' 1102 Mexico, 25 196 98,
legorret@data.net.mx
Planner Moore Ruble Yudell, 933 Pico
Boulevard, Santa Monica, California 90405,
T: 310-450-1400, www.moorerubleyudell.com
Planner Duany Plater-Zyberk & Co., 1023
SW 25 Avenue, Miami, Florida 33135,
T: 305-844-1023, www.dpz.com
Planner EDAW, Inc., 17875 Von Karman
Avenue, Suite 400, Irvine, California 92614,
T: 949-660-8044, www.edaw.com
Planner Roma Design Group, 1527 Stock-
ton Street, San Francisco, California 94133,
T: 415-788-8728, www.roma.com
Planner Moule & Polyzoides, 180 East
California Boulevard, Pasadena, California
91106, T: 626-844-2400, www.mparchi
tects.com

Land Use
Acres (Hectares), Percent of Site
Open Space 500 (202), 46%
Recreation/Amenities 340 (138), 31%
Other 247 (100), 23%
Total 1,087 (440), 100%

Residential Information
Number Units Planned/Number Units Built
Single-Family Detached 180/NA
Townhouses 450/NA
Multifamily Condominiums 1,100/NA
Apartments 1,500/NA
Total Units 3,230/1,385

Commercial Space Information
Square Feet (Meters) Approved/Square Feet
(Meters) Built
Retail 600,000 (55,742)/10,000 (929)
Office 5–6 million
(464,515–557,418)/240,000 (22,297)
**Total 5.6–6.6 million
(520,257–613,160)/ 250,000
(23,226)**

Development Schedule
Planning Started 1976
Construction Started 2000
Sales Started Late Summer 2002
Number of Phases 2
Phases Completed 0
Percentage Completed 15%
Estimated Date of Completion
2012–2017

Stapleton
Denver, Colorado

Development Team
Developer Forest City Development, 1401
17th Street, Suite 510, Denver, Colorado
80202, T: 303-382-1800
Master Planner Calthorpe Associates,
739 Allston Way, Berkeley, California 94710,
T: 510-548-6848, www.calthorpe.com
Planner/Design/Landscape EDAW,
Inc., 1809 Blake Street, Suite 200, Denver,
Colorado 80202, T: 303-595-4522,
www.edaw.com
Engineer BRW, Inc./URS Corporation,
1225 17th Street, Suite 200, Denver, Col-
orado, T: 303-293-8080, www.urscorp.com
Engineer Matrix Design Group, 1601
Blake Street, Suite 508, Denver, Colorado
80202, T: 303-572-0200, www.matrix
designgroup.com

Land Use
Acres (Hectares), Percent of Site
Residential 1,120 (453), 24.8%
Town Centers 145 (59), 3.2%
Open Space 1,116 (452), 24.8%
Public and Civic Facilities 134 (54), 3.0%
Recreation/Amenities 108 (44), 2.4%
Trunk Roads/Parking 907 (367), 20.2%
Other* 970 (393), 21.6%
Total 4,500 (1,902), 100%
*Includes commercial uses outside of town
centers and 400 acres of industrial ware-
housing not being developed by Forest City.

Residential Information
Number Units Planned/Number Units Built
Single-Family Detached 5,500/NA
Single-Family Attached 2,500/NA
Apartments 4,000/NA
Total Units 12,000/NA

Commercial Space Information
Square Feet (Meters) Approved/Square
(Meters) Built
Retail 3,000,000 (278,709)/0
Office 10,000,000 (929,030)/0
Total 13,000,000 (1,207,740)/0

Total Project Development Cost
Site Acquisition Cost $150 million
Site Improvement Cost $2.9 billion
Soft Costs $950 million
Total Cost $4 billion

Development Schedule
Site Purchased May 2001 (First 270
acres)
Planning Started 1989
Construction Started May 2001
Sales Started January 2002
Number of Phases Multiple
Phases Completed 0
Percentage Completed 1%
Estimated Date of Completion 2025

Verrado
Buckeye, Arizona

Development Team
Developer DMB Associates, Inc., 7600 East
Doubletree Ranch Road, Suite 300, Scotts-
dale, Arizona 85258, T: 480-367-7000
Planner EDAW, Inc., 17875 Von Karman
Avenue, Suite 400, Irvine, California 92614,
T: 949-660-8044, www.edaw.com
Architect Dale Gardon Design, 8160
North Hayden Road, Suite 108, Scottsdale,
Arizona 85258, T: 480-948-9666
Architect William Hezmalhalch Associates,
17875 Von Karman Avenue, Suite 401,
Irvine, California 92614, T: 949-250-0607
Civil Engineer Wood Patel & Associates,
2051 W. Northern Avenue, Suite 100,
Phoenix, Arizona 85021, T: 602-335-8500,
www.woodpatel.com
Golf Course Architect John Fought
Design, 24333 NE Airport Road, Aurora,
Oregon 97002, T: 503-678-4330
Landscape Architect Vollmer & Associ-
ates, 5685 North Scottsdale Road,
Suite E-120, Scottsdale, Arizona 85250,
T: 480-945-9555, www.vollmer.com

Land Use
Acres (Hectares), Percent of Site
Residential 2,700 (1,093), 31%
Mixed-Use/Town Center 300 (121), 3%
Open Space 3,900 (1,578), 44%
Public and Civic Facilities 220 (89), 3%
Recreation/Amenities 240 (97), 3%
Golf Facilities 800 (324), 9%
Roads/Parking 430 (174), 5%
Other (Resort) 210 (85), 2%
Total 8,800 (3,561), 100%

Residential Information
Number Units Planned/Number Units Built
Single-Family Detached 7,200/0
Townhouses 1,900/0
Apartments 900/0
Total Units 10,000/0

Commercial Space Information
Square Feet (Meters) Approved
Retail 1,500,000 (139,355)
Office 2,300,000 (213,677)
Light Industrial 200,000 (18,580)
Total 4,000,000 (371,612)

Development Schedule
Site Purchased Development agreement
with Caterpillar Trust 1999
Planning Started 1999
Construction Started Projected 2002
Sales Started Projected 2003
Number of Phases 7
Phases Completed 0
Percentage Completed 0
Estimated Date of Completion 2018

WaterColor
Seagrove Beach, Florida

Development Team
Developer Arvida, 1701 E. County Hwy.
30A, Suite 101, Seagrove Beach, Florida
32459, T: 850-231-6500, www.arvida.com
**Town Planner/Design Architect Town
Center and Beach Club**
Cooper, Robertson & Partners, 311 West
43rd Street, New York, New York 10036,
T: 212-247-1717, www.cooperrobertson.com
Architect of Record/Town Center
Looney Ricks Kiss, 175 Toyota Plaza, Suite
600, Memphis, Tennessee 38103, T: 901-
521-1440, www.lrk.com
Pattern Book Consultant Urban Design
Associates, 707 Grant Street, 31st Floor,
Pittsburgh, Pennsylvania 15219, T: 412-263-
5200, www.urbandesignassociates.com
Architect/Housing Historical Concepts,
430 Prime Point, Suite 103, Peachtree City,
Georgia 30269, T: 770-487-8041,
www.historicalconcepts.com
Design Architect/Inn Rockwell Group,
5 Union Square West, New York, New York,
T: 212-463-0334, www.rockwellgroup.com
**Design Architect/Beachfront Condo-
minium Bldg.**
Graham Gund Architects, 47 Thorndike
Street, Cambridge, Massachusetts 02141,
T: 617-250-6800, www.grahamgund.com
**Architect of Record/Beach Club, Inn,
and Beachfront Residential Condo**
Glover Smith Bode, 1140 NW 63rd Street,
Suite 500, Oklahoma City, Oklahoma
73166, T: 405-949-9549, www.gsb-inc.com
Architect/Bait and Boat House
Christ & Associates, 35 Clayton Lane, Santa
Rosa Beach, Florida, 32459, T: 850-231-
5538
Landscape Architect Nelson-Byrd Land-
scape Architects, 408 Park Street, Charlottes-
ville, Virginia, 22902, T: 804-984-1358

Land Use
Acres (Hectares), Percent of Site
Residential 207 (84), 42%
Town Center 5 (2), 1%
Open Space 248 (100), 50%
Public and Civic Facilities 5 (2), 1%
Recreation/Amenities 16 (7), 3%
Other 18 (7), 3%
Total 499 (202), 100%

Residential Information
Number Units Planned/Number Units Built
Single-Family Detached TBD/0
Townhouses TBD/8
Multifamily Condominiums 102/95
Apartments TBD/0
Other TBD/0
Total Units 1,140/103

Commercial Space Information
Square Feet (Meters) Approved/Square Feet
(Meters) Built
Retail 80,000 (7,432)/30,000 (2,787)
Office 20,000 (1,858)/10,000 (929)
**Total 100,000 (9,290)/40,000
(3,716)**

Development Schedule
Site Purchased 1927
Planning Started 1997
Construction Started 1999
Sales Started 2000
Number of Phases Up to 4
Phases Completed Part of Phase One
Estimated Date of Completion 2010

Illustration Credits

Preliminaries Frontispiece, Alex Kosich, Jr.; title page, Tom Lamb; 7, EDSA; 10, © Jim Kirby

The Art of Creating Communities 14–16, Alexander Garvin; 17, Alexander Garvin (top), courtesy of the National Park Service, Frederick Law Olmstead National Historic Site (bottom); 18–19, Alexander Garvin; 20, from Clarence Stein, *New Towns for America*, 1966, courtesy of MIT Press (top left), Alexander Garvin (top right); 21–22, Alexander Garvin; 23, Alexander Garvin (top left), The Celebration Co. (top right); 24–25, Alexander Garvin; 27, The Olin Partnership; 28, Development Design Group, Inc.; 29, Alexander Garvin

Contemporary Communties 30–31, Tom Lamb

Beacon Cove 32–39, courtesy of Mirvac

Bonita Bay 40–49, courtesy of The Bonita Bay Group

Celebration 50–51, © Peter Aaron/Esto/The Celebration Co.; 52, The Celebration Co. (top), EDSA (bottom); 53, © Peter Aaron/Esto/The Celebration Co.; 54, The Celebration Co. (top left), © Peter Aaron/Esto/The Celebration Co. (top middle), The Celebration Co. (top right), © Peter Aaron/Esto/The Celebration Co. (bottom left and right); 55, Smith Aerial Photography/The Celebration Co. (top left), Peter Aaron/Esto/The Celebration Co. (top right, bottom left, bottom right); 56, © Alex S. MacLean/Landslides (top), The Celebration Co. (bottom); 57, Alexander Garvin (top), © Peter Aaron/Esto/The Celebration Co. (bottom); 58, courtesy of Urban Design Associates; 59, courtesy of Urban Design Associates

DC Ranch 60–61, Dino Tonn; 62–63, Swaback Partners; 64, Gary Ward; 65, Dino Tonn (top left), Lonna Tucker (top right), Dino Tonn (bottom left), DMB Associates (top right); 66, Dino Tom (top left and right), Gary Ward (bottom); 67, Render This (left), Gary Ward (right)

Fairview Village 69, Rick Holt; 70, William L. Dennis Architecture & Town Design (top), Rick Holt (bottom); 71, Lennertz & Coyle Architects & Town Planners (top), Rick Holt (bottom); 72–75, Rick Holt; 76, Rick Holt (top), William L. Dennis Architecture & Town Design (bottom); 77, Rick Holt (top left), Sienna Architects & Co. (top right), John Hughel Photography (bottom)

Harbor Town 78, © Alex S. MacLean/ Landslides; 80, Looney Ricks Kiss; 81, Jim Hilliard Photography (top), Looney Ricks Kiss (bottom left), Jeffrey Jacobs/ Architectural Photography, Inc. (bottom right); 82–83, Henry Turley Co. (top left), Jeffrey Jacobs/ Mims Studio (top middle and right), Looney Ricks Kiss (bottom); 84–85, Jeffrey Jacobs/Mims Studio (top and bottom left), Henry Turley Co. (bottom middle), Jeffrey Jacobs/ Architectural Photography, Inc. (bottom right); 86–87, Jeffrey Jacobs/Mims Studio (top), Jeffrey Jacobs/Architectural Photography, Inc. (bottom)

I'On 90–91, Gary Coleman; 92, Seaman Whiteside and Associates (left), Gary Coleman (right); 93–97, Gary Coleman

The Irvine Ranch 98–100, Tom Lamb; 101, The Irvine Co.; 102–104, Tom Lamb; 105, The Irvine Co.; 106, Tom Lamb (top and middle), John Connell (bottom); 107, Phillip Channing

Karrow Nord 108, Werner Huthmacher; 110, Moore Ruble Yudell; 111–117, Werner Huthmacher

Kentlands 118–119, Laurence Aurbach; 120, © Alex S. MacLean/Landslides; 121, Duany Plater-Zyberk & Co.; 122, courtesy of Great Seneca Development Corp. (top row), courtesy of Great Seneca Development Corp. (bottom left), Duany Plater-Zyberk & Co. (bottom middle), courtesy of Great Seneca Development Corp. (bottom right); 123, courtesy of Great

Seneca Development Corp. (top), courtesy of Great Seneca Development Corp. (bottom left), Duany Plater-Zyberk & Co. (bottom middle), courtesy of Great Seneca Development Corp. (bottom right); 124, Duany Plater-Zyberk & Co.; 125, Duany Plater-Zyberk & Co. (top), courtesy of Great Seneca Development Corp. (bottom)

Ladera Ranch 126, Tom Lamb; 128–129, EDAW, Inc.; 130–131, Tom Lamb; 132–133, EDAW, Inc. (left), Dave Smith (middle top), Tom Lamb (middle bottom, top right, bottom right); 134, EDAW, Inc.; 135, Tom Lamb (top), EDAW, Inc. (bottom)

McKenzie Towne 136–138, Carma Developers Ltd.; 139, Jayman Master Builders and Cedarglen Homes (top), Carma Developers Ltd. (bottom); 140–141, Carma Developers Ltd.; 142, Jayman Master Builders (top left), Carma Developers Ltd. (top right), Jayman Master Builders (bottom); 143, Carma Developers Ltd.

Orenco Station 145, Fletcher Farr Ayotte Architects; 146, Fletcher Farr Ayotte Architects (top left), Costa Pacific Homes (top right), Fletcher Farr Ayotte Architects (bottom); 147, Fletcher Farr Ayotte Architects; 148, Fletcher Farr Ayotte Architects (top and bottom left), Pacific Realty Associates (bottom right); 149, Costa Pacific Homes; 150–151, Fletcher Farr Ayotte Architects

Park DuValle 152–155, Urban Design Associates; 156, Urban Design Associates (top row), Paul Rocheleau (bottom row); 157, Urban Design Associates; 158, Paul Rocheleau; 159, Urban Design Associates (top), David Aschkenas (bottom)

Poundbury 160, © Mark Fiennes/Duchy of Cornwall; 162, © Duchy of Cornwall; 163, © Duchy of Cornwall (left), Erling Okkenhaugh (right); 164–165, © Mark Fiennes/Duchy of Cornwall (top left), Erling

Okkenhaugh (bottom left), © Mark Fiennes/Duchy of Cornwall (middle and top right), Erling Okkenhaugh (bottom right); 166, © Mark Fiennes/Duchy of Cornwall (top), Erling Okkenhaugh (bottom); 167, © Mark Fiennes/Duchy of Cornwall; 168, © Mark Fiennes/Duchy of Corwall; 169, Erling Okkenhaugh (top left), © Mark Fiennes/Duchy of Cornwall (top right), Erling Okkenhaugh (bottom)

Rancho Santa Margarita 170–171, Tom Lamb; 172, PBR; 173, Rancho Santa Margarita Joint Venture; 174, Rancho Santa Margarita Joint Venture (top), Tom Lamb (bottom); 175, Rancho Santa Margarita Joint Venture; 176–177, Tom Lamb; 178, Tom Lamb (top), Rancho Santa Margarita Joint Venture (bottom row); 179, Tom Lamb; 180, Dixi Carillo (left), PBR (right); 180, Dixi Carillo

Reston 183, © Jim Kirby; 184, courtesy of Terrabrook; 185, © Alex S. MacLean/ Landslides (top), Dean Hawthorne (bottom left), © Jim Kirby (bottom middle and right); 186, © Jim Kirby (top), © Alex S. MacLean/ Landslides (bottom left), © Jim Kirby (bottom right); 187, Llewellyn (left), © Jim Kirby (middle and right); 188, courtesy of Terrabrook; 189, © Jim Kirby (top and middle), © Alex S. MacLean/Landslides (bottom and right)

Summerlin 190, OpulenceStudios, Inc.; 192, EDAW, Inc.; 193–194, OpulenceStudios, Inc.; 195, EDAW, Inc. (top), Alex Kosich, Jr. (bottom); 196, The Galloway Group (left), OpulenceStudios, Inc. (right); 197, OpulenceStudios, Inc. (right); 198, PBR (top), OpulenceStudios, Inc. (bottom); 199, OpulenceStudios, Inc.

The Woodlands 201, Ted Washington/The Woodlands Operating Co., L.P.; 202–203, The Woodlands Operating Co., L.P. (left), Ted Washington/The Woodlands Operating Co., L.P. (middle, top right, bottom right);

204–205, Ted Washington/The Woodlands Operating Co., L.P. (top left, bottom left, middle), The Woodlands Operating Co., L.P. (right); 206–207, Ted Washington/The Woodlands Operating Co., L.P.; 208, The Woodlands Operating Co., L.P. (left), Ted Washington/The Woodlands Operating Co., L.P. (top and bottom right); 209–211, The Woodlands Operating Co., L.P.

New Visions 212–213, Ralph Daniel

Civano 214–223, Moule & Polyzoides

Coffee Creek Center 224–222, William McDonough + Partners; 223, Jim Wilson/Lake Erie Land Co.

Jinji Lake 232–233, Bill Hook; 234, EDAW, Inc.; 235, EDAW, Inc. (top), Dixi Carillo (bottom left), EDAW, Inc. (bottom right); 236, Dixi Carillo; 237, Bill Hook (top), EDAW, Inc. (bottom row); 238, Bill Hook; 239, Dixi Carillo; 240–241, Bill Hook

Playa Vista 242–243, ROMA Design Group; 242, courtesy of Playa Capital Co. (top), Jim Simmons, Anette Del Zoppo Productions (bottom); 243, Focus 360 (top), Jim Simmons, Anette Del Zoppo Productions (bottom); 244, courtesy of Playa Capital Co.; 245, Paul Gleason (top), Milo Olea (middle), Jeanne LaRae Concepts (bottom); 246, Focus 360; 247, courtesy of Playa Capital Co.; 248, David A. Suplee Architectural Illustrators (top), Milo Olea (bottom); 249, Van Tilburg, Banvard & Soderbergh, AIA

Stapleton 253, courtesy of KB Homes; 254, Stan Doctor/EDAW, Inc.; 255, courtesy of Calthorpe Associates (left), Stan Doctor/EDAW, Inc.; 256, Stan Doctor/EDAW, Inc.; 257, EDAW, Inc. (top), Stan Doctor/EDAW, Inc. (bottom); 258, courtesy McStain Neighborhoods (top), courtesy Forest City Development (bottom); 259, courtesy McStain Neighborhoods (top), courtesy

Forest City Development (bottom); 260–261, courtesy Wolff Lyon Architects/EDAW, Inc. (top and middle left), courtesy of KB Homes (middle), courtesy of Trimark Communities (top and middle right), courtesy of Joh Lang Homes (bottom right)

Verrado 263, from John W. Reps, *Bird's Eye Views: Historic Lithographs of North America*, 1998, courtesy of Princeton Architectural Press; 264, EDAW, Inc.; 265, Conceptual Design; 266, EDAW, Inc.; 267, Dale Gardon Design; 268, Conceptual Designs; 269, William Hezmalhalch Architects (top and middle rows), EDAW, Inc. (bottom row)

WaterColor 271, Ralph Daniel; 272, Arvida (top), Jack Gardner (bottom); 273, Jack Gardner (top), Cooper, Robertson & Partners (bottom); 274, Ralph Daniel; 275, Michael McCann; 276, Melanie Taylor & Associates (top), Cooper, Robertson & Partners (bottom); 277, Looney Ricks Kiss (top), Historical Concepts (middle and bottom rows)

Colophon 288 [children at play in Reston, Virginia], © Jim Kirby

Index

Page numbers in italics refer to photograph captions.

The text of *Great Planned Communities* was composed in Sabon, a font designed in 1964 by Jan Tschichold, a book designer and typographer trained in calligraphy. Sabon is recognized as a strong yet restrained typeface of classical proportions.

The titling font used is Centaur, designed in 1915 by Bruce Rogers. It is derived from the 15th-century work of Venetian printer Nicolas Jenson, a pioneer in the use of the "roman" type style. Centaur maintains Jenson's original influences with elegance and remains today a great 20th-century classic typeface.

Futura, designed by Paul Renner in 1927, is used for captions and subheads. This sans serif Bauhaus-influenced typeface is based on strict geometric shapes.

Great Planned Communities was designed, typeset, and produced by Marc Alain Meadows on a Macintosh PowerBook G3 in QuarkXpress, and was printed and bound in Canada by the Friesens printing company.